For the Praise of His Glory

FOR THE PRAISE OF HIS GLORY

RANDY L ALLEN

NELLA PUBLISHING HOUSE
A Division of Nella Limited Liability Company
Tuscaloosa, Alabama

Cover: Massadona, Colorado. Photographs by Randy L. Allen unless otherwise indicated.

Unless otherwise indicated, the Scripture quotations contained herein are from the New Revised Standard Version Bible, copyright 1989, Division of Christian Education of the National Council of the Churches of Christ in the U.S.A. Used by permission. All rights reserved.

Scripture quotations labeled "NIV" contained herein are from the *The Life Application Bible, New International Version* edition published jointly by Tyndale House Publishers, Inc. and Zondervan Publishing House. Scripture taken from the HOLY BIBLE, NEW INTERNATIONAL VERSION. Copyright ©1973, 1978, 1984 by International Bible Society. Used by permission of Zondervan Publishing House. All rights reserved.

The "NIV" and "New International Version" trademarks are registered in the United States Patent and Trademark Office by International Bible Society. Use of either trademark requires the permission of International Bible Society.

For the Praise of His Glory: 52 Devotionals. Copyright © 2021 by Randy L. Allen. All rights reserved. Printed in the United States of America. No part of this book may be used or reproduced in any manner whatsoever without written permission except in the case of brief quotations in critical articles and reviews. For information address 500 Main Avenue, Suite 201, Northport, Alabama 35476.

https://RandyLAllen.com

ISBN   978-1-7344159-2-6

First Edition: July 2021

For the Praise of His Glory

Randy L Allen

Contents

1.	We Are Vapor	1
2.	Cost of Following Jesus	7
3.	Darkness and Light	14
4.	Emerging from Stone	21
5.	Fear Not	27
6.	Patience and Urgency	34
7.	Time is of the Essence	40
8.	Freed from Bondage	46
9.	Becoming Desensitized	52
10.	Transformed Into Christ's Image	57
11.	The Redeemer and the Redeemed	64
12.	Joy of Giving	72
13.	Jesus' Voice	79

14.	God's Plans for You	85
15.	The Falling of Many	92
16.	Christ's Representatives	98
17.	Angle of Approach	105
18.	Using our Gifts for God's Glory	111
19.	Questioning our Motives	117
20.	Voice for the Voiceless	122
21.	Spiritual Repair	130
22.	Clearing the Path	137
23.	Audience of One	143
24.	Separation from God	151
25.	The Fasting God Desires	158
26.	The Trouble with Success	165
27.	Relationship with God	173

28.	Recognizing God's Visitation	180
29.	Experiencing the Resurrected Christ	187
30.	God's Ways	196
31.	Mustard Seed	204
32.	Go!	210
33.	Seizing Christ's Rest	218
34.	Waking Up to Jesus Christ	225
35.	Claiming God's Promises	231
36.	I Am Barabbas	236
37.	Who is Jesus?	244
38.	What is Truth?	253
39.	Hear, Act and Do	260
40.	God's Will	269
41.	Who Are Evil	279

42.	Relationship & Prayer	286
43.	Lukewarm	294
44.	Satan's Tactics	304
45.	God's Purpose	313
46.	Transcendence	323
47.	Faith	332
48.	A Public Service Warning	340
49.	Good Trees	349
50.	Bond of Peace	357
51.	Signs, Wonders and Belief	366
52.	A Thorn for Humility	376
53.	About the Author	387
54.	Notes	390

For the Praise of His Glory

Massadona, Colorado

Randy L Allen

In Christ we have also obtained an inheritance, having been destined according to the purpose of him who accomplishes all things according to his counsel and will, so that we, who were the first to set our hope on Christ, might live for the praise of his glory. In him you also, when you had heard the word of truth, the gospel of your salvation, and had believed in him, were marked with the seal of the promised Holy Spirit; this is the pledge of our inheritance toward redemption as God's own people, to the praise of his glory.

Ephesians 1:11-14

Randy L Allen

Jesus is life. He came offering life to everyone. His life is available through faith, and faith comes from God by hearing the word of Christ Jesus. I pray this book complements your daily discipline of studying God's holy word and communing with Him in prayer and serves as a source of inspiration. May you receive His life abundant and enjoy His wholeness, peace and rest, and may you share His life, light and love with everyone you encounter. Amen.

Randy L Allen

1

WE ARE VAPOR

> COME NOW, YOU WHO SAY, "TODAY OR TOMORROW WE WILL GO TO SUCH AND SUCH A TOWN AND SPEND A YEAR THERE, DOING BUSINESS AND MAKING MONEY." YET YOU DO NOT EVEN KNOW WHAT TOMORROW WILL BRING. WHAT IS YOUR LIFE? FOR YOU ARE A MIST THAT APPEARS FOR A LITTLE WHILE AND THEN VANISHES. INSTEAD YOU OUGHT TO SAY, "IF THE LORD WISHES, WE WILL LIVE AND DO THIS OR THAT." JAMES 4:13-15

Fergie woke me by licking my nose, her way of saying she needs to go outside. It was way earlier than I would have liked. The sky was just beginning to show signs of light and a heavy fog filled the air. As the sun rose, the fog quickly disappeared revealing a bright blue cloudless sky. James says, "You are a mist that appears for a little while and then vanishes." Like the fog, we are here on earth for a little while and then we vanish.

Time is fleeting. Our life is a brief window of opportunity comprised of days and moments. We do not know how long we have, but we know the window is closing. We each must decide what we will do with each moment and each day, and the resulting life is a tapestry woven with choices made. What do you feel in response to that thought? Do you feel a sense of doom, fear or dread? Do you regret missed opportunities? Are you rejoicing and thanking God that you are here on earth today with new moments and new opportunities?

The quote from James above is a call to live with decisive urgency, yet he quickly transitions to a call for patience. Scripture calls us to balance urgency and patience. We need to patiently prepare so that when the opportunity arises we are able to act quickly and decisively. This is the plot of many love stories. Robin Williams' character in *Good Will Hunting* describes having a ticket to the greatest World Series game of all time. He was a huge fan; he went to great lengths to obtain a ticket to the big game; and as he prepared to enter the game he met a girl. He knew in that instant that he wanted to be with the girl forever, and he feared that if he left her the opportunity would be lost. In that instant he decided to stay with her and miss the game. He recognized the situation and he acted with decisive urgency.

I recently heard an entrepreneur speak about some of his investment decisions. He described hearing pitches for Facebook, Twitter and YouTube long before the names meant anything to anyone, and he knew in his gut that he needed to invest as much as he possibly could, so he did and the investments worked out very well for him. He had experienced a lot of pitches describing investment opportunities and his experience allowed him to quickly assess each pitch and act with decisive urgency.

Windows of opportunity are typically short lived. It's like a surfer waiting for the perfect wave. It takes experience to recognize what the wave will become as the swell is just beginning to rise. When the surfer sees the right wave forming, she must act at the right time to catch it, otherwise it will move past her, an opportunity missed.

Life is a brief window of opportunity comprised of moments and days. It is a fog that quickly disappears. It is a gift from God. What opportunity will you seize today? We are called to love God and to love our neighbor. May you respond with urgency to opportunities presented today to allow God's glory to shine through you.

Thoughts to Consider

1.   Read James 4 & 5. James begins chapter 4 contrasting pride and humility, and friendship with the world and submission to God. We are called to be of God while we are out in the world. We are called to be in the world serving as His light to the world. How has your friendship with the world influenced your ability to serve God? How does this lay a foundation to discuss the brevity of life?

2.   James transitions to discuss our plans for the future, the trappings of wealth, and patience. He writes, "What is your life? For you are a mist that appears for a little while and then

vanishes" (James 4:14), suggesting we should approach each moment with a sense of urgency because we do not know how many moments remain. Soon thereafter he writes, "You must also be patient. Strengthen your hearts, for the coming of the Lord is near" (James 5:8). God's holy word urges us to balance urgency with patience, acting with urgency through God's holy grace according to His calling and will, patiently waiting on God when appropriate, and praying for God's discernment to distinguish which is appropriate for the moment. How do you balance patience and urgency?

3.   Read Job 7 & 42. In chapter 7 Job talks to God. He discusses the brevity of human life on earth and asks God to stop tormenting him. Over the following 34 chapters, Job endures in agony his friends' theology, his physical suffering, and as he waits on God, he encounters Him. In chapter 42, Job describes the changes he has experienced saying, "I had heard of you by the hearing of the ear, but now my eye sees you; therefore I despise myself, and repent in dust and ashes" (Job 42:5-6). It seems that God allowed Job to marinate in his suffering so that his spirit would be transformed and he would gain eyes to see God. Job sought urgent relief, but God had other plans for him. Describe times in your life when God allowed you to patiently marinate in suffering. Did you, like Job, gain eyes to see God? If you did, in what specific ways?

4.   Read Luke 12:13-21. An unnamed man in the crowd approaches Jesus and asks Jesus to act as judge between the man and his brother regarding their inheritance. Jesus explains He has no standing to act as judge on matters such as that, then He warns about greed and tells the Parable of the Rich Fool. In the parable, a rich man harvests a bumper crop and he builds

large facilities to store the grain so that, "for many years [he may] relax, eat, drink, be merry" (Luke 12:19). Jesus concludes the parable saying, "But God said to him, 'You fool! This very night your life is being demanded of you. And the things you have prepared, whose will they be?' So it is with those who store up treasures for themselves but are not rich toward God" (Luke 12:20-21). Compared to eternity, even the longest human life is incredibly brief. We need to prudently plan as if we will live tomorrow while acting with luxurious generosity toward God. How are you generous toward God?

5. Read Psalms 39, 102 & 144. In what circumstances do the psalmists discuss the brevity of life? How are the psalms similar? What differentiates them? How do they compare with the passage from James first set forth above?

6. In the passages above, brevity of life is discussed in the context of urgency, patience, greed and suffering. As you consider the thought, what specific things should you change about your life? What steps will you take this week to begin implementing the changes?

North Window, Arches National Park, Utah

2

COST OF FOLLOWING JESUS

Then Jesus told his disciples, "If any want to become my followers, let them deny themselves and take up their cross and follow me. For those who want to save their life will lose it, and those who lose their life for my sake will find it. For what will it profit them if they gain the whole world but forfeit their life? Or what will they give in return for their life? Matthew 16:24-26

Now large crowds were traveling with him; and he turned and said to them, "Whoever comes to me and does not hate father and mother, wife and children, brothers and sisters, yes, and even life itself, cannot be my disciple. Whoever does not carry the cross and follow me cannot be my disciple. For which of you, intending to build a tower, does not first sit down and estimate the cost, to see whether he has enough to complete it? Otherwise, when he has laid a foun-

DATION AND IS NOT ABLE TO FINISH, ALL WHO SEE IT WILL BEGIN TO RIDICULE HIM, SAYING, 'THIS FELLOW BEGAN TO BUILD AND WAS NOT ABLE TO FINISH.' OR WHAT KING, GOING OUT TO WAGE WAR AGAINST ANOTHER KING, WILL NOT SIT DOWN FIRST AND CONSIDER WHETHER HE IS ABLE WITH TEN THOUSAND TO OPPOSE THE ONE WHO COMES AGAINST HIM WITH TWENTY THOUSAND? IF HE CANNOT, THEN, WHILE THE OTHER IS STILL FAR AWAY, HE SENDS A DELEGATION AND ASKS FOR THE TERMS OF PEACE. SO THEREFORE, NONE OF YOU CAN BECOME MY DISCIPLE IF YOU DO NOT GIVE UP ALL YOUR POSSESSIONS.
LUKE 14:25-33

Jesus often uses physical imagery while teaching about spiritual matters. The passages above contain some of His statements regarding the cost of following Him. While He freely offers the gift of holy grace to everyone, and it is a gift that cannot be earned or deserved, following Him involves surrender. If we truly desire to follow Him we must give ourselves to Him.

During the first century in the Roman Empire, the cross was a symbol of torture and violent death. Scripture records Jesus carrying to Golgotha the cross upon which He would be hung. So when Jesus says to His disciples "If any want to become my followers, let them deny themselves and take up their cross and follow me," the image is clear that Jesus is telling them that they need to be crucified, that they need to die. But Jesus is not calling for actual, physical death; He is using the image to make a spiritual point.

He continues saying, "For those who want to save their life will lose it, and those who lose their life for my sake will find it." Jesus uses crucifixion to explain that His disciples must leave their old lives behind; they must be spiritually transformed through Him. Whoever clings to their old, worldly ways, their old life, will miss the opportunity to live with Christ. They must abandon worldly pursuits, they must deny fleshly desires, they must lose everything associated with their old life and they must do so for Jesus. They must be transformed in spirit through Him, and through that transformation they gain new life, new desires, new perspective, and they become His disciples.

In His next teaching, after using the example of calculating the cost before starting a building project and analyzing the likelihood of success before going to battle, Jesus says, "In the same way those of you who do not give up everything you have cannot be my disciples." He urges His disciples to totally, completely surrender to Him, give up their old life and dedicate themselves to Him.

While the gift of salvation is freely offered as a gift of grace, discipleship requires an investment. Disciples must pay a price.

Jesus' teaching forces me to ponder whether I have paid any price associated with following Him. Am I allowing His holy presence to permeate and transform my being, am I really giving up worldly, fleshly desires, or am I merely engaged in intellectual pursuits as I study His holy word? Have I really surrendered while struggling with worldly desires and temptations?

I invite you to ponder questions such as these. Jesus asks us to give up all the things in our hearts that are blocking us from Him. He invites us to surrender to Him. He wants all of us. He wants all of you. And our gradual spiritual transformation, our gradual release of worldly desires marks our progression along the path of sanctification. May you continue progressing along the path, may you continue to surrender, may you continue to grow in Christ, may you continue living as His disciple.

Thoughts to Consider

1. Chapter 12 of Romans begins saying,

    > I appeal to you therefore, brothers and sisters, by the mercies of God, to present your bodies as a living sacrifice, holy and acceptable to God, which is your spiritual worship. Do not be conformed to this world, but be transformed by the renewing of your minds, so that you may discern what is the will of God—what is good and acceptable and perfect. Romans 12:1-2

God's holy word urges us to present ourselves as living sacrifices, holy and acceptable to Him. What does that entail? What steps should you take to accomplish it? The next sentence gives a hint – avoid conformance to the world and seek God's holy renewal of our minds so that we may "discern what is the will of God." We give ourselves to God so that He may fill us with Him. Isn't it awesome that God, the holy and pure One, the

Creator of the universe, the Sovereign One desires that sort of intimate relationship with us?

2. Read 1 Peter 2:18-25. Pain and suffering are part of human existence. Peter discusses pain and suffering relative to that of Jesus Christ, who was without fault, had done nothing wrong, yet was abused and tortured. In response, Jesus Christ entrusted Himself to God, "the one who judges justly" (1 Peter 2:23). Jesus surrendered Himself completely to God and it was God's will that He suffer for us and Peter writes, "For to this you have been called, because Christ also suffered for you, leaving you an example, so that you should follow in his steps" (1 Peter 2:21). He continues saying, "He himself bore our sins in his body on the cross, so that, free from sins, we might live for righteousness; by his wounds you have been healed" (1 Peter 2:24). God's holy word calls us to follow in Jesus' steps. He surrendered completely to God, and He followed through on God's will for His life. What does it mean to you to hear that you "should follow in his steps"?

3. In the passage from Luke set forth above, Jesus says, "Whoever comes to me and does not hate father and mother, wife and children, brothers and sisters, yes, and even life itself, cannot be my disciple" (Luke 14:26). Jesus begins His call for radical, total, complete commitment and surrender to Him by saying hatred of family and hatred of life itself is a prerequisite to being His disciple. However, the Ten Commandments instructs us to honor our parents (see Exodus 20:12) and Jesus said He came to fulfill the law, not to abolish it (see Matthew 5:17). How are the statements consistent? In the first statement, Jesus uses hyperbole to make His point. He does not intend for us to take the statement literally, but to understand the cost of committing

to Him. Disciples must love Jesus more than everything else. They must treasure Him even more than they treasure their children, spouse, parents, and even their own life. What have you given up because of your association with Jesus?

4. Read Matthew 22:34-40, John 8:39-47 & 1 Corinthians 16. I once heard John Piper connect the three passages. In the first Jesus describes the Greatest Commandment as the command to love God with our entire being, and the second greatest as the command to love our neighbor. In the passage from John, Jesus explains to a group of religious leaders that people who enjoy relationship with God as Father love Jesus – loving Jesus is the test of their relationship with God. 1 Corinthians 16:22 says, "Let anyone be accursed who has no love for the Lord." If we connect the three passages, we see that loving Jesus is essential to the Greatest Commandment and people who do not love Jesus are "accursed." What is the cost of following Jesus? Perhaps the more important question is, what is the cost of not loving Jesus?

For the Praise of His Glory

Napali Coast State Wilderness Park, Kauai, Hawaii

3

DARKNESS AND LIGHT

The Lord is my shepherd, I shall not want. He makes me lie down in green pastures; he leads me beside still waters; he restores my soul. He leads me in right paths for his name's sake. Even though I walk through the darkest valley, I fear no evil; for you are with me; your rod and your staff — they comfort me. Psalm 23:1-4

Again Jesus spoke to them, saying, "I am the light of the world. Whoever follows me will never walk in darkness but will have the light of life." John 8:12

"You are the light of the world. A city built on a hill cannot be hid. No one after lighting a lamp puts it under the bushel basket, but on the lampstand, and it gives light to all in the house. In the same way, let your light shine before others, so that they may see your good works and

GIVE GLORY TO YOUR FATHER IN HEAVEN. MATTHEW 5:14-16

God is with you and is actively involved in your life. Are you traveling through a dark valley? Do you feel threatened or attacked? Knowing who God is, knowing His power, knowing that nothing is beyond His ability, that He loves you and is with you, with all that in mind, know in your heart that you have nothing to fear.

Jesus is the light of the world, and as we allow His light to flow through us, we are also light of the world. We will still experience difficult times, but God is with us. In fact, it is possible that God allows us to go through the difficulty so that we are positioned to serve as beacons of light in the darkness.

As John Wesley sailed across the Atlantic returning home after his missionary trip to America, a violent storm rocked the ship. He was gripped by fear. As he cowered, he noticed a group of men singing hymns and praising God. They exhibited no evidence of fear and he wondered about the chasm separating his faith from theirs. In that dark time, they were light to the world. They were in a storm, but they were not walking in darkness – they were light revealed by the darkness around them. God allowed them to go through the storm so that they could be light for others.

While sitting with Lori watching a chemo cocktail drip into her veins, I enjoyed short conversations with others sharing a similar experience. One day each week, Pam sat near us receiving her chemo infusion. Her smile and kind words warmed the space around her, and as Lori reached her low point and was isolated in bed in a private room, Pam stopped by simply to let Lori know she was thinking about her. Pam was struggling with her own condition, yet she took the time and energy to seek Lori and to offer her compassion and kindness, and the glow of her light brought life and love into the room.

While leading a Bible study in the county jail, I have felt the presence of evil and I have seen inmates serving as beacons of light to other inmates. While in jail, while living in that dark place, they were light revealing God's glory to others.

Are you traveling through a dark place, is a storm threatening to sink your ship, are you under attack? Please know in your heart with absolute certainty that God is with you. Resist the temptation of retreating in fear; move toward God instead. Allow His light to shine through you. Through Christ Jesus, you are a beacon of light transforming the darkness around you.

THOUGHTS TO CONSIDER

1. Read Genesis 1:1-5. God created the heavens and the earth, and the formless void was covered in darkness until God spoke light into existence. When God speaks amazing things happen. He is the Creator and He creates by speaking things into existence. God transforms chaos to order. God is the source of light and light is good. What light is He creating as He speaks in and through you?

2. Read John 1:1-18. John begins his gospel writing,

> In the beginning was the Word, and the Word was with God, and the Word was God. He was in the beginning with God. All things came into being through him, and without him not one thing came into being. What has come into being in him was life, and the life was the light of all people. The light shines in the darkness, and the darkness did not overcome it. John 1:1-5

Life has come into being through Jesus Christ and "the life was the light of all people." The life is light. Jesus Christ is the light and the life, through Him we are offered new life, He illuminates darkness, and He sends His disciples out into the dark world as His beacons of light. In what way does this resonate with your experience? Have you known people who serve as Christ's beacons of light? How did they shine?

3. Read Psalm 23. While David walks "through the darkest valley," (Psalm 23:4) surrounded by evil that others fear, he does not fear because he trusts God completely. He knows he is in a dark, evil place, but he also knows God is with him and he is filled with God's holy presence to the point of overflowing, and he says, "surely goodness and mercy shall follow me all the days of my life" (Psalm 23:6). Not all fear is bad – feeling fear while standing on the edge of a tall cliff may propel you to a safer location. However, in other situations fear, worry, fretting are symptoms of failing trust. Sometimes God allows us to move through dark valleys to serve as light to others and to prepare us for future service. Describe a dark valley you have experienced. With hindsight, how did God use you as His light

during or because of your experience?

4.   Read John 3. The chapter includes the following passage in which Jesus says,

> "Indeed, God did not send the Son into the world to condemn the world, but in order that the world might be saved through him. Those who believe in him are not condemned; but those who do not believe are condemned already, because they have not believed in the name of the only Son of God. And this is the judgment, that the light has come into the world, and people loved darkness rather than light because their deeds were evil. For all who do evil hate the light and do not come to the light, so that their deeds may not be exposed. But those who do what is true come to the light, so that it may be clearly seen that their deeds have been done in God." John 3:17-21

Jesus begins by explaining that He comes offering new life to everyone in the world. He freely offers the gift of new life to everyone, but some will choose darkness not light, some will choose to continue living their old life rather than receiving the new life offered in and through Christ Jesus. Jesus does not condemn; rather, everyone who fails to choose new life in and through Christ Jesus continues in their state of death or their state of condemnation. How do you respond to this?

5.   Read John 12. At John 12:35-36 Jesus says, "The light is with you for a little longer. Walk while you have the light, so that the darkness may not overtake you. If you walk in the darkness, you do not know where you are going. While you have the light,

believe in the light, so that you may become children of light." I love the image of children of light and the image of a lamp lighting a room described in Matthew 5:15. How do others know you are a child of light? In what ways do you allow God's love, light and life to flow through you, brightening the room you are in?

Randy L Allen

Chautauqua Park, Boulder, Colorado

4

EMERGING FROM STONE

> AND WE KNOW THAT IN ALL THINGS GOD WORKS FOR THE GOOD OF THOSE WHO LOVE HIM, WHO HAVE BEEN CALLED ACCORDING TO HIS PURPOSE. FOR THOSE GOD FOREKNEW HE ALSO PREDESTINED TO BE CONFORMED TO THE IMAGE OF HIS SON, THAT HE MIGHT BE THE FIRSTBORN AMONG MANY BROTHERS AND SISTERS. AND THOSE HE PREDESTINED, HE ALSO CALLED; THOSE HE CALLED, HE ALSO JUSTIFIED; THOSE HE JUSTIFIED, HE ALSO GLORIFIED. ROMANS 8:28-30

This passage describes the path of grace. By grace, God stirs our hearts causing us to ponder life's important questions and ask about Him; He showers us with His justifying grace and as we receive it, we gain faith; and He reveals His glory through those who grow in relationship with Him. As we progress along the path of sanctifying grace, we are each being "conformed to the image of His Son."

In 1501 Michelangelo's benefactor provided a massive block of white marble and requested that he carve a statue of King David. Michelangelo started chiseling, carving and polishing, and continued for several years. Gradually the image of a thirteen-and-a-half-foot tall muscular nude young man appeared. The image is startlingly realistic. His toes and toenails are lifelike. His hands and fingers have intricate detail like protruding veins and polished nails, and they hold a sling.

We recently visited the Academy Gallery in Florence to see the remarkable work of art. As our tour guide led us down the corridor toward David, she stopped to show some unfinished statues – large rectangular marble blocks with human images just beginning to emerge. The contrast between the rough, unfinished figures and the perfectly chiseled, carved and polished image of David highlighted the master's talent.

Like the block of marble, we are being transformed. Gradually, the Master is chiseling and carving us out of the stone in which we are housed, transforming us to the image of Christ. While His holy grace showers over us, we must accept the gift and we must allow ourselves to be transformed, which is why our daily walk involves spiritual disciplines. As you study Scripture, as you pray, as you receive Sabbath rest, as you praise and worship God, as you engage in your spiritual disciplines, allow yourself to be transformed, conforming to the image of Christ.

The thought that we are housed within stone, seeking to emerge reminds me of a story our guide told as we toured the museum. Michelangelo was asked how he created the masterpiece, and he replied that he merely released the image originally formed in the stone. According to the narrative, David was there all along, trapped in the stone, and Michelangelo was merely the instrument helping him emerge. If true, his words and attitude remind me of Jesus' words at Luke 17:10: he was an unworthy servant, merely doing his duty.

We are being chiseled into the image of Christ Jesus and He calls us to help others as we each progress along the path of God's grace. As you serve, do so with compassion, gentleness and the very grace that God is bestowing upon you. May God's glory continue to be revealed through you.

Thoughts to Consider

1. Read Luke 17:1-10. Jesus instructs the disciples to be on guard against stumbling in sin, urges them to be forgiving, and discusses faith. Then He discusses the human desire for status and recognition, explaining that slaves expect no recognition or thanks for having accomplished their jobs saying, "So you also, when you have done all that you were ordered to do, say, 'We are worthless slaves; we have done only what we ought to have done!'" (Luke 17:10). Sin, forgiveness, faith and humility. How do these relate to conforming to the image of Christ?

2. Read 2 Corinthians 3. The chapter is filled with confident hope and passion in the transformation available in and through Christ Jesus. Paul explains that the church in Corinth is his resume, his letter of recommendation because its individuals are being transformed such that the church presents Christ

Jesus to the world. He concludes the chapter writing, "And all of us, with unveiled faces, seeing the glory of the Lord as though reflected in a mirror, are being transformed into the same image from one degree of glory to another; for this comes from the Lord, the Spirit" (2 Corinthians 3:18). Paul wrote the words inspired by God. If he were inspired by God to describe you today, would he write something similar? Why or why not?

3.   Read 1 Corinthians 15. The chapter begins discussing the resurrection of Christ. As foretold in God's holy word, Christ died, was buried, and on the third day He rose again. Then He appeared to many including, on one occasion, over 500 and as Paul wrote the words most of the 500 still lived, so the claim was subject to verification. Paul concludes the discussion explaining Christ's resurrection is essential to our faith saying, "If there is no resurrection of the dead, then Christ has not been raised; and if Christ has not been raised, then our proclamation has been in vain and your faith has been in vain" (1 Corinthians 15:13-14). He transitions to discuss the resurrection of the dead saying, "for as all die in Adam, so all will be made alive in Christ" (1 Corinthians 15:22), and then discusses the resurrection of the body. He discusses our physical existence and our spiritual existence and says, "Just as we have borne the image of the man of dust, we will also bear the image of the man of heaven" (1 Corinthians 15:49). The resurrection is fundamental to our faith, and through Christ Jesus we gain His likeness and His resurrection. How is the imprint of His image connected with His resurrection?

4.   Read Colossians 3:1-17. Paul describes new life in Christ Jesus. As we are transformed in Christ, as a result of His holy transformation we should put away earthly desires and

emotions, and replace them with heavenly desires and emotions. As part of Paul's appeal he writes,

> But now you must get rid of all such things – anger, wrath, malice, slander, and abusive language from your mouth. Do not lie to one another, seeing that you have stripped off the old self with its practices and have clothed yourselves with the new self, which is being renewed in knowledge according to the image of its creator. Colossians 3:8-10

As an individual is transformed in the image of Christ Jesus, inward transformation should reveal itself through behavioral shifts. In what specific ways is this consistent with your experience?

North Shore, Oahu, Hawaii

5

Fear Not

"Do not fear, for I am with you, do not be afraid, for I am your God; I will strengthen you, I will help you, I will uphold you with my victorious right hand." Isaiah 41:10

"For this reason I remind you to rekindle the gift of God that is within you through the laying on of my hands; for God did not give us a spirit of cowardice, but rather a spirit of power and of love and of self-discipline." 2 Timothy 1:6-7

Our daily news is filled with evidence of evil and at times the world seems like a scary place. Folks executed while shopping for groceries. Others killed because they gathered to worship God. Others targeted for broadcasting their opinions. Frightening realities may trigger fear-filled responses, but God urges us to fear not, and Scripture provides many examples of God's people responding to worldly threats by boldly moving forward.

Peter and John were arrested for preaching the Gospel. While ordering their release, the judicial council told them to stop preaching. Peter and John rushed to gather with other believers and prayed that God would enable them to "speak [God's] word with great boldness" (Acts 4:29). As he preached, Paul was threatened time and time again, yet he continued to boldly proclaim the good news of Jesus Christ. Rather than cower in response to worldly threats, they responded with powerful boldness.

What is the key to faith like theirs?

God is really God. He is sovereign, He is really with us, and He showers us with His holy grace. When we struggle, when we doubt, when we succumb to fear, He calls out to remind us that He is truly God, is truly with us, truly loves us, and is working on our behalf. When we know in the depth of our souls that the statements are true, any fear we once felt should melt away and be replaced with a spirit of boldness; yet, as another example of the battle waged within us, in certain situations we still experience fear. Like the good Coach, good Teacher, or good Shepherd, God continues urging us to focus on Him, trust in Him, release fear and discover His power.

Scripture is filled with passages quoting God as He encourages both pillars of faith and ordinary people, urging them to release their fear because He is with them and acting on their behalf. God explains to Abram, "Do not be afraid. I am your shield, your very great reward" (Genesis 15:1). One night God appeared to Isaac saying, "I am the God of your father Abraham. Do not be afraid for I am with you…" (Genesis 26:24). As Jacob traveled to Egypt, God spoke to him saying, "I am God, the God of your father. Do not be afraid to go down to Egypt for I will make you into a great nation there" (Genesis 46:3). God spoke through Isaiah saying, "So do not fear, for I am with you; do not be dismayed, for I am your God" (Isaiah 41:10).

Over and over God urges us to relinquish fear because He is really here, really with us and really acting on our behalf. In a very similar fashion, Matthew concludes the gospel bearing his name with Jesus proclaiming, "And surely I am with you always, to the very end of the age" (Matthew 28:20). Jesus drops the mic after assuring us of His continuous presence. He is and always will be God with us.

Please know in your heart, in the depths of your soul that God is really God, He is truly all-powerful, He truly loves you, He is acting on your behalf, and He is urging you to replace fear with the boldness of His power. May God's glory continue to be revealed through you.

THOUGHTS TO CONSIDER

1.   Is fear ever good? At a younger age I was on a quest to hike each mountain in Colorado taller than 14,000 feet. At certain points along each hike I had to assess how to proceed safely and whether it was possible to do so. On a couple, very near

the top, after hiking for hours, with the goal fifty or hundred feet away, I mean it was right there, a cliff separated me from the goal, and I considered the prospect of slipping and falling and incurring serious injury so far from people without any way of even attempting to seek help, and rather than attempting to scale the cliff without proper equipment, I chose to turn around and descend the mountain. Fear of bodily harm prevented me from moving forward. Similarly, fear prevents me from walking across a busy highway, swimming in the Gulf when sharks are in the area, standing outside during a lightning storm, and engaging in all sorts of other dangerous activities. In certain situations, fear reminds me of my responsibility to make prudent choices, to assess the situation and be safe. In other situations, fear is an indication that we fail to trust God. What distinguishes the two? What separates good fear from bad fear? A wise man once told me to focus on the things within my control and to leave the rest to God.

2. Read Acts 4. Before considering chapter 4 directly, please turn to Acts 23:8. Paul is once again on trial before the council, this time he is accused of false teaching and defiling the temple. While presenting his defense, he raises the matter of resurrection, stating "I am on trial concerning the hope of the resurrection of the dead" (Acts 23:6), and that statement divided the council because Pharisees believe in the resurrection, angels and spirit, but Sadducees do not. So we see division between Jewish denominations on theological matters.

With that, let's go back to chapter 4. The chapter begins with Peter and John preaching in the temple about Jesus, His resurrection, and "that in Jesus there is resurrection of the dead" (Acts 4:2). The Sadducees are "much annoyed" with them and they arrest Peter and John (see Acts 4:1-2). The following day, Peter and John appear before the council with a man they had healed, and the council orders them to stop speaking or teaching "at all in the name of Jesus" (Acts 4:18). Peter and John answer, "Whether it is right in God's sight to listen to you rather than to God, you must judge; for we cannot keep from speaking about what we have seen and heard" (Acts 4:19-20).

The council releases them, and they go to their friends and together they all pray. The prayer ends as follows:

> "And now, Lord, look at their threats, and grant to your servants to speak your word with all boldness, while you stretch out your hand to heal, and signs and wonders are performed through the name of your holy servant Jesus." When they had prayed, the place in which they were gathered together was shaken; and they were all filled with the Holy Spirit and spoke the word of God with boldness. Acts 4:29-31

In response to threats from people in power who ordered them to stop preaching the name of Jesus, they prayed asking God to grant them boldness to speak His holy word and they asked God to heal, and to perform signs and wonders through Jesus' holy name. In response to their prayer, the building shook and they were filled anew with the Holy Spirit.

Given the choice of following God or humans, they chose God and they asked God to grant them boldness. Describe a time you were forced to make a decision like that. What did you do? If you have never been in a situation like that, try to imagine how you would feel and how you would respond.

3.   Read Genesis 15. In chapter 14 Abram rescued Lot, his servants and possessions from captivity in Dan. On his way back home, Abram met the King of Sodom and the priest of God Most High, Melchizedek of Salem. They shared bread and wine, praised God and Abram gave Melchizedek one tenth of the plunder (see Genesis 14:17-24). After this, God appeared to Abram in a dream saying, "Do not be afraid, Abram, I am your shield; your reward shall be very great" (Genesis 15:1). Why did God begin the conversation by discussing fear? What was Abram's reward? In what ways might fear have hindered Abram's ability to receive the reward?

Jenny Creek, Colorado

6

PATIENCE AND URGENCY

"BE STILL, AND KNOW THAT I AM GOD! I AM EXALTED AMONG THE NATIONS, I AM EXALTED IN THE EARTH." PSALM 46:10

NOW THE ELEVEN DISCIPLES WENT TO GALILEE, TO THE MOUNTAIN TO WHICH JESUS HAD DIRECTED THEM. WHEN THEY SAW HIM, THEY WORSHIPED HIM; BUT SOME DOUBTED. AND JESUS CAME AND SAID TO THEM, "ALL AUTHORITY IN HEAVEN AND ON EARTH HAS BEEN GIVEN TO ME. GO THEREFORE AND MAKE DISCIPLES OF ALL NATIONS, BAPTIZING THEM IN THE NAME OF THE FATHER AND OF THE SON AND OF THE HOLY SPIRIT, AND TEACHING THEM TO OBEY EVERYTHING THAT I HAVE COMMANDED YOU. AND REMEMBER, I AM WITH YOU ALWAYS, TO THE END OF THE AGE." MATTHEW 28:16-20

Jesus teaches us to be patient as we grow in relationship with Him, and to act with urgency. Patience and urgency may not readily fit together in our minds, yet He calls us to patient preparation and urgent action.

Jesus planned to be in Jerusalem for Passover. He knew the time had come for Him to give Himself up for us that weekend – He had an appointment with destiny – and He knew God's glory would be revealed through it all. Two days before Passover He visited the temple before walking to the Mount of Olives, where He sat and taught the disciples through the long discourse filling Matthew chapters 24 & 25.

Jesus explains that He will return, discusses vigilant preparation and diligent faith, and teaches about final judgment. Throughout the teaching Jesus warns His listeners. He warns that people will seek to deceive, teaching us that we must learn God's holy word and seek the benefit of His discerning Spirit to guard against deception; and He urges us to stay vigilant as we anticipate His return. Jesus peppers the statements with words like "watch out … keep watch … be ready … keep watch …" (see Matthew 24:4, 42, 44; 25:13).

He describes a group of bridesmaids waiting to join a wedding celebration. The ones who are prepared and who act when the opportunity arises are allowed to enter the party. Others are excluded – they are unable to act because they failed to prepare. It is a parable about being prepared, being still and alert, seeing opportunities and, when the time arises, acting urgently.

Spiritual preparation requires intentional focus on Him. Keeping watch requires being still while observing the world around us. They each require discipline, focus and patience.

"Be ready ... keep watch." The teaching is reminiscent of the psalm in which God instructs us, "Be still, and know that I am God!" (Psalm 46:10).

After the Passover meal, Jesus surrenders to guards and gives His life for us. After His resurrection, He appears for forty days teaching the disciples and many others, and then He ascends to heaven. As Jesus prepares to ascend, Matthew records Jesus' final words. As part of the final paragraph of Matthew's gospel, Jesus says, "Go therefore and make disciples of all nations" (Matthew 28:19). Jesus orders His disciples to "Go ... and make...." He orders urgent action.

How are we to "Be still" and "Go"?

We are called to patiently practice our spiritual disciplines, to enjoy our stillness with Him and allow our relationship with Christ to grow. We are called to patiently prepare our spiritual beings so that, when opportunities arise, we are able to see them and are ready to act with urgency. We meditate on Scripture, pray, seek God, and open ourselves to be transformed to His image, so that we have eyes to see, ears to hear, and His power and courage to act.

We patiently prepare and urgently act. May God's perfect discerning Spirit fill you, transform you and make you whole.

Thoughts to Consider

1. Read Psalm 46. The psalm begins saying, "God is our refuge and strength, a very present help in trouble. Therefore we will not fear, though the earth should change, though the mountains shake in the heart of the sea; though its waters roar and foam, though the mountains tremble with its tumult" (Psalm 46:1-3). The world continuously changes; even things that seem stable, like mountains, continuously change; however, God is constant. He does not fluctuate. He does not change and He is the perfect refuge and source of strength. How does certainty in God build the foundation for being still and exalting God among the nations?

2. Robert Alter translates the passage first set forth above as, "Let go, and know that I am God. I loom among the nations, I loom upon earth" (Psalm 46:11).[1] "Be still" becomes "Let go." In the context of warfare, it suggests a command to relax, stop striving, stop fighting and allow God to serve as the fortress that He is. And "exalted" becomes "loom," which transforms the image of being lifted up in praise to a ghostly, shadowy figure hovering in the fog. God is everywhere, He sees all and knows all, He is sovereign, He is in control. Does the combination of translations help you better understand God's holy word? Does this understanding inspire you to behave differently than the passage as translated first above? How so?

3. Read John 13 &15. Jesus says, "I give you a new commandment, that you love one another. Just as I have loved you, you also should love one another. By this everyone will know that you are my disciples, if you have love for one another" (John 13:34-35). A little while later He says, "This is my com-

mandment, that you love one another as I have loved you. No one has greater love than this, to lay down one's life for one's friends" (John 15:12-13). If disciples of Christ Jesus are people who follow Him and who love just as Jesus loves, and if He calls His disciples to "go and make disciples of all nations," can you call yourself His disciple? If not, what specific things should you change?

4. Read Matthew 25. Jesus describes the judgment that will take place when He returns. All nations will be gathered. Jesus will separate goats and sheep based on who helped people in need (see Matthew 25:31-46). How does this passage influence your view of serving as a disciple of Christ Jesus, and your view of those in need you regularly encounter? Read in the context of Matthew 28, doesn't this make you want to go to everyone in the world to tell them about Christ Jesus and His love, and to encourage them to truly be His disciples with His love flowing through them? While that may seem like an unlikely or impossible goal (or possibly not in this digital age), what might a more realistic goal be for you today, tomorrow, this year?

Uncompahgre Peak, Colorado

7

TIME IS OF THE ESSENCE

> BUT THIS IS WHY I HAVE LET YOU LIVE: TO SHOW YOU MY POWER, AND TO MAKE MY NAME RESOUND THROUGH ALL THE EARTH. EXODUS 9:16

> REJOICE ALWAYS, PRAY WITHOUT CEASING, GIVE THANKS IN ALL CIRCUMSTANCES; FOR THIS IS THE WILL OF GOD IN CHRIST JESUS FOR YOU. I THESSALONIANS 5:16-18

> KEEP AWAKE THEREFORE, FOR YOU DO NOT KNOW ON WHAT DAY YOUR LORD IS COMING. MATTHEW 24:42

Time is one of the elements distinguishing our existence from God's. While God is spirit, we are part physical. As such, we are part of His glorious creation bound by time and space, and time – each day, each hour, each breath – is a gift from God. He showers us with His holy grace, He surrounds us with His love, He designs each of us with a purpose, and He calls us into His glorious service.

Time is a precious gift. We are capable of living one moment at a time – no more and no less – and we do not know how many moments on earth we will have, but we know that this moment is a glorious gift. I urge you to pray, "Father, how are you calling me to use this moment, this hour, this day?"

God invites us to live continuously in a state of spiritual communion with Him. At times we sense God urging us to enjoy Sabbath rest, while at other times He presents the opportunity to act urgently on His behalf, allowing His light to flow through us illuminating darkness. Life becomes a mosaic of prayerful communion, Sabbath rest and urgent action.

This should be true while we are out living in the world. Jesus calls us to be salt and light (Matthew 5:13-16). He calls us to go and make disciples (Matthew 28:19). He calls us to serve other people in the world. He calls us to action by placing opportunities to serve along our daily walk. If your workplace seems dark, fill it with light. If you frequently encounter angry people, shower them with love. When you encounter people in need, help as you are able.

For reasons I struggle to comprehend, He employs people to achieve His purposes on earth. God could have snapped His spiritual fingers and delivered His people from slavery in Egypt, but He chose to employ Moses as His servant. And so it is with each of us each day. He designed you for a purpose. Through relationship with Christ Jesus, through the spiritual transformation available in Him, by dwelling in Him and living His purpose, we discover wholeness.

Time is of the essence. May you have eyes to see, ears to hear, and a heart that is fertile soil for His seed to grow.

Thoughts to Consider

1. God uses His people who seek Him into His glorious service. He also reveals His glory through people with hardened hearts. In the first passage above, God sends Moses to speak God's words to Pharaoh. Here is the full paragraph:

> Then the Lord said to Moses, "Rise up early in the morning and present yourself before Pharaoh, and say to him, 'Thus says the Lord, the God of the Hebrews: Let my people go, so that they may worship me. For this time I will send all my plagues upon you yourself, and upon your officials, and upon your people, so that you may know that there is no one like me in all the earth. For by now I could have stretched out my hand and struck you and your people with pestilence, and you would have been cut off from the earth. But this is why I have let you live: to show you my power, and to make my name resound through all the earth. You are still exalting yourself against my people, and will not let them go. Tomorrow at this time I will cause the heaviest hail to fall that has ever fallen in Egypt from the day it was founded until now. Send, therefore, and have your livestock and everything that you have in the open field brought to a secure place; every human or animal that is

> in the open field and is not brought under shelter will die when the hail comes down upon them.'" Those officials of Pharaoh who feared the word of the Lord hurried their slaves and livestock off to a secure place. Those who did not regard the word of the Lord left their slaves and livestock in the open field. Exodus 9:13-21

God is revealing who He is to Pharaoh, to the people of Egypt, to all the earth, and also to Moses and the Israelites. And He uses Pharaoh, hardened heart and all, as a means through which He reveals His power and sovereign authority. He easily could have killed Pharaoh and all of Egypt, "But this is why I have let you live: to show you my power, and to make my name resound through all the earth" (Exodus 9:16). We do not need to be perfectly holy for God to employ us into His glorious service. How might God be positioning you to reveal His glory through you and your situation?

2. Read 1 Thessalonians 5. We do not know how much time we have, but we know the task before us. The chapter begins saying,

> Now concerning the times and the seasons, brothers and sisters, you do not need to have anything written to you. For you yourselves know very well that the day of the Lord will come like a thief in the night. 1 Thessalonians 5:1-2

God's holy word continues urging us to live as children of the light, rejoicing, filled with peace, seeking God, praying all the time, and seeking His holiness. As you consider the brevity of life and the uncertainty of time remaining for each of us, what is your response to the exhortations in verses 12-25?

3. Read Matthew 24:36-44, Matthew 25:1-13 and Luke 21:34-38. Time and time again Jesus discusses the brevity of life and our uncertainty regarding the amount of time remaining. He urges us to be alert, be on guard, to watch out, to be ready. What does this mean to you? What steps are you taking to be ready? Is there anything in your life that you need to change? If so, what? What specific steps will you take this week to begin the process of change?

For the Praise of His Glory

Polihale Beach, Kauai, Hawaii

8

FREED FROM BONDAGE

THEN JESUS SAID TO THE JEWS WHO HAD BELIEVED IN HIM, "IF YOU CONTINUE IN MY WORD, YOU ARE TRULY MY DISCIPLES; AND YOU WILL KNOW THE TRUTH, AND THE TRUTH WILL MAKE YOU FREE." JOHN 8:31-32

BUT MOSES SAID TO THE PEOPLE, "DO NOT BE AFRAID, STAND FIRM, AND SEE THE DELIVERANCE THAT THE LORD WILL ACCOMPLISH FOR YOU TODAY; FOR THE EGYPTIANS WHOM YOU SEE TODAY YOU SHALL NEVER SEE AGAIN. THE LORD WILL FIGHT FOR YOU, AND YOU HAVE ONLY TO KEEP STILL." EXODUS 14:13-14

THE ISRAELITES SAID TO THEM, "IF ONLY WE HAD DIED BY THE HAND OF THE LORD IN THE LAND OF EGYPT, WHEN WE SAT BY THE FLESHPOTS AND ATE OUR FILL OF BREAD; FOR YOU HAVE BROUGHT US OUT INTO THIS WILDERNESS TO KILL THIS WHOLE ASSEMBLY WITH HUNGER." EXODUS 16:3

After God delivers you, do not go back to bondage. The new path charted for you by God may not be easy, in fact, it may be extremely difficult, but the journey along His path provides wholeness and it leads to His glory. Is God delivering you from sickness, from addiction, from associations with bad influences, from pornography, from some other bondage? After He delivers you, continue seeking Him. Stay on the path of freedom. Avoid the temptation of returning to bondage.

I recently had the privilege of walking in the Sinai desert on the land of the Exodus. Before experiencing the land, I read Exodus 14 describe God miraculously delivering the Israelites from slavery and then, at chapter 16, only six weeks later, the former slaves complained about the difficulties of their new path and longed to return to their old life. I wondered how anyone could desire slavery over freedom. But as I walked the dry, rocky, lifeless landscape, I wondered how anyone could survive there for six weeks, how anyone could walk across the rock wearing Exodus-era footwear, and how they made it six weeks before grumbling. I suddenly imagined how difficult their new path must have been. It was the path leading to the Promised Land, to God's glory, to a whole life, but it was not an easy path.

Norman was stabbed thirteen times during a fight. As doctors and nurses prepped him for surgery, they urged him to sign a form authorizing them to remove his organs for donation. They were convinced that Norman would soon die and they imagined that some good might come out of his tragic loss. Norman prayed and then he refused their request. He asked God to give him his life back and he surrendered himself to Christ.

As he recovered at home, the challenges of living a new life in Christ while surrounded by the same old influences quickly became apparent. It would have been much easier for him to return to the path of darkness, but he continued seeking God and God continued giving him strength and wholeness as he traveled the new path. He soon became a beacon of light in the darkness surrounding him, and he continues to minister to everyone he encounters.

While the stories may suggest that deliverance is a once-in-a-lifetime event, it is not. We each need deliverance continuously. As we seek God, obstacles enter our life creating barriers between us and Him, trapping us and hindering our progression along His path. Each experience, each situation, each difficultly, each deliverance prepares us to serve Him in a unique new way.

After God delivers you, do not go back to bondage; continue on God's path to freedom, wholeness and satisfaction.

THOUGHTS TO CONSIDER

1.   Read Galatians 5. Galatians 5:1 says, "For freedom Christ has set us free. Stand firm, therefore, and do not submit again to a yoke of slavery." A few paragraphs later God's holy word says,

> Live by the Spirit, I say, and do not gratify the desires of the flesh. For what the flesh desires is opposed to the Spirit, and what the Spirit desires is opposed to the flesh; for these are opposed to each other, to prevent you from doing what you want. Galatians 5:16-17

What has Christ Jesus freed you from? What held you hostage in your former life? God urges you to avoid falling into the trap again – "Do not submit again to a yoke of slavery."

2.   Read 2 Corinthians 3. The Holy Spirit gives life (see 2 Corinthians 3:6) and "the Lord is the Spirit, and where the Spirit of the Lord is, there is freedom" (2 Corinthians 3:17). Consider your life before meeting Christ Jesus. How is your life different now? What specific activities once gave you pleasure that no longer seem attractive? What specific activities are clearly inconsistent with your new life in Christ, yet they continue to entice you? How do you battle the temptation? In what specific ways do you engage Jesus to help you fight the fight?

3.   Read 1 Peter 2. Peter describes our relationship with Jesus as freeing and healing saying:

> When he was abused, he did not return abuse; when he suffered, he did not threaten; but he entrusted himself to the one who judges justly. He himself bore our sins in his body on the cross, so that, free from sins, we might live for righteousness; by his wounds you have been healed. For you were going astray like sheep, but now you have returned to the shepherd and guardian of your souls. 1 Peter 2:23-25

How does this passage compliment the passages set forth above?

4.   Read Exodus 14-16. As the story of the miraculous Red Sea crossing begins, God says the events would happen to glorify God and so that "the Egyptians shall know that I am the Lord" (Exodus 14:4). God miraculously freed the Israelites and destroyed their captors, and six weeks later we see the Israelites complaining about the difficulties they faced in the wilderness. How did God respond to their complaints? He provided for them. He is full of mercy and He provided manna, quail and water. God's glory is revealed through the parting of the sea and their miraculous deliverance. His glory is also revealed through His subsequent provision. What parallels exist in your life? How has God delivered you from bondage? After you were delivered, what difficulties did you face? How did God provide? How does He continue to provide for you? How have you personally experienced God's mercy?

Fiery Furnace, Utah

9

BECOMING DESENSITIZED

> SO GOD CREATED HUMANKIND IN HIS OWN IMAGE, IN THE IMAGE OF GOD HE CREATED THEM; MALE AND FEMALE HE CREATED THEM. GENESIS 1:27

> AH, YOU WHO CALL EVIL GOOD AND GOOD EVIL, WHO PUT DARKNESS FOR LIGHT AND LIGHT FOR DARKNESS, WHO PUT BITTER FOR SWEET AND SWEET FOR BITTER! AH, YOU WHO ARE WISE IN YOUR OWN EYES, AND SHREWD IN YOUR OWN SIGHT! ISAIAH 5:20-21

During a recent prayer meeting, as we each prayed individually, the word "desensitized" kept entering my thoughts. I discussed the experience with others and as I drove home the radio broadcast an interview discussing the desensitization of our society. In light of our prayer time, I was more attentive to the discussion than usual. Shortly after that, a news program included a story about a recent study focusing on the many impacts pornography is having on our culture.

Have we become desensitized to the darkness surrounding us? Since exposure to heightened forms of darkness causes darkness to seem normal, are we gradually beginning to accept darkness as the standard? It begins with small steps. An innocent-sounding video game exposes participants to the thought of taking a life without consequence or remorse, and while it may only be a game played in a virtual realm, the experience alters the mind. The bell cannot be unrung. The experience cannot be taken back and once that first step seems innocent, many desire heightened exposure to the stimulus and venture deeper into the virtual darkness. Eventually, as the mind is gradually altered, death and the thought of taking a life is no longer horrific or revolting, and it may be difficult to restrict blurred lines of moral behavior to the virtual realm.

I recently saw a movie depicting Times Square in the 1970's. It was a dark place. Homeless men slept on sidewalks, addicts crouched in corners shooting up, prostitutes walked the streets, pimps and drug dealers watched over the scene like lords fighting to control their turf. It was dark and dramatic. I believe the creators did their best to ensure that every detail accurately depicted the time and place, and I was struck by how tame the prostitutes were dressed compared to current norms. They were walking the streets soliciting clients in clothing that, by 1970's standards would have been extremely suggestive and inappropriate, yet their clothing was far less revealing than many wear out to dinner with friends today. What would have been shocking forty years ago has gradually become tame. Gradually, as a society we have become desensitized to the public display of exposed flesh.

We saw some of the impact of this transition through the #metoo movement, which revealed the tendency of some people in power to treat subordinates as objects available for their personal pleasure. In some parts of our society, the lines defining moral behavior have become blurred, possibly aided by the requirement of fashion and marketing to continuously push the envelope and discover new ways to capture attention, the influence of the multi-billion-dollar porn industry that encourages its viewers to see people as objects for personal pleasure, and our gradual desensitization to it.

I could easily have described countless other avenues through which we are being directed toward darkness and told the darkness is good. Each alters our soul, changes the way we view other people, changes our attitude toward moral norms and fundamentally alters our relationships.

As we grow in Christ, as we seek Him, as we seek to conform to His likeness, we gradually gain eyes to see as He sees. We gradually see other people as beings created in God's image whom He loves. If we see God's holy image revealed through other people we will not be able to see them as objects, we will not be able to see ourselves as superior to them, we will not be able to use them for our personal pleasure, and we will be revolted by killing, even in the virtual realm.

"Ah, you who call evil good and good evil, who put darkness for light and light for darkness, who put bitter for sweet and sweet for bitter! Ah, you who are wise in your own eyes, and shrewd in your own sight!" (Isaiah 5:20-21).

May God's glory fill you, flow through you, and may you have eyes to see others as beings created in His image whom He loves.

Thoughts to Consider

1. Read Romans 1. After offering a prayer of thanksgiving and discussing the power of the gospel, Paul discusses humanity's wickedness. In that discussion he writes:

> So they are without excuse; for though they knew God, they did not honor him as God or give thanks to him, but they became futile in their thinking, and their senseless minds were darkened. Claiming to be wise, they became fools; and they exchanged the glory of the immortal God for images resembling a mortal human being or birds or four-footed animals or reptiles. Romans 1:20-23

They had reason to know God, but they chose not to honor Him as God and they chose not to give thanks to Him. As a result, their minds were darkened and they exchanged God's glory for idols. Do the words written approximately 2,000 years ago continue to be relevant today? If so, in what way? What specific current events cause you to believe the words are relevant today?

2. Read Isaiah 5:8-23. God indicts people for pursuing personal pleasure while treating others with injustice. He con-

demns wealthy people for amassing real estate and excluding people who cannot afford it, and denounces those who choose to pursue personal pleasure day and night rather than pursuing God. He indicts humanity for refusing to accept God's truth while attempting to create their own rules, which at its heart demonstrates their desire to be god, repeating the original sin. God spoke these words thousands of years ago through Isaiah. Do you see evidence of the passage's relevance today? If so, what specifically is happening that mirrors God's statements?

3. Read Malachi 2. God speaks a similar message through the prophet Malachi. A portion of the passage says:

> You have wearied the Lord with your words. Yet you say, "How have we wearied him?" By saying, "All who do evil are good in the sight of the Lord, and he delights in them." Or by asking, "Where is the God of justice?" Malachi 2:17

4. In what specific ways have you become desensitized to darkness? In what specific ways have you begun to accept evil as good? If you are becoming desensitized, what specific steps will you take to resolve the situation?

5. Read Genesis 1. The passage first set forth above tells us that humans are created in God's holy image. Does this truth make you see yourself differently? Does it cause you to see people you encounter differently? How so?

10

TRANSFORMED INTO CHRIST'S IMAGE

> AND ALL OF US, WITH UNVEILED FACES, SEEING THE GLORY OF THE LORD AS THOUGH REFLECTED IN A MIRROR, ARE BEING TRANSFORMED INTO THE SAME IMAGE FROM ONE DEGREE OF GLORY TO ANOTHER; FOR THIS COMES FROM THE LORD, THE SPIRIT. 2 CORINTHIANS 3:18

As we contemplate the Lord's glory we are being transformed into His image. We are *being transformed*. The process of sanctification is gradual.

My dear friend shared her testimony and, because it illustrates this point, gave me permission to share it with you. She said that early in her marriage she prayed for God to change her husband. She prayed and prayed for God to work in his life so that he might be transformed into the person she imagined he should be. She prayed for her husband to conform to her wishes, a self-centered prayer disguised as intercession.

Massadona, Colorado

For months she prayed urgently, desperately. One day she experienced God's voice speaking directly to her spirit. He told her that she needed to focus on herself, that she needed to be transformed into Christ's image to enable her to see God's image in other people. As she conveyed the story, she revealed how the revelation stunned her. It shook her at her core and drove her to her knees in repentance.

Her prayer changed. She prayed that she might be transformed into Christ's image, and she regained eyes to see the good qualities in her husband. Rather than focusing on the negative, she saw his good qualities in a new light and this changed her entire demeanor toward him and their relationship changed and gradually, in response to the love surrounding him, he changed.

We are called to pray without ceasing. We are called to intercede for others in prayer. We are even called to pray for our enemies, but if we pray for other people to be conformed to the people we imagine they should be – a self-centered prayer disguised as intercession – we might want to reconsider our prayer, focusing on our need for transformation instead.

We each need to unveil our face before the Lord. We need to approach Him with absolute transparency and humility as we contemplate His glory, praying that we might be transformed into His image. May God's glory shine upon you, may His indwelling Spirit make you whole, may His love flow through you, may you have eyes to see other people as beings created in God's image.

Thoughts to Consider

1. Read John 17. After the Last Supper and before surrendering Himself for us, Jesus prays this amazing chapter-long prayer recorded as John 17. He prays for Himself, He prays for the disciples, and then He prays for us, believers who would come to know Him through the disciples' words. As He prays for us He says,

> As you, Father, are in me and I am in you, may they also be in us, so that the world may believe that you have sent me. The glory that you have given me I have given them, so that they may be one, as we are one, I in them and you in me, that they may become completely one, so that the world may know that you have sent me and have loved them even as you have loved me. John 17:21-23

Christ Jesus gives us the glory that God gave Him. Wow! That is amazing! Why would He possibly do that? He does that so that we might be one in the same way the Holy Trinity is one – one God in three persons – so that the world will know that Jesus is Lord. Jesus gives us glory to glorify God. How do you respond to that truth? Does it cause you to see your relationship with Christ Jesus through different eyes?

2. Read Romans 8. The chapter is a remarkable distillation of the gospel. In it, Paul writes:

> We know that all things work together for good for those who love God, who are called according to his

> purpose. For those whom he foreknew he also predestined to be conformed to the image of his Son, in order that he might be the firstborn within a large family. And those whom he predestined he also called; and those whom he called he also justified; and those whom he justified he also glorified. Romans 8:28-30

People who love God are called according to His purpose and are being conformed to the image of Christ Jesus. Through His Holy Spirit, He dwells within you. You are His holy temple. How do you respond to these truths?

3. Read Romans 12. After discussing theology, Paul transitions to discuss Christian life in practice writing,

> I appeal to you therefore, brothers and sisters, by the mercies of God, to present your bodies as a living sacrifice, holy and acceptable to God, which is your spiritual worship. Do not be conformed to this world, but be transformed by the renewing of your minds, so that you may discern what is the will of God – what is good and acceptable and perfect. Romans 12:1-2

Under the Law of Moses, sacrificial offerings were mandated to atone for sin. As followers of Christ, we offer ourselves to Him as holy, living sacrifices. But we are not holy. Only God is holy. So how might we do that? We continue progressing toward the image of Christ Jesus by allowing Him to transform our spirits and minds. How do you position yourself to allow your transformation?

4. Read Philippians 2:1-11. "Let the same mind be in you

that was in Christ Jesus..." (Philippians 2:5). How might we possibly do that? The only way is through Christ Jesus with His indwelling Holy Spirit transforming our spirits, souls and minds.

5.   As Christ Jesus transforms our souls, our worldview changes and the way we see others changes. God's holy word says,

> From now on, therefore, we regard no one from a human point of view; even though we once knew Christ from a human point of view, we know him no longer in that way. So if anyone is in Christ, there is a new creation: everything old has passed away; see, everything has become new! 2 Corinthians 5:16-17

Is this consistent with your experience?

For the Praise of His Glory

Hilton Head Island, South Carolina

11

THE REDEEMER AND THE REDEEMED

But now, apart from law, the righteousness of God has been disclosed, and is attested by the law and the prophets, the righteousness of God through faith in Jesus Christ for all who believe. For there is no distinction, since all have sinned and fall short of the glory of God; they are now justified by his grace as a gift, through the redemption that is in Christ Jesus, whom God put forward as a sacrifice of atonement by his blood, effective through faith. He did this to show his righteousness, because in his divine forbearance he had passed over the sins previously committed; it was to prove at the present time that he himself is righteous and that he justifies the one who has faith in Jesus. Romans 3:21-26

In [Jesus Christ] we have redemption through his blood, the forgiveness of our trespasses, according to the riches of his grace that

HE LAVISHED ON US. EPHESIANS 1:7-8

Why do we sometimes struggle accepting that people closest to us, the ones who caused us personal anguish, have been redeemed?

We live in a realm characterized by tremendous contrast. We see evidence of evil around us, yet we also see evidence of God's glory revealed through His creation, through loving relationships, through compassionate interaction, through His people. God's light shining through His people erases darkness in the world. We know this and we know that redemption is available to everyone through Jesus Christ. This drives us to spread the Gospel to everyone willing to listen, to support missionaries in foreign countries, to send mission teams across the globe, to worship outside the walls of our church building, to minister to inmates, and so much more.

No one is beyond God's holy grace. Redemption is available to everyone. Through faith in Jesus Christ, people who have done horrific things are redeemed, cleansed, set free, saved … transformed. No matter what you have done, God loves you, He desires relationship with you, He wants to commune with you. Through Jesus Christ, redemption is available to everyone.

Paul's story clearly depicts this. He persecuted Christians. He oversaw the group who murdered Stephen by stoning because Stephen dared to preach the Gospel, yet Paul met Jesus and was redeemed. He changed immediately and his actions reflected his new life in Jesus Christ. Paul writes,

> For I am the least of the apostles, unfit to be called an apostle, because I persecuted the church of God. But by the grace of God I am what I am, and his grace toward me has not been in vain. On the contrary, I worked harder than any of them – though it was not I, but the grace of God that is with me. 1 Corinthians 15:9-10

Intellectually we understand that murderers, rapists, terrorists are candidates for redemption. If we believe Jesus Christ offers redemption to everyone, why is it difficult to accept that people closest to us, the ones who caused us personal anguish, may also be redeemed?

May God fill you with His Spirit of forgiveness, may He transform you fully, may He give you eyes to see fellow recipients of His holy, redemptive grace as brothers and sisters in Christ. May your relationships be characterized by God's light, life and love, and may the bonds of unity, trust and fellowship be renewed.

Thoughts to Consider

1. The passage first set forth above provides the following. God's holy grace is a gift. We can never earn it. He offers justification through the redemption that is in Christ Jesus, which is effective through faith. Please pause and read that again. Faith,

redemption and justification merge through Christ Jesus.

If salvation is effective through faith, does that mean that we earn it by our faithfulness? Absolutely not! Faith is a gift from God. Faith is available by God's holy grace. Addressing this question, God's holy word says,

> But God, who is rich in mercy, out of the great love with which he loved us even when we were dead through our trespasses, made us alive together with Christ – by grace you have been saved – and raised us up with him and seated us with him in the heavenly places in Christ Jesus, so that in the ages to come he might show the immeasurable riches of his grace in kindness toward us in Christ Jesus. For by grace you have been saved through faith, and this is not your own doing; it is the gift of God – not the result of works, so that no one may boast. For we are what he has made us, created in Christ Jesus for good works, which God prepared beforehand to be our way of life. Ephesians 2:4-10

We are saved by grace through Christ Jesus effective by faith. How does that influence your thinking?

2. Read Colossians 1. Paul prays for his brothers and sisters in Colossae. As part of his prayer he says,

> May you be made strong with all the strength that comes from his glorious power, and may you be prepared to endure everything with patience, while joyfully giving thanks to the Father, who has enabled you to share in the inheritance of the saints in the light. He has res-

cued us from the power of darkness and transferred us into the kingdom of his beloved Son, in whom we have redemption, the forgiveness of sins. Colossians 1:11-14

Some focus on redemption and forgiveness exclusively as a ticket to heaven granting entry after a person breathes their last breath on earth; however, God's holy word includes amazing promises of new life to be enjoyed while we continue living here on earth. We have redemption, the forgiveness of sins, in Christ Jesus. We have been rescued from the power of darkness and delivered to the kingdom of God. He gives us His power and strength enabling us to endure everything with patience. Does Paul's prayer in Colossians influence your view of redemption? How so?

3. What prerequisites exist before a person is qualified to receive redemption through Christ Jesus? Nothing except faith in Him. Redemption is available to everyone who believes making it incredibly inclusive. Everyone is invited.

Early in the life of the church, leaders met in Jerusalem to discuss whether people needed to be in good standing in the Jewish church as a prerequisite to being considered a Christian. Peter and Paul had been ministering to Gentiles across the region of Roman occupation and they experienced Gentiles being filled with the Holy Spirit and transformed in spirit, soul and action, causing them to know with certainty that Jewishness was not a prerequisite. As they discussed the matter Peter said,

> "My brothers, you know that in the early days God made a choice among you, that I should be the one through whom the Gentiles would hear the message of the good

> news and become believers. And God, who knows the human heart, testified to them by giving them the Holy Spirit, just as he did to us; and in cleansing their hearts by faith he has made no distinction between them and us. Now therefore why are you putting God to the test by placing on the neck of the disciples a yoke that neither our ancestors nor we have been able to bear? On the contrary, we believe that we will be saved through the grace of the Lord Jesus, just as they will." Acts 15:7-11

Through God's holy grace we are saved by faith in Christ Jesus. Everyone is eligible to receive God's holy grace. No matter who your parents are, what you have done, how sinful your life has been, God loves you and redemption through Christ Jesus is available to you. Some struggle mightily to accept that truth while others struggle with the other side of it – the same redemption is available to people who caused you pain and suffering. Which is more difficult for you to accept? Why?

4. Read Isaiah 53. Through the prophets, God foretold the coming Messiah. In Isaiah 53, God lays out the gospel of redemption through Christ Jesus. The passage includes the following:

> All we like sheep have gone astray; we have all turned to our own way, and the Lord has laid on him the iniquity of us all.
>
> …
>
> Yet it was the will of the Lord to crush him with pain. When you make his life an offering for sin, he shall see his offspring, and shall prolong his days; through him the will of the Lord shall prosper. Out of his anguish

he shall see light; he shall find satisfaction through his knowledge. The righteous one, my servant, shall make many righteous, and he shall bear their iniquities. Isaiah 53:6 & 10-11

To some extent, apart from Christ Jesus, each human is separated from God. Everyone has strayed from God, turned away from God, sinned, committed iniquity. God placed our iniquity on Jesus, the perfect, sinless One. Do Old Testament messianic prophecies influence your acceptance of Jesus as the Christ? If they do, in what specific ways?

Zarlengo Ranch, Colorado

12

Joy of Giving

I rejoice in the Lord greatly that now at last you have revived your concern for me; indeed, you were concerned for me, but had no opportunity to show it. Not that I am referring to being in need; for I have learned to be content with whatever I have. I know what it is to have little, and I know what it is to have plenty. In any and all circumstances I have learned the secret of being well-fed and of going hungry, of having plenty and of being in need. I can do all things through him who strengthens me. In any case, it was kind of you to share my distress. You Philippians indeed know that in the early days of the gospel, when I left Macedonia, no church shared with me in the matter of giving and receiving, except you alone. For even when I was in Thessalonica, you sent me help for my needs more than once. Not that I seek the gift, but I seek the profit that accumulates to your account. Philippians 4:10-17

What tangible evidence reveals that you are growing in Christ?

While Paul was imprisoned in Rome his friend, Epaphroditus, visited delivering gifts from the church in Philippi. When Epaphroditus arrived, Paul rejoiced and as his friend prepared to return home, Paul wrote a letter for him to deliver to their friends in Philippi, which is preserved in the Bible as the book of Philippians.

Compared to thank you notes today, it is an odd thank you note. Paul explains that he is content in all situations, even living in chains with nothing. He is content while starving and content with plenty because he knows true spiritual fullness, the full life that comes through abiding in Jesus Christ. His contented state has nothing to do with the physical condition surrounding him and has everything to do with his spiritual abode. Paul discusses his contented state and explains that he did not want the gifts (did I mention it is a strange thank you note?), yet he rejoiced when he saw the gifts. At first glance, this makes no sense. If he did not want the gifts, why did they generate joy?

Paul felt joy, not because he wanted the stuff, but because the gifts were tangible evidence of the spiritual growth being experienced by his friends in Philippi. He felt joy because his friends received spiritual benefits associated with giving. Spiritual transformation creates the desire to give, and giving enhances spiritual transformation, so Paul rejoiced when he saw tangible evidence of his friends' spiritual condition.

Paul's response is similar to parents rejoicing when they see evidence of their child's development. The first word, first step, first personal decision to say no to harmful influences, personal decision to accept Christ Jesus as their person Lord and Savior, first job, first budget, first decision to lead a Bible study … as we see evidence of our children growing physically, intellectually and spiritually we rejoice. Paul rejoiced because he saw evidence of his children growing in faith and he knew they were receiving spiritual rewards.

Similarly, Jesus praised a widow for placing two small copper coins in the offering saying, "Truly I tell you, this poor widow has put in more than all of them; for all of them have contributed out of their abundance, but she out of her poverty has put in all she had to live on." (Luke 21:3-4). He lifted her up, not because the church needed the gift, but because the gift revealed the beautiful state of her spirit.

Paul recognized giving as an important spiritual discipline that, similar to worship, prayer, studying Scripture, self-examination, hospitality and other forms of spiritual discipline, is worthy of regular practice. He urged believers to give each week in proportion to their income (1 Corinthians 16:2). For Paul, the spiritual benefits associated with giving were so important that on his last missionary journey he traveled from church to church across what is now Greece and Turkey urging them to give gifts, even out of their poverty, to help their brothers and sisters in Jerusalem. The Holy Spirit told Paul that he would be arrested when he returned to Jerusalem but recognizing the importance of the task he carried on, and as promised, he was arrested while delivering the love offering. Giving is evidence of God's love flowing through us. It also generates spiritual growth, and for Paul, promoting the discipline of giving within the budding Christian community was worth risking his freedom.

While chained in Rome Paul writes, "Not that I seek the gift, but I seek the profit that accumulates to your account" (Philippians 4:17). He sees evidence of his friends' spiritual transformation and he desires that they continue growing in faith, advancing toward Christ, and gaining little-by-little the attributes of Christ's holy image.

God did not need their money and He does not need ours; He desires our hearts. What tangible evidence reveals that you are growing in Christ? What will you do today that causes Jesus to rejoice because of the beautiful state of your spirit?

May you know contentment in all situations. May your life be filled with tangible evidence of your giving spirit, your sacrifice and your Christ-like love. May the image of Jesus Christ continue to grow in you.

THOUGHTS TO CONSIDER

1.   Read Malachi 1:6-14. God speaks judgment through the prophet Malachi. God is angry with the priests because they are dishonoring Him by accepting sacrifices unworthy of being offered to Him, such as sick, lame or blind livestock. Under the Law of Moses, people offered sacrifices to God to atone

for their sins. They offered livestock, birds and grain to God, who is a spiritual being. Why did God ask His people to give Him gifts that He did not need and could not use? And if He could not use the gifts, why did it matter whether the gifts were blemished?

God desires our hearts. God wants us to choose Him and to desire relationship with Him. He knows we need food to survive – He created us that way. By asking His people to give back to Him that which they need to survive, He is asking them to demonstrate faith in a real and tangible way. And by asking that they give the most valuable portion of their holdings, He demands the honor, respect and reverence He deserves. What parallels do you see between the sacrificial system set forth in the Law of Moses and joyful giving today?

2. Read 2 Corinthians 9. Paul writes to his friends in Corinth, urging them to participate in the love offering he is collecting for the church in Jerusalem, but he asks for much more than simply their coins. He wants them to desire to give. He wants their giving to flow out of their spirits transformed through Christ. He wants them to give with a joyful heart, joyful through the indwelling Holy Spirit and happy because they are able to give. He says, "Each of you must give as you have made up your mind, not reluctantly or under compulsion, for God loves a cheerful giver" (2 Corinthians 9:7).

Consider your giving. Which gifts do you give out of a sense of obligation and which do you give because you really want to give? What creates the difference? How does your giving reveal your growth in Christ?

3.	Read Galatians 5. As the Holy Spirit fills us and transforms us, we take on increasingly more of Christ Jesus' image. God's holy word describes tangible evidence that we are being transformed to the image of Christ as "fruit of the Spirit" (Galatians 5:22). The full paragraph says:

> By contrast, the fruit of the Spirit is love, joy, peace, patience, kindness, generosity, faithfulness, gentleness, and self-control. There is no law against such things. And those who belong to Christ Jesus have crucified the flesh with its passions and desires. If we live by the Spirit, let us also be guided by the Spirit. Let us not become conceited, competing against one another, envying one another. Galatians 5:22-26

Joy and generosity are two of the attributes listed in the passage. Jesus demonstrated His love, kindness, generosity and faithfulness in many ways, including the time He washed the disciples' feet (see John 13). He revealed what the joy of giving looks like. As joy and generosity are two characteristics of fruit of the Holy Spirit and Jesus is the source of satisfaction, it makes sense that we would experience greater satisfaction from giving than receiving. Is that consistent with your experience?

Randy L Allen

Tuscaloosa, Alabama

13

JESUS' VOICE

> SO THE JEWS GATHERED AROUND HIM AND SAID TO HIM, "HOW LONG WILL YOU KEEP US IN SUSPENSE? IF YOU ARE THE MESSIAH, TELL US PLAINLY." JESUS ANSWERED, "I HAVE TOLD YOU, AND YOU DO NOT BELIEVE. THE WORKS THAT I DO IN MY FATHER'S NAME TESTIFY TO ME; BUT YOU DO NOT BELIEVE, BECAUSE YOU DO NOT BELONG TO MY SHEEP. MY SHEEP HEAR MY VOICE. I KNOW THEM, AND THEY FOLLOW ME." JOHN 10:24-27

Jesus explains that His sheep listen to His voice. A seemingly infinite variety of voices scream for our attention throughout each day – unread emails littering the inbox, continuous news alerts lighting up the phone, the constant ping of social media updates, work responsibilities, chores at home … the list goes on and on. With so many voices demanding our attention, do we hear Jesus, do we discern His voice from the clutter, do we listen to Him?

"My sheep hear my voice. I know them, and they follow me." As so often happens with Jesus' teaching, His simple sentence sends shock waves through my soul. Do I hear His voice? Am I really following Him?

Please don't get me wrong – I am not questioning my salvation or redemption. By faith, by belief, by accepting His holy gift of grace I have been cleansed and adopted as a child of God. I know this because God's Truth promises it. But I wonder whether I am continuing along the path leading to holiness. Am I allowing my relationship with Jesus Christ to grow, am I allowing Him to be my Shepherd, am I hearing His voice, listening to His voice, understanding it and following Him?

How do we go about hearing His voice? When I was young all the kids from the neighborhood gathered to play baseball, football, kickball or some other activity every afternoon. As each family's dinnertime approached, a specific signal was transmitted alerting each kid it was time to go home. For several the signal was a certain, unmistakable whistle. For others it was a mother's call. For one it was a loud bell. We each new our signal and when we heard it, no matter what was happening in the game, we went home. We each had ears to hear our parents' sound and when we heard the call we responded.

Similarly, we need ears to hear Jesus' voice. We need to experience His voice frequently so it becomes familiar, then we will be able to distinguish His voice from all the others. This takes time and relationship. Scripture is filled with His voice speaking to us. We have an amazing opportunity each day to spend time studying and mediating on His holy word – we have access to

Scripture and the freedom to commune with Him through it; to commune with Him in prayer, opening our spirits and souls to His holy presence; and to bask in His presence through public and private worship. Through the regular practice of these and other spiritual disciplines our relationship with Him grows, we progress along the path leading to Him, our ability to perceive His voice grows and we become conditioned to follow Him.

An infinite variety of voices scream for our attention. You are the Good Shepherd's sheep. You are redeemed. Your sins are forgiven. You are a child of God. With this wonderfully gracious, loving, hope-filled assurance in mind, simply allow Him to be your Shepherd. Focus on Jesus' voice, listen to Him and follow Him. May God's glory continue to be revealed through you.

Thoughts to Consider

1. Jesus says, "I have told you…." When and how did Jesus say He is the Messiah? When Jesus spoke with the Samaritan woman at the well, she mentioned the Messiah and Jesus said, "I am he, the one who is speaking to you" (John 4:26). So Jesus told her plainly that He is the Messiah, but religious leaders were not part of that conversation. When did He tell them?

In John chapter 5, Jesus speaks with religious leaders in Jerusalem and He explains that His words and actions proclaim that He is the Messiah. Religious leaders acknowledge that Jesus' claim of unique Sonship to the Father are claims that He is equivalent to

God (see John 5:18), and in verses 5:19-47 Jesus explains that He is the Son revealed through Scripture and through His miraculous signs and wonders. His statements include the following: "The works that the Father has given me to complete, the very works that I am doing, testify on my behalf that the Father has sent me" (John 5:36); "You search the scriptures because you think that in them you have eternal life; and it is they that testify on my behalf" (John 5:39); and "If you believed Moses, you would believe me, for he wrote about me" (John 5:46).

In terms His audience uniquely understood, Jesus claimed to be the Messiah. How did they respond? Did they believe? No. Scripture says, "For this reason the Jews were seeking all the more to kill him, because he was not only breaking the sabbath, but was also calling God his own Father, thereby making himself equal to God" (John 5:18).

For additional claims of Messiahship, see John 8:21-38, John 10:14-18 and John 17:5.

2. Jesus says, "Very truly, I tell you, the hour is coming, and is now here, when the dead will hear the voice of the Son of God, and those who hear will live" (John 5:25). Apart from Jesus, people are spiritually dead. Through Jesus we gain spiritual life, new life, abundant life, eternal life. Those who hear gain life.

3. Faith is a holy mystery. It begins with God, but we must respond. The passage first set forth above presents the holy mystery of God's initiating grace and our corresponding responsibility. Jesus explains that the religious leaders to whom He speaks at the time do not believe because they do not hear and they do not belong to His fold (John 10:25-27). However,

His sheep hear His voice and follow (John 10:27). The ability to hear depends on God's initiating grace, but we must choose to listen and follow. Pray for ears to hear and eyes to see. Continuously seek God. Continuously desire God. May you know Him wholly, fully and completely.

4.   Read John 6:35-51. Jesus says, "This is indeed the will of my Father, that all who see the Son and believe in him may have eternal life; and I will raise them up on the last day" (John 6:40). People who see and believe have eternal life. In the next breath Jesus says, "No one can come to me unless drawn by the Father who sent me; and I will raise that person up on the last day" (John 6:44). How do you react to this mysterious interplay between God's holy initiating grace and our responsibility to respond?

Randy L Allen

Hoosier Pass, Colorado

14

God's Plans for You

"For I know the plans I have for you," declares the Lord, "plans to prosper you and not to harm you, plans to give you hope and a future. Then you will call on me and come and pray to me, and I will listen to you. You will seek me and find me when you seek me with all your heart. I will be found by you," declares the Lord, "and will bring you back from captivity." Jeremiah 29:11-14 (NIV)

I want you to know, beloved, that what has happened to me has actually helped to spread the gospel, so that it has become known throughout the whole imperial guard and to everyone else that my imprisonment is for Christ; and most of the brothers and sisters, having been made confident in the Lord by my imprisonment, dare to speak the word with greater boldness and without

FEAR. PHILIPPIANS 1:12-14

Are you searching for your purpose in life? Seek God. Live for Jesus Christ. He is the source of satisfaction, the source of life abundant, and the source of your purpose.

God has plans for you. Isn't that amazing? Even more amazing, He plans for you to flourish, and if you allow Him, He will reveal His glory through your current situation. No matter how the world may seem to be crumbling around you, no matter what you have done, no matter what choices you have made, no matter how hopeless your situation may seem when viewed through your current perspective, God has plans for you. Stop for a moment and let that sink in. God created the universe by speaking; He is infinite with power beyond our ability to understand; He knows you, your needs, and your heart; He desires relationship with you; and He wants to fill you with His life, His love and His light. He wants to shine His light through you. He has plans for you.

Jeremiah wrote the first passage above to fellow Israelites who had been taken captive and transported to Babylon. He urged them to settle in Babylon, to make the place their home and to worship, praise and seek God during their time of captivity because God was preparing them for the future. Why should we praise God during times of tremendous difficulty? Because God is God; He is worthy of our praise always and everywhere; He is with us; His promises are true; and He has plans for us to flourish.

Paul wrote the second passage while imprisoned in Rome. He rejoiced that his imprisonment "actually helped to spread the gospel." Because he was in prison, the good news of Jesus Christ was spreading faster and farther than before. That was not how Paul planned it. He envisioned preaching in Rome, then traveling to Spain to spread the good news there (see Romans 15:23-24), but God had other plans. God used Paul's imprisonment to advance the Gospel, and Paul rejoiced. He continued to be faithful to his Lord and Savior Jesus Christ, and God continued to employ Paul in His holy service. While in prison, God employed Paul to write words that continue speaking to us today. God's plans for Paul were bigger than Paul likely imagined.

What is holding you captive? How might God be positioning you to serve Him in ways you never imagined possible? People who have experienced addiction and are now clean are able to minister to people struggling with addiction in ways impossible for others to replicate. People who have experienced prison and who are now free are able to minister to inmates in ways others cannot. People who have experienced the ugliness of chemotherapy are uniquely positioned to minister to patients with cancer. People who have grieved deeply are able to minister to suffering friends in ways impossible for others to replicate. How are your experiences positioning you to serve God and help others?

God has plans for you and His plans are for you to flourish. Continue worshiping, praising and seeking God. Continue trusting that His promises are true. As you seek God, as you live for Jesus Christ, the source of satisfaction, the source of life abundant, and the source of your purpose, may His plans for you each day become clear.

Thoughts to Consider

1. Read Psalm 40. God bends down to listen to our prayers, and He responds. He has done amazing things on our behalf and His plans for us are numerous and amazing. "Happy are those who make the Lord their trust..." (Psalm 40:4).

The psalmist says the Lord, "drew me up from the desolate pit, out of the miry bog, and set my feet upon a rock, making my steps secure. He put a new song in my mouth, a song of praise to our God" (Psalm 40:2-3). This means that for a time, God allowed the psalmist to struggle in the miry bog and allowed him to have some other song on his lips. Ultimately, God lifted him up, set him on solid ground, made his steps secure and revealed new plans for him. How is God preparing you? What struggle, what miry bog is He allowing, for a time, to prepare you for the plans He has for you?

2. Read Isaiah 55. God promises life abundant, joy, peace and song. Through Isaiah, God explains that He purposefully speaks words, and His words accomplish their intended purposes on earth. In Genesis chapter 1 we see that when God speaks things happen. He transforms chaos into order by speaking, He transforms darkness into light by speaking, and through Isaiah He explains that all His words have intended purposes on earth

saying, "so shall my word be that goes out from my mouth; it shall not return to me empty, but it shall accomplish that which I purpose, and succeed in the thing for which I sent it" (Isaiah 55:11).

Immediately after making that promise, God says, "For you shall go out in joy, and be led back in peace; the mountains and the hills before you shall burst into song, and all the trees of the field shall clap their hands" (Isaiah 55:12). Through His holy word God makes a variety of promises, but these are very specific. Prayerfully consider these promises. What do they mean to you?

3. Read Zechariah 13. The passage contains a painful prophecy for the people of Israel. Through the prophet Zechariah, God explains that they will be scattered and two-thirds will perish and the third that survives will suffer greatly as God prepares them for their future purpose. Through Zechariah God says,

> And I will put this third into the fire, refine them as one refines silver, and test them as gold is tested. They will call on my name, and I will answer them. I will say, "They are my people"; and they will say, "The Lord is our God."
> Zechariah 13:9

4. Read 2 Timothy 4. Paul knows he is nearing the end of his life (see 2 Timothy 4:6) and he urges Timothy to continue his mission of delivering the good news to the world. As he concludes the letter, at verse 16 Paul mentions difficulties with his defense and he continues saying,

> But the Lord stood by me and gave me strength, so that through me the message might be fully proclaimed and all the Gentiles might hear it. So I was rescued from the lion's mouth. The Lord will rescue me from every evil attack and save me for his heavenly kingdom. To him be the glory forever and ever. Amen. 2 Timothy 4:17-18

Paul was imprisoned and he continued to endure hardship, but he never lost faith. He knew with certainty that God was with him and that God's plan would ultimately be accomplished. In what specific way does Paul's unwavering faith in the face of great distress give you hope, faith and assurance?

North Shore, Oahu, Hawaii

15

The Falling of Many

> THEN SIMEON BLESSED THEM AND SAID TO HIS MOTHER MARY, "THIS CHILD IS DESTINED FOR THE FALLING AND THE RISING OF MANY IN ISRAEL, AND TO BE A SIGN THAT WILL BE OPPOSED SO THAT THE INNER THOUGHTS OF MANY WILL BE REVEALED — AND A SWORD WILL PIERCE YOUR OWN SOUL TOO." LUKE 2:34-35

Eight days after Christmas, Mary and Joseph carried Jesus to the temple to be consecrated for God. The Holy Spirit led Simeon to the temple for a divine appointment with the Messiah. As he held the baby, Simeon declared Jesus to be the Messiah and said, "This child is destined for the falling and rising of many…"

Simeon mentioned "rising" and "falling." As God Incarnate, Jesus is the standard by which everyone else is judged. He is holy, pure, divine … perfect, and no other human has ever or will ever come close. When we abide in Him and allow Him to abide in us, we gain benefits of His new life and are lifted up through the transformative influence of His indwelling Holy Spirit. Focusing on the glorious riches He offers, we often see Jesus as the Provider of exclusively positive things – He is the Redeemer, Savior and Prince of Peace. We focus on the "rising" and fail to consider the "falling." We focus on His love and fail to consider how His brilliance, the brightness of His holy light, reveals the depths of our darkness and the unrighteousness of our inner beings.

He exposes us for who we are and because of this He is "a sign that will be opposed…." Isaiah foretold that Jesus' holiness shines a light on people's worldly condition and exposes our stumbling (see Isaiah 8:14). Paul writes that preaching "Christ crucified" is "a stumbling block to the Jews and foolishness to Gentiles," but it is the power and wisdom of God to those with ears to hear (see 1 Corinthians 1:23). Similarly, Jesus reveals that the world will be divided over Him and that He causes division saying,

> "See, I am sending you out like sheep into the midst of wolves; so be wise as serpents and innocent as doves…. Brother will betray brother to death, and a father his child, and children will rise against parents and have them put to death; and you will be hated by all because of my name…. "Do not think that I have come to bring peace to the earth; I have not come to bring peace, but a sword. For I have come to set a man against his father, and a daughter against her mother, and a

daughter-in-law against her mother-in-law; and one's foes will be members of one's own household. Matthew 10:16, 21-22 & 34-36

God Incarnate reveals our hearts, the darkest depths of our souls. Some are attracted to the light; others flee from it seeking refuge in the shadows. In response to the Holy One, some rise while others fall. May you continue to rise in Him.

Thoughts to Consider

1. Read Isaiah 8. Isaiah declares a prophecy of doom for Judah and as the flood that inspires terror rises around us, we find Immanuel, God with us. God is with us, even when we stray, even when we fall, and He will ultimately deliver us. Isaiah writes,

> For the Lord spoke thus to me while his hand was strong upon me, and warned me not to walk in the way of this people, saying: Do not call conspiracy all that this people calls conspiracy, and do not fear what it fears, or be in dread. But the Lord of hosts, him you shall regard as holy; let him be your fear, and let him be your dread. He will become a sanctuary, a stone one strikes against; for both houses of Israel he will become a rock one stumbles over—a trap and a snare for the inhabitants of Jerusalem. And many among them shall stumble; they shall fall and be broken; they shall be snared and taken.

Isaiah 8:11-15

God warns Isaiah not to "walk in the way of this people...." God urges him to focus on God, to fear God and not the things of this world, and to regard only God as holy, promising that God alone will become either a sanctuary or a stumbling stone. In your experience, have you known times when God has been a stumbling stone? What happened? How did you recover?

2.   Read Matthew 10. The chapter begins with Jesus preparing the twelve disciples to be sent out as missionaries to "the lost sheep of the house of Israel" (Matthew 10:6). He instructs them to preach "the good news, 'The kingdom of heaven has come near.' Cure the sick, raise the dead, cleanse the lepers, cast out demons" (Matthew 10:7-8), and then He warns about persecution. Jesus sends the disciples to God's chosen people, the people of Israel, yet He warns about persecution.

In a message reminiscent of Isaiah's message, Jesus urges them not to fear their persecutors saying,

> "So have no fear of them; for nothing is covered up that will not be uncovered, and nothing secret that will not become known. What I say to you in the dark, tell in the light; and what you hear whispered, proclaim from the housetops. Do not fear those who kill the body but cannot kill the soul; rather fear him who can destroy both soul and body in hell. Matthew 10:26-28

The message of Jesus Christ is divisive. While delivering life to some it seals death to others. It causes some to stumble while lifting others up. What does this mean to you?

3.   Read I Corinthians 1. Paul says the good news of Jesus Christ is either foolishness or the power of God. It is either one or the other, black or white, without any middle-of-the-road grey option. He says, "For the message about the cross is foolishness to those who are perishing, but to us who are being saved it is the power of God" (I Corinthians 1:18).

Jesus claims to be the Messiah, the anointed One, the Son of God, God. If the claims are false, He is insane. If the claims are true, everything about the world changes. Every person must decide for himself or herself and, consciously or not, does decide whether Jesus' claims are true or false. This is the most divisive choice because each person will choose and their decision leads to either life or death. While the gift of life is available to everyone, humanity is divided into two groups – those who receive the gift of life and those who refuse it. How do you respond to this? Do you think I am overstating the point? If so, why?

Canyonlands National Park, Utah

16

CHRIST'S REPRESENTATIVES

> AT THAT TIME THE DISCIPLES CAME TO JESUS AND ASKED, "WHO IS THE GREATEST IN THE KINGDOM OF HEAVEN?" HE CALLED A CHILD, WHOM HE PUT AMONG THEM, AND SAID, "TRULY I TELL YOU, UNLESS YOU CHANGE AND BECOME LIKE CHILDREN, YOU WILL NEVER ENTER THE KINGDOM OF HEAVEN. WHOEVER BECOMES HUMBLE LIKE THIS CHILD IS THE GREATEST IN THE KINGDOM OF HEAVEN. WHOEVER WELCOMES ONE SUCH CHILD IN MY NAME WELCOMES ME. MATTHEW 18:1-5

Entrance to the kingdom of heaven requires that we revert back to the way we used to be. We used to be children. Jesus begins by saying, "truly I tell you," which is Jesus code to get our attention because something extremely important is coming. He continues explaining that we need to change back to childlike faith, humility, selflessness, transparency and simplicity.

Pablo Picasso is credited with saying, "Every child in an

artist. The problem is how to remain an artist once he grows up."² Picasso suggested that life, along with its obligations and intellectual and material pursuits, squeezes artistic freedom out of people as they mature. Jesus suggests something similar happens to our faith. He urges us to reclaim what we once possessed, and He suggests two steps to begin doing so: humble ourselves and welcome others in His name.

If Jesus knocks on your door tonight, will you let Him in?

Jesus says, "Listen! I am standing at the door, knocking; if you hear my voice and open the door, I will come in to you and eat with you, and you with me" (Revelation 3:20). He refers to the doors blocking our souls and spirits from Jesus. He knocks on the doors of our hearts seeking entry into the dark recesses to shine His light and cleanse our spiritual beings. Viewed from this perspective, He continuously knocks.

We know this is happening, but this is not the kind of knock meant by my question. What if Jesus appears and physically knocks on the physical front door of your home. Will you let Him in? I presume we would each cherish the opportunity, we would readily invite Him in, we would feel ashamed of our dirtiness in many ways, we would have so many questions for Him, we would love to get to know Him better.

Will you respond similarly if a child knocks on your door, or perhaps an adult in need? Jesus connects humility with hospitality and calls us to extend great hospitality to people in need. Jesus says that they are His representatives here on earth. They stand in His place. When we welcome them we welcome Him.

Similarly, Jesus says, "Whoever welcomes you welcomes

me, and whoever welcomes me welcomes the one who sent me" (Matthew 10:40).

Jesus has representatives, agents, people who stand in His place here on earth and they might not look the way we expect them to look. Clouded by the worldly lenses we often see through, we might expect Jesus' representatives to bear a unique appearance. Perhaps we expect them to look like religious leaders wearing, I don't know, something like flowing robes with brightly colored stoles or possibly a fancy Pope-like hat. We might expect them to glow like an angel or have some entirely different appearance. While some of His representatives may look like that, others look like ordinary people – children and people in need. They even look like you and me.

Jesus taught a lot about the kingdom of heaven and He demonstrated its presence through miracles, signs and wonders. Here, He explains that (i) entrance to the kingdom requires that we regain qualities we previously possessed, (ii) humility is the key to greatness and (iii) when we extend genuine, welcoming hospitality to others, we welcome Him.

May you continue your transformation to the image of Jesus Christ, may you have eyes to see others as He sees them, and may you have the courage to welcome His representatives when they knock.

Thoughts to Consider

1.   Read Matthew 25. Chapter 25 begins with Jesus telling the Parable of the Ten Bridesmaids, its message dealing with the unpredictability of time, and our need to prepare while stressing the importance of individual responsibility and faith. Jesus continues His message of individual responsibility and faith in the Parable of Talents before discussing final judgment.

He describes a great gathering of everyone from all nations. Jesus separates them into two groups, the righteous and the unrighteous. He also describes the test used to make the determination – how did each person treat people in need? He says,

> Then the righteous will answer him, 'Lord, when was it that we saw you hungry and gave you food, or thirsty and gave you something to drink? And when was it that we saw you a stranger and welcomed you, or naked and gave you clothing? And when was it that we saw you sick or in prison and visited you?' And the king will answer them, 'Truly I tell you, just as you did it to one of the least of these who are members of my family, you did it to me.' Matthew 25:37-40

As presented in this passage, the test for righteousness has nothing to do with understanding Scripture or theology. It has nothing to do with church attendance, leading Bible studies, preaching sermons or memorizing Bible passages. It is about tangible acts of love to people in need.

2.   Read John 13. During the Last Supper, Jesus rose from the table, assumed the wardrobe of a slave and washed the

disciples' feet. After He had finished He said,

> "Do you know what I have done to you? You call me Teacher and Lord – and you are right, for that is what I am. So if I, your Lord and Teacher, have washed your feet, you also ought to wash one another's feet. For I have set you an example, that you also should do as I have done to you. John 13:12-15

A little later He said,

> "I give you a new commandment, that you love one another. Just as I have loved you, you also should love one another. By this everyone will know that you are my disciples, if you have love for one another." John 13:34-35

How does the new commandment compare to the standard for judgment described in Matthew 25?

3.   Read Matthew 10. Jesus says,

> "Whoever welcomes you welcomes me, and whoever welcomes me welcomes the one who sent me. Whoever welcomes a prophet in the name of a prophet will receive a prophet's reward; and whoever welcomes a righteous person in the name of a righteous person will receive the reward of the righteous; and whoever gives even a cup of cold water to one of these little ones in the name of a disciple—truly I tell you, none of these will lose their reward." Matthew 10:40-42

4. Jesus has representatives on earth. Matthew 10 indicates people welcome Jesus when they welcome His disciples, and Matthew 25 indicates people in need are His representatives on earth and we serve Him by helping them. Matthew 10 and John 13 indicate we serve Jesus by loving others. How does this influence your view of other people? Will this change how you treat people? If so, in what specific way?

Red Mountain, Colorado

17

ANGLE OF APPROACH

> AFTER HE HAD WASHED THEIR FEET, HAD PUT ON HIS ROBE, AND HAD RETURNED TO THE TABLE, HE SAID TO THEM, "DO YOU KNOW WHAT I HAVE DONE TO YOU? YOU CALL ME TEACHER AND LORD – AND YOU ARE RIGHT, FOR THAT IS WHAT I AM. SO IF I, YOUR LORD AND TEACHER, HAVE WASHED YOUR FEET, YOU ALSO OUGHT TO WASH ONE ANOTHER'S FEET. FOR I HAVE SET YOU AN EXAMPLE, THAT YOU ALSO SHOULD DO AS I HAVE DONE TO YOU. JOHN 13:12-15

Jesus knelt before the disciples and washed their feet, and He urges us to follow His example. How do we present ourselves to the ones we serve? Our angle of approach is important.

We bow before Jesus Christ in worship. We freely submit ourselves to Him, recognizing His sovereignty, power and authority. He sends us out into the world as His agents on a mission – we are to allow His love to flow through us. Jesus also says that when we serve people in need we serve Him (see Matthew 25:40). They stand in Christ's place; they are His proxy, His earthly personification.

Each individual in the scenario, the servant and the one being served, represents Christ. Isn't it amazing that Jesus Christ stands in both roles? This enables us to view our interaction with others in two distinct ways, asking: (i) do we present ourselves to the ones we serve in the way we present ourselves to Jesus Christ? and (ii) do we present ourselves the way He did, or in a manner even remotely befitting of claiming His holy name?

In the eyes of the world, people with economic means sufficient to help are often held in higher esteem than those in need, but we know every human life is sacred and in the kingdom of heaven greatness is not determined by economic status. We know that God creates each person, that He loves each person, that He blesses each person in unique ways, and that with each blessing comes great responsibility. When we are blessed with the gifts, talents and opportunities to help, we are called to administer His blessing to reveal His glory. As we do so, as we act as His representatives, our manner of approach is extremely important. We should each consider whether we convey the compassion, love and genuine concern worthy of claiming identity with Him.

Even when our intentions are pure, it is possible that our eyes, tainted by the world around us, cause us to see ourselves as holding a position higher than the people we are helping, and our attitude may be perceived as condescending, patronizing, pompous, arrogant or superior. Our angle of approach makes all the difference. Do we look down on others or do we look up? Do we talk down to others or do we seek to connect in a genuine, loving, compassionate way?

Signifying vulnerability, submission, reverence and respect, Jesus knelt. Throughout Scripture we see people kneeling before people they honor. When Abigail approached King David, she "bowed down before David with her face to the ground" (1 Samuel 25:23). A woman knelt before Jesus and begged Him to heal her daughter (see Matthew 15:25). Jairus, a synagogue leader, fell at Jesus' feet, begging Jesus to heal his daughter (see Luke 8:41). Cornelius sent his servants to escort Peter back to his home. When Peter arrived, "Cornelius met him and fell at his feet in reverence" (Acts 10:25).

Just before the Last Supper, Jesus the Christ, the Messiah, God Incarnate assumed the dress and position of a slave, and acted like one. He removed His outer clothing, wrapped a towel around His waist, knelt and washed the feet of other people. Jesus, God Incarnate, knelt as He served others. He approached them in a position of vulnerability, submission, reverence and respect, and He tells us to do the same.

May you approach people you serve in a Christ-like manner. May you have eyes to see them as beings standing in His place. May the image of our Lord Jesus Christ continue to grow in you, may you have eyes to see others as He sees them, may you seize each opportunity before you to serve as God calls you.

Thoughts to Consider

1.   Consider your day yesterday. Think about each person you interacted with. It is possible you interacted with people face-to-face, by telephone, by text message, by email, and through social media. With each interaction, what was your angle of approach? How did you demonstrate humility? How did you demonstrate your servant's heart?

2.   Think about times you have interacted with people in positions of power and authority in some way relating to you. Perhaps you appeared before a judge rendering a decision relating to you. Perhaps you interacted with the president of the company you work for. Perhaps it was a police officer, federal agent or some other governmental representative. How did you demonstrate your respect of their position?

3.   Consider times you have physically helped another person in need. How did you demonstrate your respect of their position?

4.   God's holy word is filled with His holy directive to love. He calls us to love Him with all our heart, mind, soul and strength. He calls us to love our neighbor as ourselves. He calls us love one another the way He loves us. He calls us to eradicate injustice. He calls us to be His agents of life, love and light out in the darkness surrounding us. As we seek to be His people, sharing and spreading His love to people we encounter, we must be extremely careful that we represent Him in a manner befitting of our relationship with Him. We must be careful to help and not to harm. Can you think of times when

your efforts to help may have harmed?

5.   For additional reading on this topic, please see *When Helping Hurts: How to alleviate poverty without hurting the poor – and yourself* by Steve Corbett and Brian Fikkert. Moody Publishers, Chicago (2009). ISBN 978-0-8024-5705-9.

Polihale Beach, Kauai, Hawaii

18

USING OUR GIFTS FOR GOD'S GLORY

THE END OF ALL THINGS IS NEAR; THEREFORE BE SERIOUS AND DISCIPLINE YOURSELVES FOR THE SAKE OF YOUR PRAYERS. ABOVE ALL, MAINTAIN CONSTANT LOVE FOR ONE ANOTHER, FOR LOVE COVERS A MULTITUDE OF SINS. BE HOSPITABLE TO ONE ANOTHER WITHOUT COMPLAINING. LIKE GOOD STEWARDS OF THE MANIFOLD GRACE OF GOD, SERVE ONE ANOTHER WITH WHATEVER GIFT EACH OF YOU HAS RECEIVED. WHOEVER SPEAKS MUST DO SO AS ONE SPEAKING THE VERY WORDS OF GOD; WHOEVER SERVES MUST DO SO WITH THE STRENGTH THAT GOD SUPPLIES, SO THAT GOD MAY BE GLORIFIED IN ALL THINGS THROUGH JESUS CHRIST. TO HIM BELONG THE GLORY AND THE POWER FOREVER AND EVER. AMEN. I PETER 4:7-11

FOR THIS REASON I REMIND YOU TO REKINDLE THE GIFT OF GOD THAT IS WITHIN YOU THROUGH THE LAYING ON OF MY HANDS; FOR GOD DID NOT GIVE US A SPIRIT OF COWARDICE, BUT RATHER A SPIRIT OF POWER

AND OF LOVE AND OF SELF-DISCIPLINE. 2 TIMOTHY 1:6-7

By God's grace, we each have certain gifts and talents. We are each called to use our gifts to serve God "so that God may be glorified in all things through Jesus Christ." I am continually amazed at the diversity of talent and the myriad of ways people use their talents and positions to glorify God.

I used to spend more time in airports than I desired, which meant I had the opportunity to visit many airport restrooms. The cleanest by far were in Charlotte, North Carolina where each restroom had a dedicated attendant. I visited one on many occasions and the attendant greeted each person praising God. As people entered he said something like, "What a glorious day the Lord has made! How are you today?" And as people left he said, "Have a blessed day!" or "May God bless you today!" or something similar. He used his platform as a restroom attendant to share God's glory with thousands of people each day.

I recently heard an interview of Tony Dungy, formerly the coach of the Indianapolis Colts football team. As he prepared his team to compete in the Super Bowl, he prayed one specific prayer. He did not pray for the Colts to win the big game; he did not pray for personal glory; rather, he prayed that God would use him and the international stage he was on to glorify God. His position as a coach provided a unique international platform, and he prayed that he might use it to glorify God.

A few years ago Michael Belk, a fashion photographer, published a book of photographs depicting scenes from the

Bible. The images bring Jesus' teaching to life in evocative ways. Before seeing his work I would have struggled to imagine how a fashion photographer might use his skills to glorify God, but Mr. Belk followed the path that God laid before him in remarkable ways.

I recently spoke with an accountant who uses his knowledge to help Christian NGO's work in foreign lands. I encountered a mechanic who helps people in need in the name of Jesus Christ. I met an art gallery owner who uses her platform to spread the good news of Jesus Christ. And I have encountered many others who each use their unique gifts and position to reveal God's glory to others.

Where has God placed you? What ignites your passion? What talents and skills do you possess? What brings you joy? God made you the way He did with a purpose in mind. He has given you a platform. May you have eyes to see the opportunities before you, and may you have the courage to use your gifts, talents and position to glorify Him.

Thoughts to Consider

1. Read Romans 12. What does new life in and through Christ Jesus look like? If Christ Jesus has made us new, washed us clean and redeemed our spirits, and if He is continuing to transform us into His holy image, how should we behave? How should we act out in the world?

In Romans 12 we see a description of piety in action. We see aspects of holiness, of being set apart from the world in pursuit of spiritual perfection. We also see people out in the world interacting with strangers, interacting with people who persecute them, rejoicing and weeping and showing hospitality. God's holy word says,

> Let love be genuine; hate what is evil, hold fast to what is good; love one another with mutual affection; outdo one another in showing honor. Romans 12:9-10

In what specific ways do you pursue piety? How do you demonstrate your love of Christ Jesus to the world?

2. Read 1 Corinthians 4. Paul writes, "Think of us in this way, as servants of Christ and stewards of God's mysteries" (1 Corinthians 4:1). Christ's servant or slave is a steward, manager, advisor, guardian, trustee or overseer of precious property, God's mysteries. In what ways are you Christ's servant? How do you serve as overseer of God's mysteries? Do others see you in the same light?

3. Read 2 Timothy. It is a short letter from Paul to his young protégé. Paul begins by reminding Timothy of God's anointing. God filled Timothy with faith and His spirit of power, love and self-discipline (see 2 Timothy 1:5-7), and Paul urges him to live a life consistent with his anointing. Similarly, God lives within you. His Holy Spirit dwells within you the moment you first believe, transforming you, calling you, anointing you into His holy service. He has not given you a spirit of fear, but of power and love and self-discipline. What will you do as His servant today?

4.   Read 1 Peter 4. Peter urges his readers to act "like good stewards of the manifold grace of God" (1 Peter 4:10). He urges his readers to constantly love others, to be hospitable and to serve one another "so that God may be glorified in all things through Jesus Christ" (1 Peter 4:11). As you consider the world around you, in what specific ways do you see God glorified through Jesus Christ? How might you glorify God through Jesus Christ? Can you imagine a world in which all things glorify God through Jesus Christ?

Eagle River, Colorado

19

QUESTIONING OUR MOTIVES

> Now when Simon saw that the Spirit was given through the laying on of the apostles' hands, he offered them money, saying, "Give me also this power so that anyone on whom I lay my hands may receive the Holy Spirit." But Peter said to him, "May your silver perish with you, because you thought you could obtain God's gift with money! You have no part or share in this, for your heart is not right before God. Repent therefore of this wickedness of yours, and pray to the Lord that, if possible, the intent of your heart may be forgiven you. Acts 8:18-22

As a talented sorcerer, Simon was respected and admired in his Samaritan community. When Philip came to town preaching the gospel of Jesus Christ, Simon followed Philip, listening and watching. He was amazed at the miracles, signs and wonders that God performed through Philip. He professed faith in Jesus Christ and was baptized.

John and Peter joined Philip in Samaria. As John and Peter placed their hands on people and prayed, those prayed for received the Holy Spirit. Simon was astounded at what he believed to be a new, remarkable magic trick. Like magicians sharing secrets of the trade, he offered to pay John and Peter to teach him how to perform the trick.

Peter rebuked Simon because Simon wanted to possess the skill, not God. Simon publicly professed faith in Jesus Christ, but he misunderstood the source of the power he saw flowing through John and Peter. He believed the apostles' signs and wonders were like other magic tricks, only better. He sought improved skills to elevate his position, earn greater respect, and make more money. He sought what is of God for personal use and pleasure, and he did not even afford God the reverence necessary to ask Him for His blessing – Simon asked the apostles, underscoring the view that he did not really understand who God is, he did not seek God, and he did not desire to glorify God. He desired to glorify himself. In response he received Peter's rebuke, not God's blessing.

Simon's story causes me to ponder my prayer life and my motives. How often do I ask God for blessings while intending to use His blessings for my purposes and pleasure? While I may cloak them in all the right language, are my prayers really efforts to glorify myself, not God? Do we seek God, or do we really seek personal benefits associated with the blessings He bestows?

Jesus promises, "But seek first his kingdom and his

righteousness, and all these things will be given to you as well" (Matthew 6:33). He also says, "And I will do whatever you ask in my name, so that the Son may bring glory the Father" (John 14:13). We are to seek God, not personal benefits flowing from Him. Truly asking in Jesus' name necessitates seeking God and God's glory.

Simon sought God's blessing for personal glory. At times I have been guilty of doing the same thing. If you find yourself following this pattern, please join me and together we can turn away from our affront to God. As we pray, may we each seek first God and may we each seek to be an instrument conforming to His will and revealing His glory. Amen.

Thoughts to Consider

1.   Read Daniel 5. As Nebuchadnezzar's son, Belshazzar, drank wine from cups taken from the temple and praised gods of gold and silver, a hand appeared and with the party watching, wrote words on the palace wall. Belshazzar brought in all the wise men from the kingdom to interpret the words, but none knew what the words meant. He then summoned Daniel. He offered to pay Daniel a purple robe, gold chain and the third ranking position in the kingdom if he could interpret the inscription. Daniel said, "Let your gifts be for yourself, or give your rewards to someone else! Nevertheless I will read the writing to the king and let him know the interpretation" (Daniel 5:17).

Daniel knew he was merely the Lord's instrument, and if he was able to interpret the words it would be God speaking, not him. He could not sell what was not his.

2. Read 2 Kings 5. Naaman was the commander of the Aramean army. He suffered with leprosy. Naaman heard from his wife's servant that the king of Israel could cure his leprosy, so he carried lots of gold, silver and garments to Israel offering to pay for a cure. The king knew Naaman was asking for what only God could give.

The prophet Elisha offered to handle the request for the king, and he did. He never saw Naaman, but he sent word for Naaman to wash seven times in the Jordan River. Naaman was insulted, but he followed Elisha's advice and was cured.

He then went to Elisha to thank him. He offered Elisha gifts but Elisha refused saying, "As the Lord lives, who I serve, I will accept nothing!" (2 Kings 5:16). Elisha could not accept payment for God's blessing, and we see that God is willing to heal people who seek His blessing.

3. We see a few people in Scripture attempting to purchase God's blessing. God desires us. He wants our hearts. He wants relationship with us. He wants us to want Him. God's holy word directs us to seek God first, to love God with all of our being and "by the mercies of God, to present your bodies as a living sacrifice, holy and acceptable to God, which is your spiritual worship" (Romans 12:1). Have you ever desired God's blessing more than you desired God? In light of God's holy word, how do you feel about that?

For the Praise of His Glory

White Rim Canyon, Utah

20

VOICE FOR THE VOICELESS

AFTER A LONG TIME THE KING OF EGYPT DIED. THE ISRAELITES GROANED UNDER THEIR SLAVERY, AND CRIED OUT. OUT OF THE SLAVERY THEIR CRY FOR HELP ROSE UP TO GOD. GOD HEARD THEIR GROANING, AND GOD REMEMBERED HIS COVENANT WITH ABRAHAM, ISAAC, AND JACOB. GOD LOOKED UPON THE ISRAELITES, AND GOD TOOK NOTICE OF THEM....THEN THE LORD SAID, "I HAVE OBSERVED THE MISERY OF MY PEOPLE WHO ARE IN EGYPT; I HAVE HEARD THEIR CRY ON ACCOUNT OF THEIR TASKMASTERS. INDEED, I KNOW THEIR SUFFERINGS, AND I HAVE COME DOWN TO DELIVER THEM FROM THE EGYPTIANS, AND TO BRING THEM UP OUT OF THAT LAND TO A GOOD AND BROAD LAND, A LAND FLOWING WITH MILK AND HONEY, TO THE COUNTRY OF THE CANAANITES, THE HITTITES, THE AMORITES, THE PERIZZITES, THE HIVITES, AND THE JEBUSITES. EXODUS 2:23 & 3:7-8

I CONSIDER THAT THE SUFFERINGS OF THIS

PRESENT TIME ARE NOT WORTH COMPARING WITH THE GLORY ABOUT TO BE REVEALED TO US.... WE KNOW THAT THE WHOLE CREATION HAS BEEN GROANING IN LABOR PAINS UNTIL NOW; AND NOT ONLY THE CREATION, BUT WE OURSELVES, WHO HAVE THE FIRST FRUITS OF THE SPIRIT, GROAN INWARDLY WHILE WE WAIT FOR ADOPTION, THE REDEMPTION OF OUR BODIES.... LIKEWISE THE SPIRIT HELPS US IN OUR WEAKNESS; FOR WE DO NOT KNOW HOW TO PRAY AS WE OUGHT, BUT THAT VERY SPIRIT INTERCEDES WITH SIGHS TOO DEEP FOR WORDS. AND GOD, WHO SEARCHES THE HEART, KNOWS WHAT IS THE MIND OF THE SPIRIT, BECAUSE THE SPIRIT INTERCEDES FOR THE SAINTS ACCORDING TO THE WILL OF GOD. WE KNOW THAT ALL THINGS WORK TOGETHER FOR GOOD FOR THOSE WHO LOVE GOD, WHO ARE CALLED ACCORDING TO HIS PURPOSE. ROMANS 8:18, 22-23, 26-28

God's holy word says that all of creation is held in "bondage to decay" and is "groaning in labor pains." In this world, suffering is ubiquitous. We each experience suffering and some form of bondage.

We know that God hears our prayers just as we know that God heard the groans and cries of His people who were held in bondage in Egypt. He heard their wordless prayers, their cries, their groans, and responded by sending a man to rescue them. What holds you in bondage? What suffering causes you to groan and cry out to God?

Please know that God hears your prayers, and you are not alone. Even if your pain is so severe that you are unable to pray, the Holy Spirit is interceding for you. He prays for you "with sighs too deep for words." Every person knows some form of suffering, and no matter how alone you might feel in this moment, other people share your pain and the Holy Spirit is praying for you. You are not alone. God hears your prayers; He prays for you and He will respond by sending His people to rescue you.

Parents of addicts know a unique form of torture. They silently grieve the gradual loss of sons or daughters, wondering what they should have done differently, wondering whether they can do anything to help, wondering whether their help is causing greater harm. Like a foggy day with hints of sunshine piercing through, their lives are clouded with grief, punctuated by moments of hope. They grieve in silence because the foundational problem is not really their own – discussing the problem involves talking about another person, which is tricky and sensitive at best. It is a special form of torture skillfully devised by the master torturer.

Earlier this week I noticed a long train crossing the wooden rail trestle in downtown Northport. Graffiti marked boxcars slowly passed by. Most were marked with a few words or symbols that looked as if they took little time to produce, but one stood out as an artfully crafted mural. Against the original yellow background an artist covered the side with large, curved, flowing letters in a bright display of colors – various hues of red, blue, green, black and white. I pondered the time, energy and expense someone invested to produce the work of art, just for it to travel from place to place, likely never to be seen again by the person who painted it. And I'm not condoning vandalism; rather I am noting the universal need to have a voice, to be noticed, to be needed, to be loved.

I imagine a person who felt as if they had no voice, a person who was not being heard or noticed amidst the chaos swirling around them, but through a colorful mural on a boxcar they were suddenly made visible. By transforming the dark world around them into a more beautiful place and stamping their creative energy on something that would last and be seen and be noticed, they were suddenly seen and heard. They moved from shadows into light. They discovered a voice.

It was a symbol of our need to connect. It was cry for help. We know that God hears our cries for help. Just as He heard His people's cry for help in Egypt and responded, He hears our cries for help. He hears you and He prays with you. And if we look to the Exodus to see one example of how God responds, He responds by sending His people to help.

As you cry out to God, as you groan unable to put your agony into words, as you continue seeking God, receive His Holy Spirit in your heart in a new and refreshed way, allow His spiritual transformation to fill the cracks of your heart, and stay open to receiving His help through the people He is sending into your life.

May you know in your heart His peace, His comfort, His rest.

THOUGHTS TO CONSIDER

1. Read Romans 8. The chapter is filled with amazing promises.

    > When we cry, "Abba! Father!" it is that very Spirit bearing witness with our spirit that we are children of God, and if children, then heirs, heirs of God and joint heirs with Christ – if, in fact, we suffer with him so that we may also be glorified with him. Romans 8:15-17

    > We know that all things work together for good for those who love God, who are called according to his purpose. Romans 8:28

After stating amazing promise after amazing promise, the chapter concludes as follows:

> What then are we to say about these things? If God is for us, who is against us? He who did not withhold his own Son, but gave him up for all of us, will he not with him also give us everything else? Who will bring any charge against God's elect? It is God who justifies. Who is to condemn? It is Christ Jesus, who died, yes, who was raised, who is at the right hand of God, who indeed intercedes for us. Who will separate us from the love of Christ? Will hardship, or distress, or persecution, or famine, or nakedness, or peril, or sword? As it is written,

> "For your sake we are being killed all day long;
> we are accounted as sheep to be slaughtered."
>
> No, in all these things we are more than conquerors through him who loved us. For I am convinced that neither death, nor life, nor angels, nor rulers, nor things present, nor things to come, nor powers, nor height, nor depth, nor anything else in all creation, will be able to separate us from the love of God in Christ Jesus our Lord. Romans 8:31-39

He who gave up His Son for us, will He not give us everything else? If He is for us, who can possibly be against us? Nothing can separate us from the Love of God in Christ Jesus!

2.   Read Job 38-42. God finally speaks to Job and his friends, directing their attention to the wonders of nature that God created and controls, and of their relative nothingness in comparison. After hearing from God, Job says, "I had heard of you by the hearing of the ear, but now my eye sees you; therefore I despise myself, and repent in dust and ashes" (Job 42:5-6). The Book of Job presents God in His awesome glory as the all-powerful, all-knowing, Creator of the universe, and His Holy Spirit dwells within us and prays for us. Pause for a moment and let that sink in. How do you respond to that?

3.   Read Psalm 34. The psalmist writes,

> The eyes of the Lord are on the righteous, and his ears are open to their cry....When the righteous cry for help, the Lord hears, and rescues them from all their troubles.

The Lord is near to the brokenhearted, and saves the crushed in spirit. Psalm 34:15 &17-18

Take some time to rewrite the psalm as your personal prayer, seizing God's promises for yourself.

For the Praise of His Glory

North Shore, Kauai, Hawaii

21

SPIRITUAL REPAIR

> TO SET THE MIND ON THE FLESH IS DEATH, BUT TO SET THE MIND ON THE SPIRIT IS LIFE AND PEACE. ROMANS 8:6

> FOR SURELY YOU HAVE HEARD ABOUT HIM AND WERE TAUGHT IN HIM, AS TRUTH IS IN JESUS. YOU WERE TAUGHT TO PUT AWAY YOUR FORMER WAY OF LIFE, YOUR OLD SELF, CORRUPT AND DELUDED BY ITS LUSTS, AND TO BE RENEWED IN THE SPIRIT OF YOUR MINDS, AND TO CLOTHE YOURSELVES WITH THE NEW SELF, CREATED ACCORDING TO THE LIKENESS OF GOD IN TRUE RIGHTEOUSNESS AND HOLINESS. EPHESIANS 4:22-23

We breathe in the aroma of new life in Christ, but we fail to fully experience it because we cling to our former ways. We are each, to some extent, divided beings and in our divided state we feel dissatisfied. We suffer. We seek wholeness.

Paul contrasts old life and new life, flesh and spirit, worldly and holy desires, life separated from God versus life pursuing God, and he places our minds on the fence making a choice. Which will govern? We are part spiritual and part physical. We have spirits, souls and bodies. Our bodies are remarkable mechanisms designed by God in truly amazing ways, but what we do with them is directed by our minds, our desires, our emotions, our character … our spiritual selves. We have the source of satisfaction, the Holy Spirit, dwelling within us the moment we first believe, and He starts working to transform our spiritual selves, but we continue living in this world surrounded by unholy influences, and so long as any part of ourselves clings to unholy, worldly desires, we will be divided and we will continue experiencing dissatisfaction.

When Paul uses the word "flesh," he refers to the part of our spiritual selves still beholden to worldly, carnal, unholy desires, still tainted by the desire to move away from God, not yet grasping the power of God, not yet transformed into the image of Christ Jesus. In contrast, when he discusses "Spirit," he refers to the Holy Spirit and that part of us that has been transformed by His indwelling. The moment we first believe, the moment we accept Jesus Christ as our Lord and Savior, the Holy Spirit takes up residence within us and part of us becomes holy. We each have His holiness within us, but how much do we have? How much of Him have we allowed in?

When we are hurting, when we feel a void and cannot quite identify the source or cause, we often look for cures in the physical realm. Driven by science, our society conditions us to do so. When we are sick we go to a doctor who diagnoses physical ailments and prescribes chemicals and procedures to help. They focus on the physical realm. Similarly, sometimes we feel a void, we feel emptiness, we feel dissatisfied, we seek satisfaction, wholeness and peace, but we do not know what is causing the void, so we look for solutions in the physical realm. We have a spiritual problem, but we misdiagnose it, and in response some seek fulfillment through physical or chemically induced mental pleasure responses, like those created by porn, sex, alcohol, a variety of increasingly powerful drugs, extreme exercise ... there is an infinite variety of places people look for physical solutions to spiritual problems, and none of them work.

Spiritual holes require spiritual repair. Spiritual needs require spiritual solutions. They require a fresh dose of the Holy Spirit. "You were taught to put away your former way of life, your old self, corrupt and deluded by its lusts, and to be renewed in the spirit of your minds, and to clothe yourselves with the new self, created according to the likeness of God in true righteousness and holiness." "To set the mind on the flesh is death, but to set the mind on the Spirit is life and peace."

May you know, deeply in your heart, the life and peace available through the indwelling Holy Spirit, may you allow Him to renew the spirit of your mind, and may you clothe yourself in the likeness of Christ Jesus.

Thoughts to Consider

1.   Read Colossians 3. God's holy word urges us to focus on Godly influences as we extinguish worldly influences from our lives. Paul writes,

> So if you have been raised with Christ, seek the things that are above, where Christ is, seated at the right hand of God. Set your minds on things that are above, not on things that are on earth, for you have died, and your life is hidden with Christ in God. Colossians 3:1-3

2.   Read Philippians 2. God the Father, Jesus Christ, the Holy Spirit is at work within you. Isn't that incredibly awesome? Paul urges us to continue advancing along the path toward sanctification saying,

> Therefore, my beloved, just as you have always obeyed me, not only in my presence, but much more now in my absence, work out your own salvation with fear and trembling; for it is God who is at work in you, enabling you both to will and to work for his good pleasure. Philippians 2:12-13

3.   Read 1 Corinthians 2. A theme running through Paul's writing is our continuous spiritual transformation in and through Christ Jesus. We are saved and that begins our lifelong process of sanctification. Paul contrasts people who focus on worldly things with those who focus on Godly things writing,

> Those who are unspiritual do not receive the gifts of God's Spirit, for they are foolishness to them, and they

are unable to understand them because they are spiritually discerned. Those who are spiritual discern all things, and they are themselves subject to no one else's scrutiny. "For who has known the mind of the Lord so as to instruct him?" But we have the mind of Christ. I Corinthians 2:14-16

4. Read Romans 7. The passages above present Christ Jesus working in us, transforming us, combined with individual responsibility. While He is working we must make good choices. Ideally we are each in the boat with Him, paddling in the same direction.

We live in this in-between state. We are partially holy, cleansed through Christ Jesus and purified by His indwelling Holy Spirit. We are being transformed, but we are not yet perfect and we still live in the flesh, subjected to sinful influences around us. Paul was a holy and righteous man. He dedicated his life to sharing the good news of Christ Jesus and God moved through him in remarkable ways. God healed people in response to Paul's prayers and in response to touching his handkerchief, yet he discusses his inner turmoil saying, "I do not understand my own actions. For I do not do what I want, but I do the very thing I hate" (Romans 7:15). Compared to most people, Paul was a righteous human; yet even he was sinful. How do you feel about your inner conflict in light of Paul's confession?

5. Read Romans 12. I know, I have asked you to read this chapter a lot recently, but it so full of richness, beginning with this:

> I appeal to you therefore, brothers and sisters, by the

mercies of God, to present your bodies as a living sacrifice, holy and acceptable to God, which is your spiritual worship. Do not be conformed to this world, but be transformed by the renewing of your minds, so that you may discern what is the will of God – what is good and acceptable and perfect. Romans 12:1-2

San Juan Range, Colorado

22

CLEARING THE PATH

> BUT YOU ARE A CHOSEN RACE, A ROYAL PRIESTHOOD, A HOLY NATION, GOD'S OWN PEOPLE, IN ORDER THAT YOU MAY PROCLAIM THE MIGHTY ACTS OF HIM WHO CALLED YOU OUT OF DARKNESS INTO HIS MARVELOUS LIGHT. ONCE YOU WERE NOT A PEOPLE, BUT NOW YOU ARE GOD'S PEOPLE; ONCE YOU HAD NOT RECEIVED MERCY, BUT NOW YOU HAVE RECEIVED MERCY. BELOVED, I URGE YOU AS ALIENS AND EXILES TO ABSTAIN FROM THE DESIRES OF THE FLESH THAT WAGE WAR AGAINST THE SOUL. I PETER 2:9-11

As we seek God and progress along the path toward Him, we encounter obstacles along the way. When we come upon things blocking our progress, we must clear the path. What in your life hinders your growth toward God?

To complete a recent task, I had to get to the other side of a basement, but the place was full of furniture, boxes, scraps of lumber, bags of concrete, paint cans and other stuff. To get to the other side I created a path by moving things. As I did, I slowly stepped forward, tripping a few times along the way. In many ways, my life is like a crowded basement.

One of my roommates during college graduated as a geophysical engineer. He accepted a job with a large international company that sent him to Bolivia to work on a seismic crew. On a typical day he and another worker laid seismic cable across the jungle floor. A few months later he was back in Denver. He said, "I carried a spool of cable on my back, and we used machetes to hack our way through the jungle laying line. The worst was when we crossed wet areas, hacking through vines in waist-deep water. The guy in front of me pointed out snakes dropping from branches into the water around us saying, 'Don't worry about that one, he's not bad. Watch out for that one…'" My friend, a cowboy from Colorado, did not last long in that job.

Some days I feel as if I am hacking my way toward God watching out for snakes around me, stumbling along the way. But have you noticed that sometimes stumbling makes us move faster? Have you ever been walking along, and one foot gets caught on something and you stumble, and as you stumble your feet move really fast to help you recover, so you end up running a few steps until you regain balance? Sometimes, just after stumbling, we actually move much faster than we were moving before. As we move toward God, we stumble along the way, and sometimes our stumbling causes us to move toward God at a faster pace.

At other times we stumble and fall, and as we lie on the

ground hurt and humiliated, we cry out to God as never before. Like the prodigal in the pigpen, stumbling forces us to realize we cannot move forward until we surrender, discover humility and truly seek Him. Eventually we must get back up and continue moving forward.

We are each hacking our way through this world, stumbling along the way toward God. If you are struggling, do not allow yourself to think you are alone in your struggle. You are not alone. And if your life is going smoothly at the moment, please know that others around you need help. Please look for opportunities to help because we are each clearing a path toward God, moving obstacles out of our way, and stumbling toward holiness.

May you continue to allow God's holy light, His life, His love to flow through you as you live your life in the world.

Thoughts to Consider

1. Read Luke 15. Jesus tells the Parable of the Lost Sheep, the Parable of the Lost Coin, and the Parable of the Prodigal and His Brother. In each, something is lost and then found, and each discovery causes joyful celebration (see Luke 15:7, 15:10 and 15:23-24).

In the Parable of the Prodigal and His Brother, both brothers are lost but one does not know it. The prodigal squanders his inheritance on poor choices, and as he starves while working hard, he decides to swallow his pride and return home. His father has been constantly watching for his return, and while he still in the distance his father sees him and rushes out to greet, welcome and hug him. And he throws a party to celebrate his son's return.

The father's behavior reveals the other son's bitterness. The brother who stayed at home working, doing the right thing, playing by the rules was angry. He was angry with his father for rewarding the prodigal's return. He seems angry with the prodigal as well, but perhaps it was actually jealousy. In any event, he had the gift that the prodigal missed out on – he had time with his father, working together, building relationship, enjoying life together. He had what could never be replaced, but as the story unfolds, he is blind to the truth.

We are each, to some extent, lost. We each have characteristics of both brothers. When we make poor choices and struggle, we must acknowledge our rebellion, repent and return home to our Father. Similarly, when we are convinced we are doing everything right, playing by the rules, obediently going through the motions yet failing to experience joy, perhaps we are missing out on the true gift of relationship with our Father. If that describes you, I urge you to acknowledge your rebellion, repent and return home to your Father so the joyful celebration in heaven might ensue.

2. Read I Peter 1. Peter was the first disciple to proclaim Jesus to be the Messiah and he was the rock upon whom Jesus built His church (see Matthew 16:13-20). He was with Jesus on the mountain when God transfigured Jesus (see Matthew 17:1-13), and after Peter denied knowing Jesus three times in rapid succession, Jesus tracked Peter down in Capernaum to call

him back to ministry (see John 21). Peter had experienced so much, and it amazes me that the same person who experienced life with Jesus during His earthly ministry wrote the words we now read as 1 Peter and 2 Peter.

As you read 1 Peter 1, realize it is Peter who wrote the words. With this firmly in your mind, read 1 Peter 1:13-25. Peter urges us to make holy choices, to "love one another deeply from the heart" (1 Peter 1:22), and to live lives worthy of our new birth in Christ Jesus. Can you think of things in your life that may be preventing you from following through on the life Peter urges you to live? If so, what will you do to remove those things from your life?

3. As John the Baptist paved the way for the coming Messiah, he preached a message of repentance saying, "Repent for the kingdom of heaven has come near" (Matthew 3:2). When Jesus started His ministry He traveled around Galilee preaching, "Repent, for the kingdom of heaven has come near" (Matthew 4:17). What role does repentance play as God prepares your heart to receive the gospel? What role does repentance play as you live your life as a disciple? Does the nature of repentance change as your heart changes? If so, how?

Waimea Canyon State Park, Kauai, Hawaii

23

AUDIENCE OF ONE

"Beware of practicing your piety before others in order to be seen by them; for then you have no reward from your Father in heaven. So whenever you give alms, do not sound a trumpet before you, as the hypocrites do in the synagogues and in the streets, so that they may be praised by others. Truly I tell you, they have received their reward. But when you give alms, do not let your left hand know what your right hand is doing, so that your alms may be done in secret; and your Father who sees in secret will reward you. And whenever you pray, do not be like the hypocrites; for they love to stand and pray in the synagogues and at the street corners, so that they may be seen by others. Truly I tell you, they have received their reward. But whenever you pray, go into your room and shut the door and pray to your Father who is in secret; and your Father who sees in secret will reward you." Matthew 6:1-6

> "AND WHENEVER YOU FAST, DO NOT LOOK DISMAL, LIKE THE HYPOCRITES, FOR THEY DISFIGURE THEIR FACES SO AS TO SHOW OTHERS THAT THEY ARE FASTING. TRULY I TELL YOU, THEY HAVE RECEIVED THEIR REWARD. BUT WHEN YOU FAST, PUT OIL ON YOUR HEAD AND WASH YOUR FACE, SO THAT YOUR FASTING MAY BE SEEN NOT BY OTHERS BUT BY YOUR FATHER WHO IS IN SECRET; AND YOUR FATHER WHO SEES IN SECRET WILL REWARD YOU." MATTHEW 6:16-18

For many the broad, immediate net cast by social media has created a mindset focusing on and deeply concerned with posts, each carefully designed to cast an image of perfection. Driven by this mindset, some orchestrate life to win praise from other people, with their sense of belonging and self-worth linked to the number of positive responses earned by each post. The mindset creates a vicious cycle of continuously seeking approval, often from mere acquaintances or people we do not even know.

In chapter 6 of his presentation of the gospel, Matthew records a portion of the Sermon on the Mount. Jesus teaches about personal holiness and our relationships with God and people in need, telling us not to undertake acts of faith to impress other people. He urges us to genuinely pursue God, to lead lives of faith, and to demonstrate faith through acts of righteousness, but to do so as matters exclusively between us and God. Acts of faith should not be intended to win social acclaim or twisted into theatrical productions for other people, and because doing so is so bad, Jesus urges us to practice our acts of holiness in ways that will not even be noticed by others.

As an example, I have a number of friends who are each engaged in prison ministry. As far as I know, none of them have any idea the others serve inmates. They each, on their own, go to a jail or prison to lead ministry. Some go to a jail or prison to pray. Others lead Bible studies. Some go into prisons to minister as part of larger groups. They each serve God by ministering to inmates, but they do not advertise their acts of righteousness.

Ideally, as we seek God, as our relationship with Him grows, as we direct our attention toward Him, we will naturally become less concerned with what other people think about us. Ideally, we bow to pray seeking God, unconcerned with what other people may think. When we serve, ideally, we deflect praise from ourselves so that God receives all praise. When we look inwardly seeking to grow closer to God, focusing on our own spiritual needs, seeking continued transformation, we should need no approval from other people. We should tie our sense of belonging and self-worth to the only absolute source of peace, comfort and rest. By making God our focus and priority, we live for an audience of one.

In the world today, with digital versions of our lives on full public display, secretly practicing acts of righteousness and living for an audience of one may seem counterintuitive. But Jesus urges us to seek God first so that we might grow closer to Him, not to win praise from others.

May you have the courage to break the cycle of the seeking approval from others. May you truly seek God first.

Thoughts to Consider

1.   Read Matthew 23. Jesus viciously attacks religious leaders in this chapter-long verbal assault, and the main thing He calls them out for is acting better than they are to receive approval from others. Here are few of Jesus' statements:

> "They do all their deeds to be seen by others; for they make their phylacteries broad and their fringes long. They love to have the place of honor at banquets and the best seats in the synagogues, and to be greeted with respect in the marketplaces, and to have people call them rabbi." Matthew 23:5-7

> "Woe to you, scribes and Pharisees, hypocrites! For you clean the outside of the cup and of the plate, but inside they are full of greed and self-indulgence. You blind Pharisee! First clean the inside of the cup, so that the outside also may become clean." Matthew 23:25-26

> "Woe to you, scribes and Pharisees, hypocrites! For you are like whitewashed tombs, which on the outside look beautiful, but inside they are full of the bones of the dead and of all kinds of filth. So you also on the outside look righteous to others, but inside you are full of hypocrisy and lawlessness." Matthew 23:27-28

A popular image of Jesus is that He is always sweet, always flowing kindness and compassion to everyone, but chapter 23 shows a different side of the Messiah. He brutally assaults people in positions of authority who abuse the power of their position, are arrogant, and put on a show to be praised by people. We are each at risk of falling into the same trap. Can you think of situations where that might be true of you?

2.   Read John 7. The chapter includes the following passage:

> About the middle of the festival Jesus went up into the temple and began to teach. The Jews were astonished at it, saying, "How does this man have such learning, when he has never been taught?" Then Jesus answered them, "My teaching is not mine but his who sent me. Anyone who resolves to do the will of God will know whether the teaching is from God or whether I am speaking on my own. Those who speak on their own seek their own glory; but the one who seeks the glory of him who sent him is true, and there is nothing false in him. John 7:14-18

We must each consider whose glory do we seek? Do we seek glory for ourselves or glory for God?

3.   Read Acts 3. As they were on their way to the temple to pray, John and Peter encountered a man who had been lame since birth. Peter took the man by the hand and he was healed. Everyone who saw it was astonished and they told others and soon a crowd gathered looking at Peter and John. Peter spoke to the crowd. He understood that the crowd looked at Peter and John as if they had done something remarkable, and he was

quick to point out it was not them, rather it was the power of Christ Jesus working through them. He explained that God raised Jesus from the dead and that "by faith in his name, his name itself has made this man strong, whom you see and know; and the faith that is through Jesus has given him this perfect health in the presence of all of you" (Acts 3:16).

Peter and John were out in the world allowing the light, love and life of Christ Jesus to flow through them, and they made sure that Christ Jesus was glorified, not them.

4.   Read Matthew 5. The Sermon on the Mount is recorded as chapters 5-7 of Matthew. Jesus begins the sermon by giving the Beatitudes, a series of short statements of blessing. Immediately after the Beatitudes, Jesus says,

> "You are the salt of the earth; but if salt has lost its taste, how can its saltiness be restored? It is no longer good for anything, but is thrown out and trampled under foot.
>
> "You are the light of the world. A city built on a hill cannot be hid. No one after lighting a lamp puts it under the bushel basket, but on the lampstand, and it gives light to all in the house. In the same way, let your light shine before others, so that they may see your good works and give glory to your Father in heaven." Matthew 5:13-16

He urges us to do good works so that God will be glorified. God is light, love and life. We may be created in His image, but when we do good works it is really His goodness flowing through us, it is His light shining not ours. So it is appropriate that the world exalts Him, not us. It is appropriate that we exalt

Him for the opportunity to serve Him and the relationship we enjoy with Him, because He is who He is.

When you are out in the world serving others, how do you direct others to give glory to God because of your good deeds?

Lake City, Colorado

24

SEPARATION FROM GOD

> WHO WILL SEPARATE US FROM THE LOVE OF CHRIST? WILL HARDSHIP, OR DISTRESS, OR PERSECUTION, OR FAMINE, OR NAKEDNESS, OR PERIL, OR SWORD? AS IT IS WRITTEN, "FOR YOUR SAKE WE ARE BEING KILLED ALL DAY LONG; WE ARE ACCOUNTED AS SHEEP TO BE SLAUGHTERED." NO, IN ALL THESE THINGS WE ARE MORE THAN CONQUERORS THROUGH HIM WHO LOVED US. FOR I AM CONVINCED THAT NEITHER DEATH, NOR LIFE, NOR ANGELS, NOR RULERS, NOR THINGS PRESENT, NOR THINGS TO COME, NOR POWERS, NOR HEIGHT, NOR DEPTH, NOR ANYTHING ELSE IN ALL CREATION, WILL BE ABLE TO SEPARATE US FROM THE LOVE OF GOD IN CHRIST JESUS OUR LORD. ROMANS 8:35-39

I recall coaches rallying our team before big games. With the team dressed, crowding the locker room, preparing to run onto the field, the coach spoke with passion igniting the team's emotion, building our confidence, and encouraging our will to fight. The hard work of preparation was finished; this was time to charge forward in confidence. Our coach passionately urged us forward instilling the knowledge, belief and confidence that we would win the game. Paul concludes chapter 8 of Romans with a pre-game rallying cry.

Nothing will be able to separate us from the love of God that is in Christ Jesus. Nothing. We will face trouble, hardship, pain and danger, but none of that will be able to separate us from God unless of course we grant it that power.

God gives His spiritual life here and now. He offers His life to us now, while we still walk around this world in these bodies. He offers life now. All we need to do is receive His holy gift of grace. We often talk about God and we should. We say and we understand intellectually that He created all things by speaking, that He breathes the breath of life into each of us, that He is infinite, He is everywhere all at the same time, that He is unbound by time, that He has power beyond anything we can ever comprehend.

And while He creates life, He also conquered death. Through Jesus Christ, He conquered death and He built a bridge spanning the chasm separating us from Him. We often discuss His incomprehensible power. As I stop to ponder the power necessary to conquer death, I realize that is truly incomprehensible power and authority. That is sovereignty.

And His Holy Spirit dwells within us. The Spirit of the sovereign One abides in you. And Jesus promises, "You will receive power when the Holy Spirit has come upon you…" (Acts

1:8). God is all-powerful, and you have His power within you the moment you first believe.

But we continue to struggle. We have each, the moment we first believe, received God's holy gift of redemption. We are children of God, we are brothers and sisters in Christ, we have the Holy Spirit dwelling within us. But we still struggle because we continue to live in this dark realm, we continue to be influenced by evil desires and we are still blindsided by evil forces. Sometimes we invite them in through our choices, but at other times they appear through no wrongdoing of our own.

We exist in the in-between state – we have experienced some of His glory but we have not yet experienced it fully. It's like walking in the house on Thanksgiving and smelling the aroma of the amazing food, but not yet feasting on it. The aroma wets our appetite; it makes us want more; yet we continue to live in this realm where everyone experiences hardship and trouble.

Sometimes hardship is caused by our own poor decisions, but sometimes it is thrust upon us from wholly outside faceless forces like famine. Rain stops falling, crops stop growing, agricultural communities falter and people starve. Here, today, we discuss global economic downturns leading to the downward spiral of layoffs, homelessness and starvation – hardship thrust upon people from outside forces.

At other times, evil has a face. As we move through the world we brush elbows with various forms of evil, and we know that people acting under the influence of evil commit horrific acts deeply scarring innocent victims every day. Innocence is lost, trust is shattered and pain ripples through families and communities.

When evil is thrust upon us, we are forced to make a choice – how will we respond? Will we seek God in response to the unexpected and undeserved pain, or will we allow it to drive a wedge between us and God?

Paul discusses suffering and hardship as certainties, not just for humans but for all of creation (see Romans 8:22). God's holy word proclaims that the Holy Spirit dwells in us, that He knows us, that He knows our needs and that He prays for us. When we know this in the depths of our souls, how can any hardship separate us from God? Like a good coach, Paul urges us to conclude that nothing can separate us from God. He urges us to make use of God's power within us, to know that the Holy Spirit is praying for us, to know that He is with us, and to use pain and suffering as tools to grow closer to the Source of love.

Know in your heart, in the depths of your soul that no horrific evil thrust upon you, no sickness, no hunger, no addiction, nothing can separate you from the love of God that is in Christ Jesus. Nothing.

THOUGHTS TO CONSIDER

1.   Read Psalm 46. God promises that He is with us and He helps us during our times of need. He does not promise to make our lives trouble free, in fact, it might be possible to read the psalm as confirmation that we will each experience trouble. But He is with us. He is our refuge. The psalmist writes:

> God is our refuge and strength, a very present help in trouble. Psalm 46:1
>
> The Lord of hosts is with us; the God of Jacob is our refuge. *Selah* Psalm 46:7
>
> "Be still, and know that I am God! I am exalted among the nations, I am exalted in the earth." The Lord of hosts is with us; the God of Jacob is our refuge. *Selah* Psalm 46:10-11

2. Read Isaiah 41. God speaks through the prophet Isaiah to His people saying,

> But you, Israel, my servant, Jacob, whom I have chosen, the offspring of Abraham, my friend; you whom I took from the ends of the earth, and called from its farthest corners, saying to you, "You are my servant, I have chosen you and not cast you off"; do not fear, for I am with you, do not be afraid, for I am your God; I will strengthen you, I will help you, I will uphold you with my victorious right hand. Isaiah 41:8-10

3. Read Zephaniah 3. God speaks through the prophet Zephaniah to His people saying,

> The Lord, your God, is in your midst, a warrior who gives victory; he will rejoice over you with gladness, he will renew you in his love; he will exalt over you with loud singing as on a day of festival. Zephaniah 3:17-18

4.   No matter what you are going through, He is with you. Nothing can separate you from His love in Christ Jesus our Lord. How do you respond to God's many assurances that He is with you?

Prichett Canyon, Utah

25

THE FASTING GOD DESIRES

SHOUT OUT, DO NOT HOLD BACK! LIFT UP YOUR VOICE LIKE A TRUMPET! ANNOUNCE TO MY PEOPLE THEIR REBELLION, TO THE HOUSE OF JACOB THEIR SINS. YET DAY AFTER DAY THEY SEEK ME AND DELIGHT TO KNOW MY WAYS, AS IF THEY WERE A NATION THAT PRACTICED RIGHTEOUSNESS AND DID NOT FORSAKE THE ORDINANCE OF THEIR GOD; THEY ASK OF ME RIGHTEOUS JUDGMENTS, THEY DELIGHT TO DRAW NEAR TO GOD. "WHY DO WE FAST, BUT YOU DO NOT SEE? WHY HUMBLE OURSELVES, BUT YOU DO NOT NOTICE?" LOOK, YOU SERVE YOUR OWN INTEREST ON YOUR FAST DAY, AND OPPRESS ALL YOUR WORKERS. LOOK, YOU FAST ONLY TO QUARREL AND TO FIGHT AND TO STRIKE WITH A WICKED FIST. SUCH FASTING AS YOU DO TODAY WILL NOT MAKE YOUR VOICE HEARD ON HIGH. IS SUCH THE FAST THAT I CHOOSE, A DAY TO HUMBLE ONESELF? IS IT TO BOW DOWN THE HEAD LIKE A BULRUSH, AND TO LIE IN SACKCLOTH AND ASHES? WILL YOU CALL THIS A FAST, a day acceptable to the Lord?

Is not this the fast that I choose: to loose the bonds of injustice, to undo the thongs of the yoke, to let the oppressed go free, and to break every yoke? Is it not to share your bread with the hungry, and bring the homeless poor into your house; when you see the naked, to cover them, and not to hide yourself from your own kin? Then your light shall break forth like the dawn, and your healing shall spring up quickly; your vindicator shall go before you, the glory of the Lord shall be your rear guard. Then you shall call, and the Lord will answer; you shall cry for help, and he will say, Here I am. Isaiah 58:1-9

We know how to do church and we do it well. We go to church most Sundays, we worship God, we praise Jesus Christ and the Holy Spirit, we sing worship songs, we give when the offering plate is passed, and we fast during Lent. We pray and study Scripture, and we each practice regular spiritual disciplines allowing us each to connect with God. While the practices are good and right, and they position us to receive God's holy transformative gift of grace in increasing measure, if we stop there, we will not experience the fullness of God's glory available to us. God calls us to allow Him to transform our spirits and souls so that we are able to go out into the world as His servants shining His light on the darkness we encounter.

Isaiah spoke to a congregation that did church well but stopped progressing along the path toward God. They longed to know God; they went to church worshiping Him; they humbled themselves before God; they fasted; and they presented themselves as righteous people; yet they continued to feel a distance between themselves and God. They sensed that God was not pleased with their worship; they failed to experience the fullness of God's blessing on their lives; and they wondered why.

God encouraged them and encourages us to view our lives through holistic lenses. He desires relationship with us and He also desires that we join our brothers and sisters in the wholeness of true relationship. While the Israelites worshiped God, they failed in their relationships with other people – they allowed injustice to continue oppressing people around them; they failed to share their excess food with hungry people; they failed to share their excess space with people in need of shelter; they failed to love their neighbors in need through tangible action.

He connects the word "fast" with a call to eliminate injustice in the world. I normally think of fasting as an inwardly focused endeavor undertaken to enhance my connection with God. I think of it as something exclusively between God and me. The passage above encourages us to see that acting in the world to end injustice and to help people in need are also forms of fasting. In fact, according to the passage, it is the form of fasting God desires.

I recently read Martin Luther King Jr.'s book *Why We*

Can't Wait in which he details the thoughts and strategies behind the Birmingham boycotts that took place during the summer of 1963. He discussed the "black church" and the "white church" as two separate entities. According to King, most white Christians in Alabama saw that their black brothers and sisters lived in poorer circumstances with fewer opportunities for advancement and fewer freedoms than they had; yet they were oblivious to the horrors inherent in the situation and the need for change. The scene they saw had become normal. They were unable to see the situation as an opportunity to act, so they failed to act. They did not help; they did not speak up; they sat back in silence.

I wonder what events swirl around me that I fail to see? What opportunities to be an agent of change in the world am I failing to act upon? Who am I failing to help? What injustice is standing, hidden in plain view because I am too oblivious to see it for what it is?

We are called to seek first God. We are called to allow His holy grace to transform our spirits and souls. We are called to practice spiritual disciplines regularly. And we are called to act in the world as His salt and light. We are called to help people in need and "to loose the bonds of injustice, to undo the thongs of the yoke, to let the oppressed go free, and to break every yoke."

May God fill us with His holy discerning spirit. May God enlighten our eyes to see the injustice around us, may He open our minds to see the avenues available for us to help, may He fill us with His power, courage and strength that we might act as His people making a difference in the world.

THOUGHTS TO CONSIDER

1. Read Amos 5. God laments Israel's condition. After describing His sorrow, God urges His people to seek Him, to do good and to hate evil. And He says,

> I hate, I despise your festivals, and I take no delight in your solemn assemblies. Even though you offer me your burnt offerings and grain offerings, I will not accept them; and the offerings of well-being of your fatted animals I will not look upon. Take away from me the noise of your songs; I will not listen to the melody of your harps. But let justice roll down like waters, and righteousness like an ever-flowing stream. Amos 5:21-24

Apparently, His people went to church, recognized the holy festivals, praised God through appropriate song and offered God sacrifices and offerings, but God lamented because injustice prevailed in the land. Do you see similarities today? If you do, make a list, naming each.

2. Read Malachi 2. God expresses His unhappiness with priests at the time for giving poor instruction, causing people to stumble and not keeping God's ways. At the conclusion of the chapter God says,

> You have wearied the Lord with your words. Yet you say, "How have we wearied him?" By saying, "All who do evil are good in the sight of the Lord, and he delights in them." Or by asking, "Where is the God of justice?"

Malachi 2:17

How could anyone, much less a priest, say that people who do evil are good and that God delights in people who do evil? I realize Malachi served as prophet a long time ago and God directed His voice toward priests who served at that time, but is it possible the truth of His indictment continues today? Is it possible that we continue to confuse good and evil?

3. Read Hosea 12. As God summarizes Israel's long history of rebellion, He pleads with His people to return to Him saying,

> The Lord the God of hosts, the Lord is his name! But as for you, return to your God, hold fast to love and justice, and wait continually for your God. Hosea 12:5-6

4. God sent prophet after prophet begging His people to see the errors of their ways, begging them to see injustice in their midst, begging them to love their neighbors. Jesus continued delivering the message to religious leaders of His day saying,

> "But woe to you Pharisees! For you tithe mint and rue and herbs of all kinds, and neglect justice and the love of God; it is these you ought to have practiced, without neglecting the others." Luke 11:42

Given that God's people repeated the mistake over and over, time and time again for thousands of years, how likely is it that we continue making the same mistake now? What injustice do you see in your immediate vicinity? What might you do to eradicate it?

Zuma Beach, Malibu, California

26

THE TROUBLE WITH SUCCESS

One of the dinner guests, on hearing this, said to him, "Blessed is anyone who will eat bread in the kingdom of God!" Then Jesus said to him, "Someone gave a great dinner and invited many. At the time for the dinner he sent his slave to say to those who had been invited, 'Come; for everything is ready now.' But they all alike began to make excuses. The first said to him, 'I have bought a piece of land, and I must go out and see it; please accept my regrets.' Another said, 'I have bought five yoke of oxen, and I am going to try them out; please accept my regrets.' Another said, 'I have just been married, and therefore I cannot come.' So the slave returned and reported this to his master. Then the owner of the house became angry and said to his slave, 'Go out at once into the streets and lanes of the town and bring in the poor, the crippled, the blind, and the lame.' And the slave said, 'Sir, what you ordered has been done,

AND THERE IS STILL ROOM.' THEN THE MASTER SAID TO THE SLAVE, 'GO OUT INTO THE ROADS AND LANES, AND COMPEL PEOPLE TO COME IN, SO THAT MY HOUSE MAY BE FILLED. FOR I TELL YOU, NONE OF THOSE WHO WERE INVITED WILL TASTE MY DINNER.'" LUKE 14:15-24

Can you imagine a football team so dominant that its fans grew bored and stopped attending games? During some games over the past few seasons, the University of Alabama football team played at home in a sold out but partially empty stadium. Fans were so certain of a blowout victory that they chose not to attend, allowing their tickets to go unused. The coaches assembled a group of talented players who worked day and night to improve and as they dominated opponents their fans grew bored. The privilege of watching one of the premier college football teams execute a high level of play was not enough – the fans desired drama before victory. As strange as it sounds, the program's success drove fans away. Sometimes, even success causes problems.

On a certain Sabbath day, Jesus ate in the home of a prominent religious leader. Jesus noticed a man suffering from a physical condition causing his body to swell. After healing the man Jesus questioned religious leaders about Sabbath customs asking, "If one of you has a child or an ox that has fallen into a well, will you not immediately pull it out on a Sabbath day?" (Luke 14:5). He then taught about seeking honor. In response, another invited dinner guest said, "Blessed is anyone who will eat bread in the kingdom of God!" It was a pleasant attempt to divert the conversation back to civil discourse, but it was loaded with presumption – the speaker presumed that he and the others eating at the table would be among those invited to eat bread in the kingdom of God – but Jesus would not be diverted.

Jesus responded by discussing the trappings of success. He described material blessings preventing people from experiencing the wholeness of full relationship with God. In the parable, various people were invited to a party and many chose not to attend because they were too busy with their blessings. One was busy with his land, another was busy with oxen, and a man who recently married was busy with his bride. They were blessed and their blessings kept them away from the party, but the people who, by society's standards, appear to be outcasts – the poor, crippled and lame people – heard the invitation. Jesus does not mention whether they attended, but His silence suggests that they did indeed attend. They were invited to a party they never imagined being able to attend, and they happily, joyously attended.

Do our blessings keep us away from God? Are we so busy living our lives filled with material blessing that we fail to experience spiritual wholeness?

In Steve Corbett and Brian Fikkert's book *When Helping Hurts*, the authors encourage us to see poverty through holistic eyes. While we often consider poverty as exclusively an economic condition, when viewed through a holistic lens we see poverty as economic, emotional, relational, physical and spiritual. While some people suffer from economic poverty, others suffer from poverty of human relationships, poverty of self-image, poverty of relationship with God, or many different manifestations. As friends return from mission trips to economically impoverished places, I commonly hear them express amazement at the peace and joy revealed through the people they met during their trip. The locals they encountered experienced severe economic poverty, yet they enjoyed a wealth of community and a deep spiritual connection with Christ Jesus.

It is possible that our view of success focusing on economics and our pursuit of goals driven by that view may be shoving us toward spiritual, emotional and relational poverty? Is your pursuit of economic success hindering your relationships with God and other people, is it hindering your walk towards sanctification, is it causing you to ignore God's call in your life? Is it causing you to miss the party God invites you to attend?

May you take the time to breathe in the Holy Spirit. Allow Him to fill you with His vitality and to heal you and your relationships.

Thoughts to Consider

1. Read Revelation 19:1-10. The great multitude of heavenly beings praise God saying,

> "Hallelujah! Salvation and glory and power to our God, for his judgments are true and just.... Hallelujah! For the Lord our God the Almighty reigns. Let us rejoice and

> exult and give him glory, for the marriage of the Lamb has come, and his bride has made herself ready; to her it has been granted to be clothed with fine linen, bright and pure" – for the fine linen is the righteous deeds of the saints. And the angel said to me, "Write this down: Blessed are those who are invited to the marriage supper of the Lamb." And he said to me, "These are true words of God." Revelation 19:1-2 & 6-9

The Lamb is Christ Jesus. His bride is His church, the Body of Christ. The covenant of marriage symbolizes the relationship between God and His people – it is the relationship on earth that embodies romantic love, protective love, friendship love and agape love. How wonderful would the world be if everyone were to live as His holy church in covenant with Him and each other? "Blessed are those who are invited to the marriage supper of the Lamb."

2. Jesus urges us to be ready, which involves planning and acting in preparation. In the following passage we hear Jesus speaking and He explains that slaves who are ready are blessed:

> "Be dressed for action and have your lamps lit; be like those who are waiting for their master to return from the wedding banquet, so that they may open the door for him as soon as he comes and knocks. Blessed are those slaves whom the master finds alert when he comes; truly I tell you, he will fasten his belt and have them sit down to eat, and he will come and serve them. If he comes during the middle of the night, or near dawn, and finds them so, blessed are those slaves. "But know this: if the owner of the house had known at what hour

the thief was coming, he would not have let his house be broken into. You also must be ready, for the Son of Man is coming at an unexpected hour." Luke 12:35-40

3. Jesus often discusses fellowship with God through Him as analogous to a feast in the kingdom of God. In the following passage Jesus distinguishes people who may have had passing contact with Christ from people who truly have relationship with Him:

> Jesus went through one town and village after another, teaching as he made his way to Jerusalem. Someone asked him, "Lord, will only a few be saved?" He said to them, "Strive to enter through the narrow door; for many, I tell you, will try to enter and will not be able. When once the owner of the house has got up and shut the door, and you begin to stand outside and to knock at the door, saying, 'Lord, open to us,' then in reply he will say to you, 'I do not know where you come from.' Then you will begin to say, 'We ate and drank with you, and you taught in our streets.' But he will say, 'I do not know where you come from; go away from me, all you evildoers!' There will be weeping and gnashing of teeth when you see Abraham and Isaac and Jacob and all the prophets in the kingdom of God, and you yourselves thrown out. Then people will come from east and west, from north and south, and will eat in the kingdom of God. Indeed, some are last who will be first, and some are first who will be last." Luke 13:22-30

4. The passages above are intended to cause alarm. They jolt us to question our relationship with Him, to ponder the

condition of our hearts, souls, spirits and minds, to consider our actions and motives. This is a good and healthy thing if it prods each of us to get back on track, to turn to God and renew our advance toward Him. And so long as we are breathing it is not too late, because Jesus stands at the door of your heart and mine knocking, seeking entry, desiring to enter and dine with us. Jesus says,

> Listen! I am standing at the door, knocking; if you hear my voice and open the door, I will come in to you and eat with you, and you with me. Revelation 3:20

5. No one is perfect. Only Jesus is perfect. This means we each have something or many things separating us from God. What separates you from God? Pray for eyes to see what it is. Pray for strength and courage and power to remove it from your life so that you may move closer in your relationship with God through Christ Jesus.

Randy L Allen

Tuscaloosa, Alabama

27

Relationship with God

For God so loved the world that he gave his only Son, so that everyone who believes in him may not perish but may have eternal life. Indeed, God did not send the Son into the world to condemn the world, but in order that the world might be saved through him. John 3:16-17

Listen! I am standing at the door, knocking; if you hear my voice and open the door, I will come in to you and eat with you, and you with me. Revelation 3:20

God created the universe by speaking. He spoke and substance came to be out of nothing. He speaks and chaos turns to order. He is the only holy, pure, divine One. He formed you. He has plans for you. He knows the intimate details of your life – He knows your hopes, dreams, fears, anxieties, and the secrets hidden deep within the recesses of your mind. God is love and He loves you. Pause for a moment and let that sink in. God, who created the universe, knows you and loves you and desires relationship with you. He wants you to experience His life abundant.

A few days ago as I drove, a man's voice on the radio told a story. Like many stories, it began with him sitting in a bar talking with a stranger. Their conversation wandered from topic to topic. The stranger mentioned his children who were grown and living in distant places, and tears rolled down his cheeks as he described how much he missed them. He described the love and heartache that only a parent knows. He said that he finally understood why his father called him so frequently, though it took him far too long to appreciate it, and he wished that he had taken the time to call his father back more often. The man who told the story concluded by saying, "When someone who loves you reaches out, the least you can do is take their hand."

Jesus describes God, the Creator of the universe, as our Father. Scripture describes His followers as children of God, brothers and sisters of Jesus Christ, and adopted heirs. God the Father desires relationship with you, with me, with us. Every time I pause and allow that thought to soak in, I am amazed beyond words. The Creator of the universe, the Author of life, the sovereign One desires relationship with us, with you and me.

He desires relationship with us for our benefit, not His, and He desires it so much that Jesus came to earth as a human being. He forfeited His heavenly majesty and came to earth as a mere mortal, suddenly bound by space and time, suddenly exposed to the darkness of the world, suddenly exposed to pain, suffering and sadness. And then He voluntarily submitted Himself to humiliation, torture and death on the cross, so that we might have a path to God, a way to redemption, a bridge spanning the chasm separating us from Him. He came so that we might experience the fullness of life lived in relationship with God the Father, Jesus Christ and the Holy Spirit.

Your heavenly Father, who loves you, is reaching out to you. I urge you to take His hand, but you may be asking, "How do I take the hand of a spiritual being?" We simply seek Him. We acknowledge that He is really who He says He is, we acknowledge that we need Him, we ask Him to come into our lives, we open our hearts to make room for Him, and we invite Him to cleanse the depths of our souls. We invite His light to transform our darkness and His life to make us new and whole.

The holy, divine, Creator of all things desires relationship with you so that you will experience His wholeness. Jesus says, "Listen! I am standing at the door, knocking; if you hear my voice and open the door, I will come in to you and eat with you, and you with me." This is awesome beyond words. May you have ears to hear and the courage to respond.

Thoughts to Consider

1.   Read John 3. Nicodemus, a religious leader, has heard stories of Jesus' miracles, signs and wonders. He believes Jesus

is truly a teacher sent by God and he genuinely desires to understand the message Jesus is preaching, so he meets privately with Jesus. And Jesus explains the gospel to Nicodemus, but His words are difficult to understand. For instance, Jesus says, "Very truly, I tell you, no one can see the kingdom of God without being born from above" (John 3:3), and Nicodemus struggles to understand how an adult might experience physical birth a second time. Jesus explains that He is discussing spiritual matters, but the entire conversation is difficult.

At verse 16 we read what is likely the best-known passage in the New Testament:

> For God so loved the world that he gave his only Son, so that everyone who believes in him may not perish but may have eternal life. Indeed, God did not send the Son into the world to condemn the world, but in order that the world might be saved through him. John 3:16-17

God loves the world so much that He gave His only Son, so that through His Son each person gains the possibility of communion and relationship with God and spiritual wholeness, forever.

2. Read Genesis 22. God commands Abraham to sacrifice his son, Isaac, as a burnt offering to God. Abraham and Sarah had prayed for a son for years and when Abraham was one hundred years old, Isaac was born (see Genesis 21:5). God answered their prayers and years later, when Isaac was old enough to ask questions, God asked Abraham to kill Isaac as an offering to God, and Abraham obeyed. But just before the knife fell, God intervened and stopped Abraham. God's holy word promises, "God himself will provide the lamb for the burnt offering, my

son" (Genesis 22:8) and "'The Lord will provide;' as it is said to this day, 'On the mount of the Lord, it shall be provided'" (Genesis 22:14).

The story shocks our conscience. How could God ask Abraham to slay his son? How could a loving God ask this of anyone? As horrific as the request was, God asked Abraham to do nothing more than God Himself was willing to do. God did indeed provide the offering – He offered His only Son as the final atoning sacrifice for our sins.

Does the account of Abraham and Isaac help you to see God's offering of Christ Jesus with new eyes? If so, in what specific way?

3.   Read Romans 5:1-11. Paul, the master evangelist, presents justification through Christ Jesus by faith. Our alienation from God is suddenly transformed through Christ Jesus. We are reconciled with God and through this gift of grace we receive His love "poured into our hearts through the Holy Spirit that has been given to us" (Romans 5:5). He continues writing,

> But God proves his love for us in that while we still were sinners Christ died for us. Much more surely then, now that we have been justified by his blood, will we be saved through him from the wrath of God. For if while we were enemies, we were reconciled to God through the death of his Son, much more surely, having been reconciled, will we be saved by his life. But more than that, we even boast in God through our Lord Jesus Christ, through whom we have now received reconciliation. Romans 5:8-11

We have been justified by His blood. He saves us from God's wrath that we each deserve. "But more than that ... we have now received reconciliation" (Romans 5:11). By God's holy grace we are offered the gift of reconciliation, of relationship, of communion with Him.

4.   Read John 14. In the passage set forth above from Revelation, Jesus says He stands at the door knocking. He wants to come into our hearts but we must open the door. He is here offering His holy gift of grace, but we must receive the gift, we must open it, we must act, and we do so by keeping His word, and He responds by making His home with us. He makes His home with us! God's holy word says,

> Judas (not Iscariot) said to him, "Lord, how is it that you will reveal yourself to us, and not to the world?" Jesus answered him, "Those who love me will keep my word, and my Father will love them, and we will come to them and make our home with them. Whoever does not love me does not keep my words; and the word that you hear is not mine, but is from the Father who sent me. John 14:22-24

God, the holy Creator of everything, desires relationship with you through Christ Jesus. How do you respond to that awesome truth?

For the Praise of His Glory

Massadona, Colorado

28

RECOGNIZING GOD'S VISITATION

> AS HE CAME NEAR AND SAW THE CITY, HE WEPT OVER IT, SAYING, "IF YOU, EVEN YOU, HAD ONLY RECOGNIZED ON THIS DAY THE THINGS THAT MAKE FOR PEACE! BUT NOW THEY ARE HIDDEN FROM YOUR EYES. INDEED, THE DAYS WILL COME UPON YOU, WHEN YOUR ENEMIES WILL SET UP RAMPARTS AROUND YOU, AND HEM YOU IN ON EVERY SIDE. THEY WILL CRUSH YOU TO THE GROUND, YOU AND YOUR CHILDREN WITHIN YOU, AND THEY WILL NOT LEAVE WITHIN YOU ONE STONE UPON ANOTHER; BECAUSE YOU DID NOT RECOGNIZE THE TIME OF YOUR VISITATION FROM GOD." LUKE 19:41-44

The passage above is from Luke 19. Ten chapters earlier, at Luke 9:51, we see Jesus begin His final journey to Jerusalem. Chapter 19 records the final leg of the journey, which begins at the extremely low elevation of 850 feet below sea level in Jericho, near the Jordan River as it feeds into the Dead Sea.

In Jericho, Jesus seeks out Zacchaeus, the chief tax collector, and invites Himself to eat with Zacchaeus in his home. The crowd cannot believe Jesus would eat with a sinner like Zacchaeus, but over their meal Zacchaeus repents. Afterward, Jesus says to the crowd, "Today salvation has come to this house, because he too is a son of Abraham. For the Son of Man came to seek out and to save the lost" (Luke 19:9-10).

Jesus explains His mission – He came to "seek out and to save the lost." Speaking to the same crowd, Jesus tells the Parable of the Ten Pounds about personal responsibility and judgment. Through the parable Jesus reveals that He knows He has enemies, He will soon be leaving for a time, but when He returns He will have greater authority, and during His absence He calls His followers to continue doing His business (He had just said that His business is seeking out and saving the lost). He then begins hiking up and over the mountain to Jerusalem.

When He reaches the point where the Mount of Olives separates Him from Jerusalem, He mounts a donkey colt to ride into the city. As people see Jesus riding a colt, they understand it is significant, and they talk and a crowd soon gathers. They begin placing clothing and palm branches along the path and they shout welcoming words of praise. According to Luke, "the whole multitude of the disciples began to praise God joyfully with a loud voice for all the deeds of power they had seen, saying, 'Blessed is the king who comes in the name of the Lord! Peace in heaven, and glory in the highest heaven!'" (Luke 19:37-38).

It is a massive celebration. Adoring crowds welcome Him into town while praising God. They say the right words and their joyful enthusiasm is infectious and the crowd swells and everything seems wonderful, yet Jesus weeps.

He sits on the Mount of Olives, looking over the city, and He weeps over the city. He knows that although the crowd says the right words, their eyes are blind to the truth. They praise God and they say that Jesus came in God's holy name, but they fail to see that through Jesus the kingdom of God is in their midst. They fail to see that He truly is God. They fail to recognize "the things that make for peace" and looking over the city He foretells its demise because "you did not recognize the time of your visitation from God," suggesting the crushing of Jerusalem might have been stopped had they only had eyes to see.

Jesus came to seek out and save the lost. He knows He has enemies who want to destroy Him, He knows the crowd's words are hollow, He knows He will not save everyone, and He knows the consequences of their failure are shocking. Jesus says, "They will crush you to the ground, you and your children within you, and they will not leave within you one stone upon another; because you did not recognize the time of your visitation from God."

They would be crushed because they failed to recognize their visitation from God. Is it possible we fall into the same trap? Is it possible we act appropriately, we praise and worship Christ with all the right words and actions, yet we fail to truly understand, we fail to receive His holy transformation, we fail to recognize the time of our visitation with God?

Jesus is God. He has always been God. While He walked the earth, He was God in their presence. And now, He is God in our presence. He is God, the Almighty, the Creator of the universe, the sovereign One. Isn't it awesome that He is here with us, continuing to seek out and save the lost, desiring relationship with us? How awesome is it that He invites us to call God "Father"? It is so amazing that we have the opportunity to engage in conversation with the holy, pure, divine, Creator of the universe.

Think about the times you have experienced His presence, when your heart burned, when you were filled with His wholeness. Perhaps tears ran down your cheeks and you laughed and His joy bubbled out of you naturally. We have experienced Him, we have recognized Him, we have felt His peace, but as I imagine Jesus weeping over the adoring crowd, I cannot help but wonder how is He responding to me?

My thoughts go in two directions. First, I think about the times I have experienced His closeness. Think about the times you have experienced Him intimately. What were you doing? What enabled you to recognize the time of your visitation from God? How often does it happen? And I wonder, what is preventing me from experiencing His wholeness all the time?

I also imagine we are part of the crowd, welcoming and adoring Jesus as He rides past on the donkey, and we see Him for who He is. We see Him and we see God. We recognize our time of visitation from God, and I wonder, because it is so awesome to see this, what am I doing to tell everyone else in the crowd about the amazing things I see? We have experienced the wholeness, the peace, the life, the light of our holy, pure, Creator. How awesome is that? Who did you last tell about your awesome, life-changing experience with Him?

May you have eyes to see and ears to hear. May your heart be fertile soil in which His seed grows.

Thoughts to Consider

1. Read Luke 19. As Jesus leaves Zacchaeus' home, He stops to talk with the crowd and He tells them the Parable of the Ten Pounds. In the parable, a nobleman plans to go to a distant place to obtain royal power for himself and then return. Before departing, he gathers ten slaves and gives them ten pounds, instructing them to "do business with these until I come back" (Luke 19:13). While he is away, enemies try to seize control and each slave makes his own choices regarding management of the pound entrusted to him. Upon his return, the nobleman rewards the slaves who performed well, took away from those who performed poorly, and executed his enemies.

We know that Jesus is returning. He has entrusted His slaves to continue His business here on earth until His return. How do you respond to the parable? Why was this the perfect time for Jesus to unveil that particular parable?

2. Read Luke 13. The scene described in the passage above is not the only time Jesus grieves Jerusalem. Luke describes an earlier occasion as follows:

> At that very hour some Pharisees came and said to him, "Get away from here, for Herod wants to kill you." He said to them, "Go and tell that fox for me, 'Listen, I am

casting out demons and performing cures today and tomorrow, and on the third day I finish my work. Yet today, tomorrow, and the next day I must be on my way, because it is impossible for a prophet to be killed outside of Jerusalem.' Jerusalem, Jerusalem, the city that kills the prophets and stones those who are sent to it! How often have I desired to gather your children together as a hen gathers her brood under her wings, and you were not willing! See, your house is left to you. And I tell you, you will not see me until the time comes when you say, 'Blessed is the one who comes in the name of the Lord.'" Luke 13:34-35

Jesus came to seek out and save the lost. He longs to gather people together "as a hen gathers her brood under her wings." He grieves because so many refuse the holy gift of grace He offers.

3. Read Psalm 118:21-29. As Jesus enters Jerusalem on a donkey, the crowd quotes Psalm 118:26 and says exactly what Jesus foretold, shouting, "Blessed is the king who comes in the name of the Lord!" (Luke 19:38). They continue saying, "Peace in heaven, and glory in the highest heaven!" (Id), which is reminiscent of the angelic announcement of Jesus' birth. Angels said, "Blessed is the king who comes in the name of the Lord! Peace in heaven, and glory in the highest heaven!" (Luke 2:38). Does this influence your view of God's sovereign hand at work through the events?

Flatirons, Chautauqua Park, Boulder, Colorado

29

EXPERIENCING THE RESURRECTED CHRIST

Now on that same day two of them were going to a village called Emmaus, about seven miles from Jerusalem, and talking with each other about all these things that had happened. While they were talking and discussing, Jesus himself came near and went with them, but their eyes were kept from recognizing him.... As they came near the village to which they were going, he walked ahead as if he were going on. But they urged him strongly, saying, "Stay with us, because it is almost evening and the day is now nearly over." So he went in to stay with them. When he was at the table with them, he took bread, blessed and broke it, and gave it to them. Then their eyes were opened, and they recognized him; and he vanished from their sight. They said to each other, "Were not our hearts burning within us while he was talking to us on the road, while he was opening

THE SCRIPTURES TO US?" LUKE 24:13-16 & 28-32

Each Easter we celebrate the most significant event in human history: Jesus conquered death and provided a bridge across the chasm separating us from God. We must each ask our self, "How will I respond?" The resurrection forever changed the world, but will we allow it to change our lives? Whether we want to or not, we each will respond. Some will ignore it, some will deny it, and others will seek Jesus Christ and experience His glory. What is your response?

Scripture records two disciples during the afternoon of the first Easter struggling to make sense of everything that had recently taken place: Jesus' arrest, torture and death, and reports of His resurrection. As they walked from Jerusalem to Emmaus, Jesus in His post-resurrection form joined them, but they did not recognize Him. They described Jesus as a prophet sent by God. They mourned His death. They thought He would redeem Israel, but religious leaders and Roman authorities joined forces to execute Him. They had believed Jesus to be the Messiah, but things had not turned out the way they expected. They were sad, confused and distraught.

The man traveling with them, who we know to be Jesus, rebuked the disciples saying, "Oh, how foolish you are, and how slow of heart to believe all that the prophets have declared!" (Luke 24:25). Then He used Scripture to explain that Jesus was indeed the Messiah and that He had to suffer and die and enter God's glory. When the three travelers reached Emmaus, the two disciples urged the man to join them for dinner. At dinner, Jesus took bread, blessed it, broke it and gave it to the disciples and in that moment their eyes were opened, and they recognized the man to be Jesus, and He suddenly vanished.

The disciples thought back over their time walking with the man. They recalled how He explained Scripture to them and how it all made so much sense and how their hearts burned as He spoke. They had just spent the afternoon with the risen Christ. They had just experienced the resurrected Christ. God Himself had just joined them as they walked from Jerusalem to Emmaus, and God Himself had just explained His holy word to them, and as He did, their hearts burned.

They got up immediately, rushed back to Jerusalem and told others what had happened. They had experienced the risen Christ and they wanted to tell everyone.

God's plans did not align with their expectations. Events had not happened the way they expected. For days they had mourned the loss of their leader, the one upon whom they had placed their hopes, and on that first Easter day confusion blended with grief. They struggled to understand the events swirling around them. As they walked home, they talked through all the events, trying to make sense of it all. They thought Jesus was the Messiah, but they did not expect the Messiah to be arrested, tortured, crucified and resurrected. Then they experienced the risen Christ, their eyes were opened to see Jesus Christ in the breaking of bread, and they were filled with joy. God ordered the events in ways they did not expect and in ways that, until Jesus explained them, they did not understand.

God's plans frequently surprise us; they are commonly different from our plans. When life veers from our script, through faith we trust that God is working out His plan.

They "urged him strongly" to stay with them. What would have happened had they not urged the man to stay and simply allowed Him to continue along the road? They would have enjoyed a nice conversation with a stranger, but they would not have seen the resurrected Christ that day. Their eyes did not open to see Him until they urged Him to stay, extended loving hospitality, shared their blessings and communed through the breaking of bread. Enjoying conversation while walking along the road involves a degree of relationship, but breaking bread in your home involves an entirely different magnitude of intimacy. When did you last open your door and strongly urge the risen Christ to join you in your home?

Jesus says, "Listen! I am standing at the door, knocking; if you hear my voice and open the door, I will come in to you and eat with you, and you with me" (Revelation 3:20). Urge Him strongly to come in and stay with you.

How are you responding to the resurrected Christ? When your heart burned in response to His holy word, when you experienced His holy presence, when He transformed your sadness and pain into joy, what did you do? Did you rush out to your friends to tell them about your experience?

God came to earth as a human. Then He died so that we might each live. This is awesome beyond words. May you have eyes to see, ears to hear and may the power of the Holy Spirit infuse you with the courage and strength to tell everyone about your experience with the risen Christ.

Thoughts to Consider

1.   A gap frequently exists between our plans and God's plans, so we each must struggle each day with whether our faith allows us to truly trust Him. Do we really believe God is who He says He is? Do we really believe He has all power and authority, that He loves us, that He hears our prayers and that He responds? Do we really believe He has plans for us? If we do, why is it so hard to trust Him when we struggle, feel pain and feel as if our life is off track? Scripture reminds us that God's knowledge and vision are all-encompassing, and His reasoning is perfect. God reminds us through Isaiah saying,

> Remember this and consider, recall it to mind, you transgressors, remember the former things of old; for I am God, and there is no other; I am God, and there is no one like me, declaring the end from the beginning and from ancient times things not yet done, saying, "My purpose shall stand, and I will fulfill my intention," calling a bird of prey from the east, the man for my purpose from a far country. I have spoken, and I will bring it to pass; I have planned, and I will do it. Isaiah 46:8-11

God has plans and He will carry them out. Do you trust Him?

2.   Read Isaiah 55. My wife, Lori, did not plan to develop cancer in her leg. She did not plan for the chemo to come

extremely close to killing her. She did not plan to develop lung cancer or break her leg requiring surgery or catch the virus that leads to COVID. But God was not surprised by any of it. He knew each event would happen and He knew how He would respond. He knew He would heal her at the perfect time. Through Isaiah, God invites us to an abundant feast, He urges us to seek Him, and He reminds us that He truly is God almighty saying,

> Seek the Lord while he may be found, call upon him while he is near; let the wicked forsake their way, and the unrighteous their thoughts; let them return to the Lord, that he may have mercy on them, and to our God, for he will abundantly pardon. For my thoughts are not your thoughts, nor are your ways my ways, says the Lord. For as the heavens are higher than the earth, so are my ways higher than your ways and my thoughts than your thoughts. For as the rain and the snow come down from heaven, and do not return there until they have watered the earth, making it bring forth and sprout, giving seed to the sower and bread to the eater, so shall my word be that goes out from my mouth; it shall not return to me empty, but it shall accomplish that which I purpose, and succeed in the thing for which I sent it. Isaiah 55:6-11

He urges us to seek Him because He is God and His ways and thoughts are superior to ours, He is near, He seeks relationship with us, and He sends His holy word to us with a purpose. Is God worthy of your worship, praise and trust?

3. Read Luke 24. As Jesus walked with two men from Jerusalem to Emmaus, He explained Scripture to them (see Luke

24:27). Later as they ate together, their eyes were suddenly opened and they realized the man was Jesus (see Luke 24:31). After Jesus left them, they rushed back to Jerusalem to tell the others what had happened. While they were talking, Jesus appeared to them all. Scripture tells us,

> Then he opened their minds to understand the scriptures, and he said to them, "Thus it is written, that the Messiah is to suffer and to rise from the dead on the third day, and that repentance and forgiveness of sins is to be proclaimed in his name to all nations, beginning from Jerusalem. You are witnesses of these things. And see, I am sending upon you what my Father promised; so stay here in the city until you have been clothed with power from on high." Luke 24:45-49

Jesus opened their minds to recognize Him and to understand Scripture and in response their hearts burned. And He sends His Holy Spirit to empower His disciples to serve as witnesses for Him. We are each His witness. If you were called to testify about the times Jesus opened your mind and your heart burned in response to His holy presence, what would you say?

4.   Read Ephesians 1. Paul prays,

> I pray that the God of our Lord Jesus Christ, the Father of glory, may give you a spirit of wisdom and revelation as you come to know him, so that, with the eyes of your heart enlightened, you may know what is the hope to which he has called you, what are the riches of his glorious inheritance among the saints, and what is the immeasurable greatness of his power for us who believe,

according to the working of his great power. Ephesians 1:17-19

Paul prays that the eyes of our hearts will be enlightened with the Holy Spirit's wisdom and revelation, and to recognize His glory, and to experience His power within us, and to know His hope. We know and trust there is power in the name of Jesus. In Jesus' holy name, may it be so. Amen.

Spider Mesa, Utah

30

God's Ways

> FOR MY THOUGHTS ARE NOT YOUR THOUGHTS, NOR ARE YOUR WAYS MY WAYS, SAYS THE LORD. FOR AS THE HEAVENS ARE HIGHER THAN THE EARTH, SO ARE MY WAYS HIGHER THAN YOUR WAYS AND MY THOUGHTS THAN YOUR THOUGHTS. ISAIAH 55:8-9

My spirit grieves in response to recent events. As I read God's words spoken through Isaiah, I ponder times when my life ventured away from the script I had written. While some were unexpectedly joyous, others destroyed me, and the totality of my experience is part of who I am today. Thinking back, I am convinced that painful episodes were seasons of spiritual growth. They forced me to rely on God in ways I had not previously known, they enabled me to see other people with new eyes, and while I desire joy and health and happiness and all the wonder possible, I realize that difficulty helps me grow closer to God.

How often have you experienced pain, sadness, grief and

confusion, and you prayed for God to take away the pain, but it continued, and you wondered why God allowed you to suffer in that manner? Have you prayed for certain outcomes, and later watched as events unfolded in ways far removed from your prayers? In my experience, pain, sadness, grief and confusion force us to turn to God, to seek Him, to surrender, trust and grow in faith.

God, speaking through the prophet Isaiah, reminds us, "For my thoughts are not your thoughts, nor are your ways my ways, says the Lord. For as the heavens are higher than the earth, so are my ways higher than your ways and my thoughts than your thoughts." God's ways frequently surprise us because we are simply not smart enough and our vision, perspective and information are not expansive enough.

I know that God knows everything and that his thoughts and thought processes are perfect and that they are far removed from mine, but when I see certain events, I cannot help wondering why. Why did God allow that to happen, or why did He structure events that way? I think about the many surprising events in Scripture. As one of many examples, consider His plan for redemption. Had I been tasked with designing the plan, I would have never imagined a plan where God comes to earth as a man, surrenders Himself to torture and execution, is resurrected, and thereby offers redemption to everyone who believes in Him. I would have imagined something much simpler, like snapping His spiritual fingers or speaking and making it so. But God's plans are higher than mine.

Similarly, I think about tragic headlines. A heavily

armed young man filled with hatred and evil enters a synagogue intent on killing people as they worship God. Another young man straps bombs to his body, walks into a crowded market and detonates the bombs. A segment of the Body of Christ, a small sliver of the Body, allows tiny seeds of disunity to grow into an all-encompassing weed of dissention, threatening to fracture that sliver of the Body. Jesus prays for unity, yet at times we foster disunity and create chaos. When God speaks, He brings order out of chaos, yet chaos continues. Do we hear His voice?

I know God respects our free will and I know that evil is a natural consequence of and, really, a requirement for free will, but my spirit grieves when I see tangible evidence of evil, especially when evil appears to be in a position to claim some form of victory. I know God is all-powerful, He is sovereign, He can do anything and everything, and I know He has a plan for each of us and a plan for the Body of Christ, and I know His ways and thoughts are higher than mine, and I know He is victorious, so I trust in His sovereign plan, I pray that I am aligned with it, and I praise His holy name. And I thank God because I know that somehow He will reveal His glory, even through situations that appear dark and ominous to us.

I also know with absolute certainty that so long as we sincerely seek Him, so long as we truly surrender to Him, and truly endeavor to serve Him in word, deed and sign, we will grow closer to our brothers and sisters in Christ who are doing the same. God breeds unity. He is love and His presence generates peace. Praise God! Praise His holy name! Jesus Christ is victorious, He is the way, truth and life, He is the resurrection, and we are each cleansed, healed and made whole by His blood. Praise God!

"For my thoughts are not your thoughts, nor are your ways my ways, says the Lord. For as the heavens are higher than the earth, so are my ways higher than your ways and my thoughts than your thoughts." I try to imagine God's eternal perspective. He is beyond time. He knows how everything in this realm bound by time and space ultimately ends. His reality is eternity. By comparison, our time here on earth is a mere instant. How might our perspective change if we had some portion of God's eternal view? How might we see the events of each day differently? Would our thoughts and priorities change?

As I consider my task list for today, attempting to view it as I imagine an eternal view might be, what on the list has eternal significance? God is eternal. Spirits and souls continue forever. Relationships might continue forever. This causes me to ask, how will I use today to grow closer to God? What will I do to build relationships or foster the spiritual growth of people I encounter? My job is certainly important – eating and maintaining a roof over our heads are important – and our jobs are gifts from God, so I am not suggesting that we stop performing our jobs and other daily responsibilities, but is it possible we could seek God and better engage others through an eternal perspective while going about our daily responsibilities? Perhaps we would spend more time praying, studying Scripture, building relationships, engaging in conversation, getting to know one another, building trust and transparency, seeing others as God's holy creation, and allowing God's love to flow through us in tangible ways.

We will not gain God's thoughts or His ways entirely, they will always be higher than ours, but consider adding matters of eternal significance to your daily task list and see how it changes your perspective. Praise God! Praise His holy name. I thank God for the work He is accomplishing through you.

May God give you eyes to see, ears to hear, and a heart that allows His seeds to grow.

Thoughts to Consider

1. Read Psalm 39. The psalmist is acutely aware of how brief life is, describing it as fleeting, the size of a few small measurements, a mere breath, and nothing compared to God. We are here for but a flash while God is eternal, existing outside of time. The thought reminds me of the words written by John Newton in the song *Amazing Grace*: "When we've been there ten thousand years, bright shining as the sun, we've no less days to sing God's praise than when we'd first begun."[3]

The psalmist writes,

> "Lord, let me know my end, and what is the measure of my days; let me know how fleeting my life is. You have made my days a few handbreadths, and my lifetime is as nothing in your sight. Surely everyone stands as a mere breath." *Selah.* Psalm 39:4-5

Only God knows how much time we have left on earth. As you consider the uncertainty and relative brevity of our lifespan, do you think about changing anything in your life? What and why?

2.   Read James 4. In his open letter to churches, James addresses a number of issues fundamental to faith. At the end of chapter 4 he addresses the brevity and uncertainty of our lifespan writing,

> Come now, you who say, "Today or tomorrow we will go to such and such a town and spend a year there, doing business and making money." Yet you do not even know what tomorrow will bring. What is your life? For you are a mist that appears for a little while and then vanishes. Instead you ought to say, "If the Lord wishes, we will live and do this or that." As it is, you boast in your arrogance; all such boasting is evil. Anyone, then, who knows the right thing to do and fails to do it, commits sin. James 4:13-17

3.   Read Psalm 6. The psalm is a prayer for deliverance and healing. How does it reflect your prayers during your time of suffering? How is it different?

4.   Read I Corinthians 15. Paul summarizes the good news of Jesus Christ writing,

> Now I would remind you, brothers and sisters, of the good news that I proclaimed to you, which you in turn received, in which also you stand, through which also you are being saved, if you hold firmly to the message that I proclaimed to you – unless you have come to believe in vain. For I handed on to you as of first importance what I in turn had received: that Christ died for

our sins in accordance with the scriptures, and that he was buried, and that he was raised on the third day in accordance with the scriptures, and that he appeared to Cephas, then to the twelve. Then he appeared to more than five hundred brothers and sisters at one time, most of whom are still alive, though some have died. I Corinthians 15:1-6

God's ways are superior to our ways. His thoughts are superior to our thoughts. He planned the path for our salvation and implemented His plan at the perfect time. How is He working in your life?

For the Praise of His Glory

North Shore, Oahu, Hawaii

31

Mustard Seed

He also said, "With what can we compare the kingdom of God, or what parable will we use for it? It is like a mustard seed, which, when sown upon the ground, is the smallest of all the seeds on earth; yet when it is sown it grows up and becomes the greatest of all shrubs, and puts forth large branches, so that the birds of the air can make nests in its shade." Mark 4:30-32.

I am amazed by the miracle of new life. I look at our grandson's tiny hands and feet. He is a tiny little human with tiny little features, yet he has everything within him necessary to grow into an adult. He as all the parts of humanity, God has encoded and programmed his cells to multiply and work together according to His wondrous plan. Given time, nutrients and support he will grow physically, and given proper spiritual nutrients and support, God's presence will grow within him as well.

Scripture often uses physical images to portray spiritual realities. In the so-called Love Chapter, Paul paints an analogy between his progression from childhood and his spiritual transformation, writing, "When I was a child, I spoke like a child, I thought like a child, I reasoned like a child; when I became an adult, I put an end to childish ways. For now we see in a mirror, dimly, but then we will see face to face. Now I know only in part; then I will know fully, even as I have been fully known" (1 Corinthians 13:11-12). Similar to our physical growth, we are growing spiritually in Jesus Christ, and as we grow we put away things from our former life. The image suggests that spiritual progression moves in a single direction – just as fully-grown adults do not revert into infants, people moving toward spiritual maturity do not revert.

Similarly, Jesus uses the image of a mustard seed to describe the growth potential of the kingdom of God. A mustard seed is a tiny little seed, and, like an infant, it contains everything necessary to grow into the largest plant in the garden. God has encoded and programmed the seed such that, given time, nutrients and support, it will grow large enough to support perching birds. It is designed to grow in a single direction – after the seed sprouts and begins to grow, it cannot revert back into a seed.

So it is with the kingdom of God. Given fertile soil, nutrients, support and time, God's holy seeds grow and our spirits are transformed and we experience His holy touch on our lives and we cannot go back. Once we experience God's holy grace, once we know with certainty that He is with us, that He is who He says He is, that He really dwells within us, we cannot go back to the place we were before. The power of the Holy Spirit is within you, me, us. Once we experience Him, we cannot go back.

May the kingdom of God grow into a mighty oak within you. May you continue on the path to spiritual adulthood. May you breathe in God's holy presence with each breath you take, may you invite Him into your heart in a new and refreshed way, may you experience His wholeness, may the kingdom of God grow within you.

Thoughts to Consider

1. Read Mark 4. The chapter begins with Jesus sitting in a boat near the shore teaching through parables to a crowd gathered nearby. He tells the Parable of the Sower and later He explains the parable to the disciples. The sower generously scatters seeds everywhere – on the path, on rocky soil, among thorns, and on good soil. Birds eat seeds from the path. Seeds on rocky soil grow but quickly wither because their roots do not grow. Seeds planted near thorns grow but are soon choked out. Seeds in good soil grow and produce an abundant crop.

Jesus explains that the seed is God's holy word. He scatters His word all over the place and the condition of the soil where it lands determines the outcome. Jesus says,

> "Do you not understand this parable? Then how will you understand all the parables? The sower sows the word. These are the ones on the path where the word

is sown: when they hear, Satan immediately comes and takes away the word that is sown in them. And these are the ones sown on rocky ground: when they hear the word, they immediately receive it with joy. But they have no root, and endure only for a while; then, when trouble or persecution arises on account of the word, immediately they fall away. And others are those sown among the thorns: these are the ones who hear the word, but the cares of the world, and the lure of wealth, and the desire for other things come in and choke the word, and it yields nothing. And these are the ones sown on the good soil: they hear the word and accept it and bear fruit, thirty and sixty and a hundredfold." Mark 4:13-20

Out of the four types of soil, only one produces a crop. God is showering us with His holy grace, are we prepared to receive it? We must contend with evil forces trying to snatch the seeds from our grasp. We must contend with personal desires and the busyness of life preventing His holy seed from producing a crop through us. We must have faith established in advance of trouble and persecution in order to respond properly to it.

What are your daily disciplines? What do you do each day to prepare your soil to receive His holy word? As you consider your daily routine, what should you change to better prepare your heart to receive Him?

2. As Jesus concludes the Parable of the Sower He says, "Let anyone with ears to hear listen!" (Mark 4:9). After explaining the parable, Jesus says,

> "Is a lamp brought in to be put under the bushel basket,

or under the bed, and not on the lampstand? For there is nothing hidden, except to be disclosed; nor is anything secret, except to come to light. Let anyone with ears to hear listen!" And he said to them, "Pay attention to what you hear; the measure you give will be the measure you get, and still more will be given you. For to those who have, more will be given; and from those who have nothing, even what they have will be taken away." Mark 4:21-25

Jesus repeats His urging for people with ears to hear to listen, and He urges us to pay attention because "the measure you give will be the measure you get...." What is He saying? What does it mean, particularly in the context of the Parable of the Sower and the Parable of the Mustard Seed?

3. Read Isaiah 61. Early in His ministry, Jesus travels to His hometown and teaches at the synagogue. He reads Scripture starting at Isaiah 61:1. After reading He says, "Today this scripture has been fulfilled in your hearing" (Luke 4:21). Jesus claims God's anointing and proclaims that He brings good news, heals, frees and comforts, and those who receive His words "will be called oaks of righteousness, the planting of the Lord to display his glory" (Isaiah 61:3). May you be a mighty oak of faith and righteousness.

For the Praise of His Glory

Prichett Canyon, Utah

32

Go!

The man from whom the demons had gone begged that he might be with him; but Jesus sent him away, saying, "Return to your home, and declare how much God has done for you." So he went away, proclaiming throughout the city how much Jesus had done for him. Luke **8:38-39**

Then Jesus called the twelve together and gave them power and authority over all demons and to cure diseases, and he sent them out to proclaim the kingdom of God and to heal. Luke **9:1-2**

After this the Lord appointed seventy-two others and sent them two by two ahead of him to every town and place where he was about to go. He told them, "The harvest is plentiful, but the workers are few. Ask the Lord of the harvest, therefore, to send out workers into his

HARVEST FIELD. GO! I AM SENDING YOU OUT LIKE LAMBS AMONG WOLVES. "WHEN YOU ENTER A TOWN AND ARE WELCOMED, EAT WHAT IS OFFERED TO YOU. HEAL THE SICK WHO ARE THERE AND TELL THEM, 'THE KINGDOM OF GOD HAS COME NEAR TO YOU.'" LUKE 10:1-3 & 8-9 (NIV)

Jesus heals, cleanses, and empowers, and then He sends transformed people out into the world as His salt and light. He is always sending people to help others. Scripture provides many examples of this. As one example He sent the twelve disciples out into the world to preach, teach, heal and cleanse. He taught them, He demonstrated God's power to them, and when they were ready, they received His transformative presence and went out into the world as His agents. Scripture says Jesus "gave them power and authority over all demons and to cure diseases, and he sent them out to proclaim the kingdom of God and to heal" (Luke 9:1-2). After that, He sent a larger group of transformed followers, seventy-two messengers, out into the world to heal the sick and to teach about the kingdom of God.

Scripture records Jesus regularly sending people away from Him to demonstrate God's love through loving action and miraculous signs, and to tell the world the good news of God's holy kingdom. He tells people to "Go!" He urges us to become engaged in God's mission in the world. He offers His holy transformation, He fills us with His love, His life, His light, and, according to His will, He empowers disciples to heal, cleanse and reveal His power and love and grace here on earth.

As I ponder this message, I am reminded of how difficult it is for most of us to reveal our inner selves to the world. We tend to keep our hearts wrapped up and hidden. Jesus Christ lives in our hearts, but we choose to keep Him to ourselves and reveal Him only to others within the safe confines of our church building. This thought causes me to ponder the safety we feel within that sacred space.

As we gather together to worship each Sunday, at times we look around, count heads and judge the effectiveness of the service by the attendance. We meet in our beautiful church building, invite others to come worship with us, and I pray we are hospitable to them when they come, and while inviting others to join us in worship and enjoying crowded, vibrant services are good things, if we consider Jesus' instruction, we might focus more on going out into the world and sharing the good news of the kingdom God than on convincing others to come to us.

I recently had the opportunity to study under Dr. Winston Worrell. He suggested that we consider church as a train station or crossroads rather than a destination. As he spoke, I envisioned church as a rural gas station. In some rural areas, the local gas station is the place where people stop briefly in the morning for a cup of coffee, a bite to eat, a moment of connection, and some fuel before they continue along their way out into the world where they live their lives. The gas station is the place people connect and refuel on their way toward their destination. If Jesus sends us out into the world as His light, should we consider our church building as a gas station rather than the destination?

Jesus promises to empower us when He sends us out. He gives power and authority to people that He sends out into the world. If we believe this, if we really believe this, how could we possibly be intimidated or fearful of following His call?

After crossing the Sea of Galilee, Jesus met a man possessed by a legion of demons. Jesus ordered demons out of the man and sent them into a herd of pigs causing the pigs to run off a cliff, fall into the sea and drown. After this miraculous experience, the newly freed man wanted to follow Jesus. He begged Jesus to allow him to follow Him and to join His group traveling with Him, but Jesus sent the man away. Jesus sent the man out into the world to tell everyone "how much God has done for (him)." The man was walking, talking, living, breathing testimony of God's holy, cleansing, healing grace. His changed appearance and behavior were miraculous signs of God's power, authority and love – the man's words merely confirmed what people could readily see before he spoke. And Jesus sent him into the world to tell others about his experience with God using a simple formula: "declare how much God has done for you."

Years ago I was in Mongolia and, as the visiting foreigner, I was asked to stand in front of a congregation and give my testimony. I was terrified. The pastor saw my deer-in-the-headlights response and he tried to encourage me saying, "it's no big deal, just explain what your life was like before meeting Jesus and what it is like now." In the moment of terror, I found much more comfort thinking that no one in the room spoke English anyway. But as we consider going out into the world as Christ's disciples, the formula is quite simple: simply explain what God has done for you.

Jesus urges His disciples to "Go!" As you go out into the world today, please remember that the formula is simple, Jesus' provision of power and authority is real, and He really does call us to serve as His light while we are out in the world. May you know His strength, power and courage dwell within you, may you seize the opportunities placed in your path to share the good news, may you grow as His disciple today.

Thoughts to Consider

1. Read Matthew 28. The final paragraph in the Gospel According to Matthew says,

> Now the eleven disciples went to Galilee, to the mountain to which Jesus had directed them. When they saw him, they worshiped him; but some doubted. And Jesus came and said to them, "All authority in heaven and on earth has been given to me. Go therefore and make disciples of all nations, baptizing them in the name of the Father and of the Son and of the Holy Spirit, and teaching them to obey everything that I have commanded you. And remember, I am with you always, to the end of the age." Matthew 28:16-20

Jesus tells His disciples to go out into the world teaching the good news, instructing everyone to obey Jesus' commands, and baptizing in the name of Father, Son and Holy Spirit. He calls us to go.

2.   Read Acts 1. For forty days after that first Easter, Jesus appeared to many and taught. According to Paul, Jesus appeared to the twelve disciples, to James, to the apostles and then to Paul (see 1 Corinthians 15:5-8). As Jesus prepared to ascend to heaven, He met with the disciples and said, "But you will receive power when the Holy Spirit has come upon you; and you will be my witnesses in Jerusalem, in all Judea and Samaria, and to the ends of the earth" (Acts 1:8). Immediately after saying that, He ascended to heaven.

Jesus promises the power of the Holy Spirit will come upon you and He calls His disciples to go out into the world as His witnesses. He calls us to go.

3.   Read 1 Peter 3. Peter witnessed and experienced so much alongside Jesus, and after Jesus ascended to heaven, Peter was in Jerusalem during that particular Pentecost celebration when God unleashed the Holy Spirit and he preached his first sermon (see Acts 2). In his first letter he urges his readers to gently and reverently serve as witnesses to the hope they have in Christ, writing,

> Now who will harm you if you are eager to do what is good? But even if you do suffer for doing what is right, you are blessed. Do not fear what they fear, and do not be intimidated, but in your hearts sanctify Christ as Lord. Always be ready to make your defense to anyone who demands from you an accounting for the hope that is in you; yet do it with gentleness and reverence. 1 Peter

3:13-16

How do you explain the hope that you have in Christ Jesus? Is your hope in Christ Jesus obvious enough for others to ask you about it?

For the Praise of His Glory

Rocky Moutain National Park, Colorado

33

SEIZING CHRIST'S REST

AT THAT TIME JESUS SAID, "I THANK YOU, FATHER, LORD OF HEAVEN AND EARTH, BECAUSE YOU HAVE HIDDEN THESE THINGS FROM THE WISE AND THE INTELLIGENT AND HAVE REVEALED THEM TO INFANTS; YES, FATHER, FOR SUCH WAS YOUR GRACIOUS WILL. ALL THINGS HAVE BEEN HANDED OVER TO ME BY MY FATHER; AND NO ONE KNOWS THE SON EXCEPT THE FATHER, AND NO ONE KNOWS THE FATHER EXCEPT THE SON AND ANYONE TO WHOM THE SON CHOOSES TO REVEAL HIM. COME TO ME, ALL YOU THAT ARE WEARY AND ARE CARRYING HEAVY BURDENS, AND I WILL GIVE YOU REST. TAKE MY YOKE UPON YOU, AND LEARN FROM ME; FOR I AM GENTLE AND HUMBLE IN HEART, AND YOU WILL FIND REST FOR YOUR SOULS. FOR MY YOKE IS EASY, AND MY BURDEN IS LIGHT." MATTHEW 11:25-29

In five short sentences, Jesus connects several amazing

nuggets worthy of prolonged meditation. God is the source of wisdom and we value education, intelligence and rational thought; yet as we pursue higher thinking and seek to be seen as clever, we might miss the simplicity of God's truth. If we seek God the Father, we find Him through Jesus Christ, the source of rest and peace. God creates order out of chaos; He is the source of life, love and wisdom; we know God the Father through Jesus Christ; and the Prince of Peace offers peace, comfort and rest.

Last Wednesday my schedule was overloaded. I started my day much earlier than usual, hurried to work and jumped into the fray, moving from project to project without taking much of a break, before rushing to the Sanctuary to set up for our prayer meeting and Holy Communion. After preparing the Sanctuary, I sat in a pew, took a few deep breaths and suddenly realized how tired I was. In my stillness, exhaustion crept in. I closed my eyes and they burned. My body was tired. My mind was tired. I needed rest. As these things began to occur to me folks began to arrive for our time together in prayer. We talked, sang hymns, shared Holy Communion and prayed, and during our time together basking in Christ's holy presence, my exhaustion disappeared. I stood after our time praying together and, amazingly, I was recharged. My eyes no longer burned, my body was no longer tired, I felt better in every possible way.

"Come to me … and I will give you rest … and you will find rest for your souls." Rest. The Greek word translated in English as "rest" is transliterated as "anapauso." The word is sometimes used in a passive sense to mean sleeping or relaxing after hard work. In the passive sense the word focuses on the subject's activity or lack of activity. But in the passage above, the word is used in an active sense focusing on the result rather than the activity, which may lead us to words like refresh or recharge. This is what I experienced. After a long, hard day I was exhausted and as I bowed before Jesus Christ worshiping Him, singing hymns and praying and seeking Him, He refreshed and recharged my body, soul and spirit. He recharged me. I experienced His anapauso, His rest.

We often discuss the revelation in Scripture of Jesus' teaching, His loving action, and God's power and authority flowing through Him by signs, miracles and wonders. While we regularly gather to study God's holy word and we regularly go out into the world as God's hands and feet serving others and fulfilling God's mission, some believe that God has discontinued the practice of revealing His presence, power and authority through miracles, sign and wonders. But His miraculous signs and wonders are all around us. We simply need eyes to see them. When we pray, He hears our prayers and He responds, when we seek Him we find Him, and He does indeed reach into our world demonstrating His holy presence in tangible ways. I know this because I trust in His promises and because I have experienced His touch – among countless other ways, on that particular Wednesday evening He refreshed me.

Our minds are gifts from God and education, higher intelligence, learning and refined clarity of thought are gifts from God and worthy pursuit; however, Jesus warns that our pursuit of cleverness might cause us to miss the simplicity of God's truth. His presence, signs and wonders surround us. Jesus Christ is the source of peace and rest. He is the truth. May you find His rest and peace, may you have eyes to see His holy hand at work all around you, and may you experience His healing touch.

THOUGHTS TO CONSIDER

1. Read Luke 8:9-27. Jesus gives three short thoughts connected by the thread of focus – is our focus on and faith in God or ourselves? First, Jesus tells a parable of two men praying, a Pharisee and a tax collector. Recall that the original listeners regarded tax collectors as so evil that they reserved a special category for them when listing so-called "sinners" (see Matthew 9:10, 11:19, 21:31; Mark 2:15; Luke 5:30, 7:34, and 15:1). The Pharisee prayed about his personal acts of righteousness, lifting himself up, while the tax collector humbled himself before God, acknowledged his sinfulness and begged God for mercy. As a result, the tax collector was justified, not the Pharisee.

Next, people brought babies to Jesus so He would bless them. When the disciples objected Jesus said, "Let the little children come to me, and do not stop them; for it is to such as these that the kingdom of God belongs. Truly I tell you, whoever does not receive the kingdom of God as a little child will never enter it" (Luke 18:16-17). Babies are transparently who they are. They are not pretentious, they do not lift themselves up, they do not seek others to acknowledge their social standing – theirs is the kingdom of God.

Finally, Jesus encounters a wealthy ruler who claims to have fulfilled God's commandments. Jesus asks him to sell his possessions, give to the poor and follow Jesus, but the man cannot do that. Jesus said, "How hard it is for those who have wealth to enter the kingdom of God! Indeed, it is easier for a camel to go through the eye of a needle than for someone who is rich to enter the kingdom of God" (Luke 18:24-25). The message cuts deeply as it exposes our heart of faith and trust – where do we truly place our trust? Do we believe God the Father loves and provides for His children? Is our focus on Him or ourselves?

2.   Read Matthew 11. Beginning at verse 20 Jesus discusses cities that apparently experienced His miraculous signs, wonders and miracles, and heard His teaching, yet failed to repent. They saw and heard God flowing through Jesus, yet they rejected Him and His message, and Jesus pronounces judgment on them saying, "For if the deeds of power done in you had been done in Sodom, it would have remained until this day. But I tell you that on the day of judgment it will be more tolerable for the land of Sodom than for you" (Matthew 11:23-24).

Jesus expresses judgment on people to whom God's glory is revealed through Jesus, but who reject Him. Immediately after that, in the context of rejection, Jesus says, "I thank you, Father, Lord of heaven and earth, because you have hidden these things from the wise and the intelligent and have revealed them to infants; yes, Father, for such was your gracious will" (Matthew 11:25-26). Some reject and some believe. Some have eyes to see the revelation of God's glory while others are blind to it. The passage also underscores God's sovereignty – Jesus says it is God who hides these things from some and reveals these things to others.

Pray for God to enlighten the eyes of your spirit. Pray for Him to open your eyes to see His glory as He reveals Himself before you and ears to hear His holy word.

3. In the next breath Jesus says, "All things have been handed over to me by my Father; and no one knows the Son except the Father, and no one knows the Father except the Son and anyone to whom the Son chooses to reveal him" (Matthew 11:27). If we truly desire to know God, to engage in relationship with God, we must go through Jesus. Jesus is the way, the truth and the life (see John 14:6).

4. It is in the context of revelation, rejection, belief and judgment that Jesus discusses the rest that He offers to weary, burden-laden souls. His "yoke is easy and [His] burden is light." How does His offer of rest fit within the context of the chapter? Given the context, does your understanding of the passage change? If so, how?

Randy L Allen

Colorado

34

WAKING UP TO JESUS CHRIST

> PRAISE THE LORD! PRAISE, O SERVANTS OF THE LORD; PRAISE THE NAME OF THE LORD. BLESSED BE THE NAME OF THE LORD FROM THIS TIME ON AND FOREVERMORE. FROM THE RISING OF THE SUN TO ITS SETTING THE NAME OF THE LORD IS TO BE PRAISED. THE LORD IS HIGH ABOVE ALL NATIONS AND HIS GLORY ABOVE THE HEAVENS.
> PSALMS 113:1-4

How do you start each day? What do you do to ensure that, before you go back out into the chaotic world, your mind is centered on Jesus Christ?

I have listened to a lot of Billy Graham's sermons over the years courtesy of YouTube. I recall him saying in one that he had a habit of starting each day by reading and meditating on five Psalms, progressing through the book every 30 days.

I recently heard a woman speaking on the radio describe how she starts each day by reciting Psalm 113:3. When she wakes, before her feet touch the floor, she proclaims, "From the rising of the sun to its setting the name of the Lord is to be praised." By doing this she sets her mind on Jesus Christ, her Lord and Savior, before doing anything else.

I need to remind myself each morning and throughout each day who God is because when I focus on His identity, praise and worship arise, and as my heart is filled with awe, wonder and praise, I am reminded of His promises, and this combination provides the foundation for the day. He is indeed the holy, pure, divine, Creator of all things. He has all power and authority in heaven and on earth, and He really does know everything about me. He knows my needs and desires. He is love and He really does love me, and He hears my prayers and He responds. We are each created in His glorious image, and through Jesus Christ we are the Father's children, adopted as heirs and redeemed, saved and freed. His Holy Spirit dwells within us, strengthening us, empowering us, convicting us.

Praise His holy name! He is holy, holy, holy, Lord God almighty! "From the rising of the sun to its setting the name of the Lord is to be praised."

God is faithful. He is constant. His love does not change. And our praise of Him should be constant as well. Regardless of what is going on in your life, regardless of the trials, pain, suffering and hardship you are facing, praise His holy name, continue to seek Him, continue to worship Him, continue to commune with Him in prayer. We continue to praise God because He continues to be God, regardless of our situation, so I do not say what I am about to say as if it is a bargain or a transaction being negotiated, it is not, but when we genuinely seek Him, when we genuinely offer Him our praise and worship, when we sincerely commune with Him, our burdens become lighter and our life improves as a result of the increase of His holy presence within us.

We are created in His holy image. May our faithfulness mirror His.

Thoughts to Consider

1. Read Psalm 113. Why do we praise and worship God? You might say we praise and worship God because He loves us, or because He blesses us, or because He answers our petitions. Those things are true, but each might also be said of other people. So those are insufficient reasons for praise and worship. He is holy, pure and divine. He is the Author of life, the Creator of all things, sovereign God with all power and authority in heaven and on earth. We praise and worship God because He is God. Do you agree? If not, why?

2. Read Psalm 141 and Revelation 5. The psalmist begins writing,

> I call upon you, O Lord; come quickly to me; give ear to my voice when I call to you. Let my prayer be counted as incense before you, and the lifting up of my hands as an evening sacrifice. Psalm 141:1-2

The line is reminiscent of John's heavenly revelation where he writes,

> Then I saw between the throne and the four living creatures and among the elders a Lamb standing as if it had been slaughtered, having seven horns and seven eyes, which are the seven spirits of God sent out into all the earth. He went and took the scroll from the right hand of the one who was seated on the throne. When he had taken the scroll, the four living creatures and the twenty-four elders fell before the Lamb, each holding a harp and golden bowls full of incense, which are the prayers of the saints. They sing a new song:
>
>> "You are worthy to take the scroll and to open its seals, for you were slaughtered and by your blood you ransomed for God saints from every tribe and language and people and nation; you have made them to be a kingdom and priests serving our God, and they will reign on earth."
>
> Then I looked, and I heard the voice of many angels surrounding the throne and the living creatures and the elders; they numbered myriads of myriads and thousands of thousands, singing with full voice,
>
>> "Worthy is the Lamb that was slaughtered to receive power and wealth and wisdom and might and honor and glory and blessing!" Revelation 5:6-12

Heavenly creatures holding golden bowls filled with incense, which are the prayers of God's people, fall at the Lamb's feet and worship Him because He is worthy of worship and praise. Why do we worship Jesus Christ? We praise and worship Him because He is worthy.

3.   Read Matthew 20. God is God, the Father, Son and Holy Spirit. God alone is worthy of our praise and worship. On top of that, God the Father gave His only Son so that we might live (see John 3:16) and Jesus surrendered Himself for us (see Matthew 20:28). Jesus says,

> When the ten heard it, they were angry with the two brothers. But Jesus called them to him and said, "You know that the rulers of the Gentiles lord it over them, and their great ones are tyrants over them. It will not be so among you; but whoever wishes to be great among you must be your servant, and whoever wishes to be first among you must be your slave; just as the Son of Man came not to be served but to serve, and to give his life a ransom for many." Matthew 20:24-28

Does the thought that Jesus surrendered His life, His blood for you, yes for you, change your view of praising and worshiping Him?

San Juan Range, Colorado

35

CLAIMING GOD'S PROMISES

FOR THE SON OF GOD, JESUS CHRIST, WHOM WE PROCLAIMED AMONG YOU, SILVANUS AND TIMOTHY AND I, WAS NOT "YES AND NO"; BUT IN HIM IT IS ALWAYS "YES." FOR IN HIM EVERY ONE OF GOD'S PROMISES IS A "YES." FOR THIS REASON IT IS THROUGH HIM THAT WE SAY THE "AMEN," TO THE GLORY OF GOD. BUT IT IS GOD WHO ESTABLISHES US WITH YOU IN CHRIST AND HAS ANOINTED US, BY PUTTING HIS SEAL ON US AND GIVING US HIS SPIRIT IN OUR HEARTS AS A FIRST INSTALLMENT. 2 CORINTHIANS 1:19-22

In Jesus Christ, "every one of God's promises is a "Yes." Let that sink in for a moment. Consider God's promises recorded in Scripture. From Genesis through Revelation, Scripture is filled with God's promises. Each and every promise made by God is "Yes" in Jesus Christ. Through Him, we are the beneficiaries of God's promises.

Consider a few:

You are my servant, I have chosen you and not cast you off; do not be afraid, for I am your God; I will strengthen you, I will help you, I will uphold you with my victorious right hand. Isaiah 41:9-10

Then the Lord said to him, "Who gives speech to mortals? Who makes them mute or deaf, seeing or blind? Is it not I, the Lord? Now go, and I will be with your mouth and teach you what you are to speak." Exodus 3:11

For surely I know the plans I have for you, says the Lord, plans for your welfare and not for harm, to give you a future with hope. Then when you call upon me and come and pray to me, I will hear you. Jeremiah 29:11-12

Ask, and it will be given you; search, and you will find; knock, and the door will be opened for you. Matthew 5:7

And remember, I am with you always, to the end of the age. Matthew 28:20

He who did not withhold his own Son, but gave him up for all of us, will he not with him also give us everything else? Romans 8:32

Scripture is filled with God's promises. You are created in God's image.[4] God is with you.[5] He has plans for you.[6] He loves you.[7] God calls you by name.[8] You are redeemed.[9] You are His.[10] You are a child of God,[11] a sibling of Jesus Christ,[12] an adopted heir.[13] The power of the Holy Spirit is within you.[14] He will strengthen you.[15] And like a bad television commercial, but wait there's more … Scripture also tells us that in Jesus Christ, "every one of God's promises is a 'Yes.'"[16] In Jesus Christ, through Jesus Christ, God's promises are yours, mine, ours.

How amazing is that? With this in mind, I urge you to scour God's holy word searching for His promises, and when you discover His truth meditate on it, and as you align your spirit, soul and body with Jesus Christ, you will know His promises. Believe and trust in them, claim them and receive them. I pray that God's promises will be real in your life. Amen.

THOUGHTS TO CONSIDER

1. Read Isaiah 43. The chapter begins, "But now thus says the Lord, he who created you, O Jacob, he who formed you, O Israel…" (Isaiah 43:1). God speaks through the prophet Isaiah. As you read the chapter note each promise God speaks. How many do you count? Which ones speak clearly to you?

2. Read I John 3. At the end of chapter 2 John writes, "As for you, the anointing that you received from him abides in you, and so you do not need anyone to teach you. But as his anointing teaches you about all things, and is true and is not a lie, and just as it taught you, abide in him" (I John 2:27). After this, he begins discussing children of God. How does it make you feel to know you are a child of God?

3. Read Psalm 91. What promises does God communicate to you through the psalm?

4. I encourage you to read back through God's promises set forth above and the Scripture cited for each. First, please develop your own understanding of each promise, and as to each, please ask the following questions. Do you believe God's promises? Do you believe they apply to you? When you read His promises, do you believe He is speaking to you through His holy word? I realize your answer may be different depending on the promise. Categorize the types of promises you truly believe and the types that you do not believe, or you do not believe apply to you. As to the promises you struggle to believe, what is it about them that causes you difficulty?

For the Praise of His Glory

Massadona, Colorado

36

I Am Barabbas

Pilate then called together the chief priests, the leaders, and the people, and said to them, "You brought me this man as one who was perverting the people; and here I have examined him in your presence and have not found this man guilty of any of your charges against him. Neither has Herod, for he sent him back to us. Indeed, he has done nothing to deserve death. I will therefore have him flogged and release him."

Then they all shouted out together, "Away with this fellow! Release Barabbas for us!" (This was a man who had been put in prison for an insurrection that had taken place in the city, and for murder.) Pilate, wanting to release Jesus, addressed them again; but they kept shouting, "Crucify him, crucify him!" A third time he said to them, "Why, what evil has he done? I have found in him no ground for the sentence of

DEATH; I WILL THEREFORE HAVE HIM FLOGGED AND THEN RELEASE HIM." BUT THEY KEPT URGENTLY DEMANDING WITH LOUD SHOUTS THAT HE SHOULD BE CRUCIFIED; AND THEIR VOICES PREVAILED. SO PILATE GAVE HIS VERDICT THAT THEIR DEMAND SHOULD BE GRANTED. HE RELEASED THE MAN THEY ASKED FOR, THE ONE WHO HAD BEEN PUT IN PRISON FOR INSURRECTION AND MURDER, AND HE HANDED JESUS OVER AS THEY WISHED. LUKE 23:13-25

Jewish historian Josephus recorded that during the time surrounding Jesus' ministry, a Jewish group known as the Zealots orchestrated many uprisings against Roman occupation. By some accounts Zealots employed a number of tactics, including concealing themselves in crowded marketplaces and stealthily attacking Roman sympathizers with daggers. In 68-70 AD, misjudging Roman resolve, they attacked the Roman army and were slaughtered.

As we think back to our nation's beginning, our forefathers fought against an occupying force, a distant government that did not understand local realities, and taxes supporting distant rulers. Barabbas was likely a Zealot who led fellow Jews to resist Roman occupation. Was he a freedom fighter zealously seeking to free his country from an occupying force? Was he a good man seeking to make his homeland a free place in which his children and grandchildren might prosper? Or was he a terrorist, a murderer, a person who disturbed the peace? The label we place upon people often depends on our perspective.

We do not know much about Barabbas. Each Gospel writer mentions him and they each mention unique details. The name Barabbas means "son of abba" or "son of father," so his name could refer to anyone. Interestingly, Matthew tells us that his full name was Jesus Barabbas, so his name was Jesus, son of father.

The passage above explains that Jesus was innocent, and Barabbas was guilty – charged, convicted and sentenced to death – yet Pilate released Barabbas and sentenced Jesus to torture and execution. Jesus Christ died in Barabbas' place. He was nailed to a cross built for Barabbas.

In many places Scripture explains that Jesus died for the sins of the world – for my sins and yours. Speaking of Jesus Christ, Peter writes,

> "He himself bore our sins in his body on the cross, so that, free from sins, we might live for righteousness; by his wounds you have been healed. For you were going astray like sheep, but now you have returned to the shepherd and guardian of your souls." 1 Peter 2:24-25

I imagine Barabbas, son of father, after his release. What does he feel? What does he think? I imagine sitting at a distance, looking on as Jesus Christ hangs dying on the cross, knowing that He is dying in my place. I imagine feeling the dust cling to my moist skin, I imagine the smells of the people around me and the charcoal cooking in the distance, I imagine the sounds of the crowd, I imagine the sun warming my body, and there

I am, knowing that I have been, by the awesome mystery of God's grace, given a new life. I am free to go home, to enjoy the evening with my family, to taste food and drink, to work, and to enjoy the way it all satisfies me. And I know that I should be hanging where Jesus Christ hangs.

I am Barabbas because I too am son of father, I too am guilty, I too have been set free, granted new life, saved because Jesus, the Christ, the Messiah, God gave Himself up for me. By His wounds I am healed. Are you son/daughter of father? Scripture reminds us, "By his wounds you have been healed."

Thoughts to Consider

1. Read Matthew 1. Matthew presents Jesus' genealogy demonstrating His ancestry traces to King David and Abraham as foretold by the prophets. He then describes Jesus' birth. As part of that narrative, an angel appears to Joseph urging him to marry Mary saying,

> "She will bear a son, and you are to name him Jesus, for he will save his people from their sins." All this took place to fulfill what had been spoken by the Lord through the prophet:"Look, the virgin shall conceive and bear a son, and they shall name him Emmanuel," which means,"God is with us." Matthew 1:21-23

Jesus is God with us and He saves His people from their sins. It is as simple as that.

2. Read I John 1-2. John begins the letter writing,

> We declare to you what was from the beginning, what we have heard, what we have seen with our eyes, what we have looked at and touched with our hands, concerning the word of life this life was revealed, and we have seen it and testify to it, and declare to you the eternal life that was with the Father and was revealed to us we declare to you what we have seen and heard so that you also may have fellowship with us; and truly our fellowship is with the Father and with his Son Jesus Christ. We are writing these things so that our joy may be complete. I John 1:1-4

John was one of the disciples who lived with Jesus and studied under Jesus, and who heard, saw and touched Jesus with his physical ears, eyes and hands. He begins his letter reminding his readers that he is describing what he gathered from personal experience with Jesus Christ. A couple paragraphs later John writes,

> My little children, I am writing these things to you so that you may not sin. But if anyone does sin, we have an advocate with the Father, Jesus Christ the righteous; and he is the atoning sacrifice for our sins, and not for ours only but also for the sins of the whole world. I John 2:1-2

We each sin. To some extent we are each separated from God. Not a single one of us is perfect. Christ Jesus, our advocate before God the Father, offered Himself as the atoning sacrifice for our sins and for the sins of every human who has and will inhabit earth. How do you respond to that truth?

3.   Read 1 Peter 1-3. Peter begins discussing the new life available "through the resurrection of Jesus Christ from the dead" (1 Peter 1:3), the joy experienced by those who know Him (see 1 Peter 1:6-9), and the purification of our souls (1 Peter 1:22). He then discusses Jesus Christ's sacrifice and suffering for us saying,

> For Christ also suffered for sins once for all, the righteous for the unrighteous, in order to bring you to God. 1 Peter 3:18

Christ Jesus was innocent, yet He suffered. We deserve God's wrath, but He endured it for us.

4.   Read Romans 3. Paul discusses salvation available in Christ Jesus as justification by God's grace through faith. He discusses justification, redemption, sacrifice and atonement writing,

> But now, apart from law, the righteousness of God has been disclosed, and is attested by the law and the prophets, the righteousness of God through faith in Jesus Christ for all who believe. For there is no distinction, since all have sinned and fall short of the glory of God; they are now justified by his grace as a gift, through the redemption that is in Christ Jesus, whom God put forward as a sacrifice of atonement by his blood, effective through faith. Romans 3:21-25

Regardless of the mechanism used as we try to wrap our minds around what Jesus did for us and offers to us, through faith we believe that He died, rose again, ascended to heaven, and through Him we gain new life, forgiveness and reconciliation with God, forever. As you convert the concepts from the abstract notion to a holy gift of grace offered to you personally, how do you respond?

For the Praise of His Glory

Laguna del Inca, Portillo, Chile

37

Who is Jesus?

> Then the kings of the earth and the magnates and the generals and the rich and the powerful, and everyone, slave and free, hid in the caves and among the rocks of the mountains, calling to the mountains and rocks, "Fall on us and hide us from the face of the one seated on the throne and from the wrath of the Lamb; for the great day of their wrath has come, and who is able to stand?" Revelation 6:15-17

When you think of Jesus, what images come to mind? Some see a flower child hippie preaching a message of love. Some see a powerful teacher or prophet. He certainly delivers powerful messages of love, forgiveness and the kingdom of God, but He is much more complex than many consider. During His ministry as a man on earth, while showing tremendous compassion and welcoming love to people on the fringe of society, He revealed sharp judgment and criticism to religious leaders, and He called people to repent.

Years ago, along with six others, Lori and I met with Reverend Brad Henderson each Sunday evening as part of his doctoral thesis work. We practiced lectio devina, an ancient prayer practice involving reading and meditating on Scripture, praying for God to speak to us through the passage, and reflecting on words, phrases or thoughts that jumped out to each of us. It was a remarkable experience. As we intentionally sought to hear God's divine voice through His holy word, He always delivered.

During our last session, Brad distributed a questionnaire for each of us to complete and return. The questionnaire ended with a probing question: "Who is Jesus to you?" I loved the class and moved quickly through the questionnaire until reaching the final question, when I suddenly found myself paralyzed with a myriad of possible answers swirling through my mind.

Who is Jesus to me? I could say friend, but He's not physically present, so is that accurate? Spiritual friend? Spiritual guide? Teacher, comforter, source of peace? All those statements are true, but each statement is severely lacking because He's unlike any mere mortal – He's also God. He is the sovereign One, the Creator of all things, the ultimate judge of all. He holds the keys to the kingdom. He has all power and authority. Then my mind drifted to the ways Jesus describes Himself – the bread of life, the light of the world, the resurrection and the life, the way, the truth and the life, the gate for the sheep, the good shepherd, and the true vine. The descriptions boggle the mind in depth and meaning, and they certainly describe who Jesus is, but do they describe who Jesus is to me? As I pondered my mind continued to spin.

My struggle answering Brad's question came to mind recently as I read John's descriptions of Jesus in the Revelation. While praying in a cave on the island Patmos, John visited heaven in the spirit. He saw Jesus in His heavenly glory. He heard Jesus' voice roar, saw heavenly beings worshiping Jesus and experienced so much more. John begins describing Jesus as follows:

> I turned around to see the voice that was speaking to me. And when I turned I saw seven golden lampstands, and among the lampstands was someone like a son of man, dressed in a robe reaching down to his feet and with a golden sash around his chest. The hair on his head was white like wool, as white as snow, and his eyes were like blazing fire. His feet were like bronze glowing in a furnace, and his voice was like the sound of rushing waters. In his right hand he held seven stars, and coming out of his mouth was a sharp, double-edged sword. His face was like the sun shining in all its brilliance.
>
> When I saw him, I fell at his feet as though dead. Then he placed his right hand on me and said: "Do not be afraid. I am the First and the Last. I am the Living One; I was dead, and now look, I am alive for ever and ever! And I hold the keys of death and Hades. Revelation 1:12-18

Wow. I try to imagine seeing Jesus in His heavenly glory. I imagine trying to reduce the wonders, the amazing heavenly images to words using our inadequate language. Jesus is God, the Living One, the First and the Last, and He has all power and authority, even over death and Hades. He is so much more than a powerful teacher and so much more than a flower child hippie preaching a message of love. He is more than we mere humans are capable of comprehending.

Later in Revelation, John describes Jesus as the bearer of wrath so severe that the most powerful people on earth flee to the mountains and beg the mountains to fall on them to hide them from Jesus. The phrase "the wrath of the Lamb" is a concise flip of the narrative. Here on earth, we do not expect lambs be the bearers of wrath; they are soft and cuddly and cute. And many on earth see Jesus in similarly unassuming and insignificant ways, and by doing so they miss the complexity and total, absolute, incomprehensible awesomeness of our Lord and Savior. He is the Lamb; we are cleansed and saved by the blood of the Lamb; but this Lamb is like no other. And would we really want to surrender ourselves to a Lord that is any less than the sovereign, almighty One?

Who is Jesus to you? God's holy word is His effort to communicate His glory to us. He is trying to reveal the glory of Father, Son and Holy Spirit to us. May you have eyes to see, ears to hear, and a heart that is fertile soil in which His seed grows.

Thoughts to Consider

1. Read Luke 8. The chapter begins saying,

   > Soon afterwards he went on through cities and villages, proclaiming and bringing the good news of the kingdom of God. The twelve were with him, as well as some women who had been cured of evil spirits and infirmities: Mary, called Magdalene, from whom seven demons had gone out, and Joanna, the wife of Herod's steward Chuza, and Susanna, and many others, who provided for them out of their resources. Luke 8:1-3

   Jesus cured the women physically and spiritually, and they traveled with and provided for Jesus and the disciples. Who was Jesus to them?

   Later in the chapter Jesus and the disciples are crossing the Sea of Galilee when a violent storm overcomes them. Water begins to fill the boat and the disciples are afraid. Jesus rebukes the wind and the waves, and the storm stops. The sea is instantly calm, and He rebukes the disciples for their failing faith. How did the disciples view Jesus after the storm obeyed Him?

   When they arrived on the eastern shore, they encountered a man enslaved by a legion of demons. Jesus ordered the demons out of the man and he was suddenly "in his right mind" (Luke 8:36). The man begged Jesus to allow him to go with Jesus, but Jesus ordered the man to return to his home and "declare how much God has done for you" (Luke 8:39). Who was Jesus to the man formerly enslaved by demons?

Jesus and the disciples returned across the sea. As Jesus walked through a crowd the following happened:

> As he went, the crowds pressed in on him. Now there was a woman who had been suffering from hemorrhages for twelve years; and though she had spent all she had on physicians, no one could cure her. She came up behind him and touched the fringe of his clothes, and immediately her hemorrhage stopped. Then Jesus asked, "Who touched me?" When all denied it, Peter said, "Master, the crowds surround you and press in on you." But Jesus said, "Someone touched me; for I noticed that power had gone out from me." When the woman saw that she could not remain hidden, she came trembling; and falling down before him, she declared in the presence of all the people why she had touched him, and how she had been immediately healed. He said to her, "Daughter, your faith has made you well; go in peace." Luke 8:42-48

Who was Jesus to the woman?

2. Read 2 Peter 1. Peter introduces his second epistle explaining that he was an eyewitness to the majesty of Jesus Christ. He presents himself as an authority regarding Christ's majesty. In support of his assertion he explains that he was present when Jesus was transfigured on the mountain (see Matthew 17:1-13) writing,

> For we did not follow cleverly devised myths when we made known to you the power and coming of our Lord Jesus Christ, but we had been eyewitnesses of his

> majesty. For he received honor and glory from God the Father when that voice was conveyed to him by the Majestic Glory, saying, "This is my Son, my Beloved, with whom I am well pleased." We ourselves heard this voice come from heaven, while we were with him on the holy mountain. 2 Peter 1:16-18

As Peter stood on the mountain watching God transfigure Jesus and listening to God proclaim Jesus to be His Son, who was Jesus to Peter?

3.   Read 2 Corinthians 12. Like John, Paul visited heaven. He is not sure whether it was a vision or a spiritual visitation, but either way, he saw and heard amazing things. He describes it as follows:

> It is necessary to boast; nothing is to be gained by it, but I will go on to visions and revelations of the Lord. I know a person in Christ who fourteen years ago was caught up to the third heaven – whether in the body or out of the body I do not know; God knows. And I know that such a person – whether in the body or out of the body I do not know; God knows – was caught up into Paradise and heard things that are not to be told, that no mortal is permitted to repeat. 2 Corinthians 12:1-4

He never revealed what he saw and heard, but we have examples of heavenly visions recorded by John and Isaiah. If Paul's experience was similar to theirs, can you imagine who Jesus was to Paul?

4.   What is your experience with Jesus Christ? How has

your experience with Him shaped who He is to you?

Near Mount Sinai, Sinai Peninsula, Eqypt

38

WHAT IS TRUTH?

Jesus said to him, "I am the way, and the truth, and the life. No one comes to the Father except through me." John 14:6

When the Spirit of truth comes, he will guide you into all truth; for he will not speak on his own, but will speak whatever he hears, and he will declare to you the things that are to come. John 16:13

Sanctify them in the truth; your word is truth. John 17:17

Pilate asked him, "So you are a king?" Jesus answered, "You say that I am a king. For this I was born, for this I came into the world, to testify to the truth. Everyone who belongs to the truth listens to my voice." Pilate asked him, "What is truth?" After he had said this, he went

OUT TO THE JEWS AGAIN AND TOLD THEM, "I FIND NO CASE AGAINST HIM." JOHN 18:37-38

In this setting, Pilate served as judge. He spoke with Jesus, the Christ, Son of God, the Truth, the holy, pure, divine One who is the judge of all, but in this setting, in his palace, surrounded by soldiers obeying his commands, Pilate served as judge. Jesus explained to Pilate that He came into the world to testify to the truth and "Everyone who belongs to the truth listens to my voice" (John 18:37).

From Jesus' prior statements we know that the truth is the source of sanctification, God's word is truth, the Holy Spirit guides us to truth, and Jesus is the truth. Truth is something fixed. It is a certainty. It is something that Jesus testifies to and it is something people are capable of belonging to. The truth is embodied in the person of Jesus Christ and God's holy word, and the Holy Spirit guides us to it, or perhaps more appropriately, to Him.

Jesus explained these things. Pilate heard the words but not the message. He focused on his problems and his primary task at hand – maintaining order as Jerusalem swelled with millions of visitors for the Passover. If he lost control of Jerusalem, he might very well lose his position and fall from power, and he was not about to let that happen. To Pilate, Jesus was not necessarily a person, He was certainly not God incarnate, He was potentially the catalyst for a massive uprising that could cost Pilate his position. Jesus was a chess piece on the board waiting for Pilate's next move. As Pilate pondered his choices, he heard Jesus speak and he muttered a rhetorical reply, "What is truth?"

Had he really desired to know the answer to his question, he would have discovered truth because the Source of truth was standing in his presence, but he did not have eyes to see and he was more concerned with his personal list of priorities.

I think about Pilate and try to assess how often I am guilty of doing the same thing. How often am I preoccupied with my agenda for the day, with my set of priorities, with my personal to-do list, and fail to see Jesus Christ standing before me? How often do I fail to hear the message being communicated by the Truth when He is speaking clearly to me?

I recently read an article about amazing technology that is becoming increasingly available – computer programs that allow people to create incredibly realistic videos of people doing and saying things they never did or said. After loading photos and voice recordings of an individual, the program allows the user to create a virtual version of that individual. The user is then capable of manipulating the virtual individual to do and say all sorts of things. Known as "deep fake," the resulting videos are realistic and believable, and the events portrayed are entirely fictional.

As a result, fictional events may look and sound like reality. I read an interview of one popular actress who said her image, without her consent or prior knowledge, has been used in countless scenes doing things she would never do. She said years ago she fought each one that came to her attention, but as she fought one, dozens more were generated, and she quickly realized that she had lost control of her image. We can no longer believe what we hear or see on any of the myriad of screens surrounding us. If we see or hear images of people doing things that we cannot imagine they would ever do, the images may be fake. And if we see video of people committing horrific acts and the video is real, they are suddenly able to claim that the video is merely deep fake and they never did what the video shows them doing. In a world in which false things look real, our confidence in everything erodes and we begin to wonder whether truth exists.

Does truth still exist or is it like the buggy whip – something that was once commonly available but now extinct? If we accept the possibility that truth exists, we may be like Pilate asking, "What is truth?"

Jesus explains that Satan, the devil "does not stand in the truth, because there is no truth in him. When he lies, he speaks according to his nature, for he is a liar and the father of lies" (John 8:44). The truth is undoubtedly under attack. This is nothing new. The tactics may be new, but the battle is timeless.

Jesus also says, "Whoever is from God hears the words of God" (John 8:47). Truth does indeed exist. It is fixed. It does not change. It is the standard. God's holy word is truth. Jesus Christ is truth. The Holy Spirit guides us to truth. And we are sanctified, made holy, made righteous, made whole in truth.

I pray that we each avoid the distractions surrounding us in this chaotic world and maintain our connection with truth. May we each stay in God's holy word, pray all the time, and seek His guidance as we set our priorities each day. May the Spirit of discernment fill you and guide you and allow you to hear the words of God and to know the Truth.

Thoughts to Consider

1.   Read John 1. John begins the gospel writing,

     In the beginning was the Word, and the Word was with God, and the Word was God. He was in the beginning with God. All things came into being through him, and without him not one thing came into being. What has come into being in him was life, and the life was the light of all people. The light shines in the darkness, and the darkness did not overcome it…. And the Word became flesh and lived among us, and we have seen his glory, the glory as of a father's only son, full of grace and truth. John 1:1-5 & 14

Jesus is the Word. He has always been. Creation came into existence through Him. He is God and He became flesh and lived on earth. The quotes first set forth above say that Jesus is truth, that God's holy word is truth, that the Holy Spirit is the Spirit of truth, and we are sanctified by truth. And Jesus is the Word. It all circles back to Jesus.

2.   Read John 13-17. The chapters provide a detailed account of the Last Supper. Jesus taught and taught and taught, and as He prepared to conclude He said, "I still have many things to say to you, but you cannot bear them now" (John 16:12).

By reading the quotes first set forth above in the full context of Jesus' teaching that evening, does your understanding of His message change? If it does, how?

3.   Read John 18, Matthew 27, Mark 15 and Luke 23. Each gospel includes an account of Jesus before Pontius Pilate. Based on your reading of the four accounts, why did Pilate not recognize the truth standing before him? Do you see parallels in your life?

For the Praise of His Glory

Glacier Bay National Park, Alaska

39

Hear, Act and Do

"Not everyone who says to me, 'Lord, Lord,' will enter the kingdom of heaven, but only the one who does the will of my Father in heaven. On that day many will say to me, 'Lord, Lord, did we not prophesy in your name, and cast out demons in your name, and do many deeds of power in your name?' Then I will declare to them, 'I never knew you; go away from me, you evildoers.'

"Everyone then who hears these words of mine and acts on them will be like a wise man who built his house on rock. The rain fell, the floods came, and the winds blew and beat on that house, but it did not fall, because it had been founded on rock. And everyone who hears these words of mine and does not act on them will be like a foolish man who built his house on sand. The rain fell, and the floods came, and the winds blew and beat against that house, and it fell — and great was its fall!" Matthew 7:21-27

Reinforcing His desire for relationship with us, Jesus urges us to hear His words, act on them and do the will of the Father. Hearing, acting and doing are essential to our relationship with Jesus Christ.

I enjoy comfort and find peace and discover hope in many things Jesus says, but Jesus' statements above cause great inner turbulence. We know belief precedes following, following requires action, and relationship with Jesus Christ is the essence of the kingdom of heaven. We also know that our words and actions reveal the crevices of our spirits and souls. With these thoughts in mind, if we claim association with Jesus Christ but our actions suggest otherwise, we should pause to consider the reality of our condition.

His words shake me to my core. I know I deserve to hear "away from me, you evildoer," but will I? The answer depends on my relationship with Jesus Christ. The questions are simple: do I hear and act on His words, am I doing God's will, does Jesus Christ know me? God is love, He showers us with His holy grace, and I pray for mercy not the justice I deserve, I pray for relationship with Jesus Christ and I trust in His promises and I know He promises that when we seek, we find. But am I genuinely seeking relationship with Him?

Relationship with Jesus Christ lies at the heart of this teaching. A few chapters later, Jesus points at the disciples and says, "Here are my mother and my brothers! For whoever does the will of my Father in heaven is my brother and sister and mother" (Matthew 12:50). Once again, He connects doing the will of the Father to relationship with Jesus Christ. Relationship with Jesus Christ is connected to and determined by our choices – whether we choose to do God's will.

Jesus explains that many people call Him "Lord," prophesy in His name, cast out demons in His name, and do all sorts of good deeds in His name; yet do not have relationship with Him. We may call ourselves Christians, carry around our Bibles, attend Bible studies, go to church all the time, do amazing deeds in His name and otherwise project the appearance of association with Him, yet still not have relationship with Him. In fact, if that describes us, Jesus calls us "evildoers."

What separates "evildoers" from people who enter the kingdom of heaven? The same choice that separates people who enjoy relationship with Jesus Christ from everyone else – whether they do God's will.

Relationship with Jesus Christ is the kingdom of heaven. When we engage in relationship with the Christ, the Messiah, the Son of God, we enter the realm of His influence, surrender to Him, receive His power and join the kingdom of heaven. Who enters the kingdom of heaven? Who has relationship with Jesus Christ? The one who *hears* Jesus' words *and acts* on them is like a house built on rock. Hearing Jesus Christ and acting on His words establish a solid foundation of faith, enable relationship, and through relationship the Father's will is revealed, opening the door to the kingdom. Who enters the kingdom? Who has relationship with Jesus Christ? The one who *does* the will of the

Father.

We should pray and study and meditate on Scripture and pray more. These are vital to lives of faith, they are vital to our relationship with Jesus Christ and essential to discerning God's will, but we must also act and do (while acting may include merely going through motions, doing entails accomplishment). We are not called to cloister ourselves away, hiding from the world in prayer and study. Jesus calls us out into the world, acting as His agents, involved in His great mission. We are called to be salt and light. We are called to be His branches connected to Him and bearing fruit. We are called to hear *and* act. We are called to *do* the will of the Father.

Each time it occurs to me that the Creator of the universe, the One unbound by time and space, the One who created all matter by speaking, almighty God desires relationship with us, I am struck again by awe and wonder. We, who are "evildoers," we who often have thoughts inconsistent with the presence of God's glory, we are objects of His holy, pure, divine desire. Jesus Christ desires relationship with us, He desires that we become holy, and that we allow His Holy Spirit to transform our minds that we may discern God's will. He urges us to seek Him and He promises that, when we do, we will find Him.

May you have eyes to see, ears to hear, and may your heart be fertile soil in which His holy seed grows. May you know His holy will and may you be filled with His holy power, courage, energy and confidence to act and accomplish His will. May your relationship with Jesus Christ grow today and each day, forever.

Thoughts to Consider

1.   Read Matthew 6. The Sermon on the Mount fills chapters 5-7 of Matthew. Jesus speaks about acts of piety – giving, praying and fasting – and warns about the potential for hypocrisy. He presumes we pray and he says the following:

> "When you are praying, do not heap up empty phrases as the Gentiles do; for they think that they will be heard because of their many words. Do not be like them, for your Father knows what you need before you ask him.
>
> "Pray then in this way: Our Father in heaven, hallowed be your name. Your kingdom come. Your will be done, on earth as it is in heaven. Give us this day our daily bread. And forgive us our debts, as we also have forgiven our debtors. And do not bring us to the time of trial, but rescue us from the evil one.
>
> For if you forgive others their trespasses, your heavenly Father will also forgive you; but if you do not forgive others, neither will your Father forgive your trespasses. Matthew 6:7-15

Jesus instructs us to pray to God the Father, asking that His will be done on earth as it is in heaven. How often do you pray that not counting the times you pray the Lord's Prayer?

2.   Read Matthew 7. Midway through the chapter Jesus begins discussing how difficult it is for people to receive His gift

of life. He says,

> "Enter through the narrow gate; for the gate is wide and the road is easy that leads to destruction, and there are many who take it. For the gate is narrow and the road is hard that leads to life, and there are few who find it." Matthew 7:13-14

A couple paragraphs later Jesus says the words first quoted above, including saying,

> "Not everyone who says to me, 'Lord, Lord,' will enter the kingdom of heaven, but only the one who does the will of my Father in heaven." Matthew 7:21

Few find the narrow path, which involves doing the will of God the Father. We should each be confident that we on it.

3. Read Micah 6. The prophet Micah writes,

> "With what shall I come before the Lord, and bow myself before God on high? Shall I come before him with burnt offerings, with calves a year old? Will the Lord be pleased with thousands of rams, with ten thousands of rivers of oil? Shall I give my firstborn for my transgression, the fruit of my body for the sin of my soul?" He has told you, O mortal, what is good; and what does the Lord require of you but to do justice, and to love kindness, and to walk humbly with your God? Micah 6:6-8

How does this passage influence your view of God's will as it relates to your life?

4. Read Ephesians 5. Early in his letter to friends in Ephesus, Paul explains that God "has made known to us the mystery of his will, according to his good pleasure that he set forth in Christ" (Ephesians 1:9), and he prays that God

> may give you a spirit of wisdom and revelation as you come to know him, so that, with the eyes of your heart enlightened, you may know what is the hope to which he has called you, what are the riches of his glorious inheritance among the saints, and what is the immeasurable greatness of his power for us who believe, according to the working of his great power. Ephesians 1:17-19

Paul begins chapter 5 urging us to imitate God, to behave as God's beloved children and to live in love. He then contrasts the way children of God should behave with the way others in the world may behave, and he continues writing,

> Be careful then how you live, not as unwise people but as wise, making the most of the time, because the days are evil. So do not be foolish, but understand what the will of the Lord is. Do not get drunk with wine, for that is debauchery; but be filled with the Spirit, as you sing psalms and hymns and spiritual songs among yourselves, singing and making melody to the Lord in your hearts, giving thanks to God the Father at all times and for everything in the name of our Lord Jesus Christ. Ephesians 5:15-20

He tells us that God makes known the mystery of His will through Christ Jesus, he prays that our minds will be enlightened to know God's will, and he urges us to act in accordance with God's will. What do you think about that?

Randy L Allen

Nile River, Eqypt

40

God's Will

And going a little farther, he threw himself to the ground and prayed, "My Father, if it is possible, let this cup pass from me; yet not what I want but what you want." Matthew 26:39

Then Jesus said to him, "Put your sword back into its place; for all who take the sword will perish by the sword. Do you think that I cannot appeal to my Father, and he will at once send me more than twelve legions of angels? But how then would the scriptures be fulfilled, which say it must happen this way? At that hour Jesus said to the crowds, "Have you come out with swords and clubs to arrest me as though I were a bandit? Day after day I sat in the temple teaching, and you did not arrest me. But all this has taken place, so that the scriptures of the prophets may be fulfilled." Then all the disciples deserted him and fled. Matthew 26:52-56

Last week we considered Jesus saying, "only the one who does the will of my Father in heaven" will enter the kingdom of heaven (Matthew 7:21). This raises vitally important questions – what is the Father's will and how do we know what it is?

After the Last Supper as Jesus prayed in the garden, and later as guards came to arrest Him, He revealed a great deal about our free will and God's will. Jesus willingly surrendered to the guards, to the Sanhedrin and to Roman authorities because He knew it was the Father's will. He could have asked legions of angels to rescue Him, but that would have been contrary to God's will, it would not have fulfilled Scripture. His prayer in Gethsemane makes it clear that Jesus had free will, He could have chosen to do what He wanted, and He freely chose to do God's will.

In this situation, Jesus knew the will of the Father. Although He does not explain how He knew it, He mentions that God revealed His will through the prophets as recorded in Scripture. So Scripture reveals God's will.

In places, Scripture reveals God fulfilling His will directly, such as in the beginning when He speaks and things happen the way He wants them to (see Genesis 1). Much more commonly Scripture shows God asking people to accomplish His will and they have the option of doing as He asks or not. For example, God employed Moses on His great mission of releasing His people from slavery, He employed prophets to deliver messages,

He asked John the Baptist to pave the way for Jesus, He engaged the Apostles to form His church, and He called and calls countless more.

As Jesus suggests twice in the passage above, Scripture reveals God's will. But we need eyes to see, ears to hear and hearts to understand. We need His holy understanding, His discerning Spirit, His wisdom. Did Jesus know God's will because He had memorized Scripture, or did He know God's will because He prayed all the time and He lived in communion with the Father, or both? Or were other factors involved?

Paul explains that our ability to discern God's will is a gift developed as our minds are transformed and renewed and sanctified by our gradual surrender to and acceptance of the indwelling Holy Spirit, writing:

> I appeal to you therefore, brothers and sisters, by the mercies of God, to present your bodies as a living sacrifice, holy and acceptable to God, which is your spiritual worship. Do not be conformed to this world, but be transformed by the renewing of your minds, so that you may discern what is the will of God – what is good and acceptable and perfect. Romans 12:1-2

Paul seamlessly blends images of our surrender, our holiness, our transformation, our separation from the world, our union with God and our ability to discern God's will – His "good and acceptable and perfect" will. He also urges us to receive our renewal, our new self in "knowledge according to the image of its creator" (Colossians 3:9); he explains that it is God's will that we each are sanctified and made holy (see 1 Thessalonians 4:3); and he continues writing:

> Rejoice always, pray without ceasing, give thanks in all circumstances; for this is the will of God in Christ Jesus for you. Do not quench the spirit. Do not despise the words of prophets, but test everything; hold fast to what is good; abstain from every form of evil. May the God of peace himself sanctify you entirely; and may your spirit and soul and body be kept sound and blameless at the coming of our Lord Jesus Christ. The one who calls you is faithful, and he will do this. 1 Thessalonians 5:18-22

It is God's will that we are each sanctified. It is God who sanctifies. Our sanctification is God's will and He does it, but we must choose to allow it. Through the passages we know that God reveals His will through His holy word and we gain discernment regarding His will as our minds are transformed and renewed and as we are made holy and sanctified. So did Jesus know God's will because He memorized Scripture, or because He prayed all the time and lived a life of communion with God? It was both. And He explains that people who believe in Him will "do the works that I do" (John 14:12), suggesting we too will know the will of the Father.

The passage first set forth above also suggests that Jesus' arrest, torture and crucifixion accomplished God's will. Jesus' death and resurrection are fundamental to our faith; yet, at first glance it is disturbing to consider that God accomplished His will by allowing horrific acts of evil – Judas' betrayal was evil, the Sanhedrin's hate-filled schemes were evil, Pilate sentencing an innocent man to die was evil. God allowed evil, He allowed His Son to suffer in awful ways, all to carry out His greater plan. Through the pain, through the agony, through the suffering, God revealed His glory and forever changed the world, but it doesn't feel quite right for God to allow evil to accomplish His plan.

Similarly, God allowed Joseph to be sold into slavery and Nebuchadnezzar to destroy Jerusalem and carry God's chosen people to Babylon as slaves – great acts of evil – all to accomplish His greater plan. As Joseph explained to his brothers, what people intended for evil God intended for good (see Genesis 50:20). God took evil and created good out of it and through it.

As my wife, Lori, suffered from an evil illness and the harmful effects of her treatment protocol, God revealed His glory time and time again through it all. We know that God is sovereign, He has all power and authority in heaven and on earth, He can do everything, yet He respects free will. We know the events of Passion Week were evil; yet God used them to accomplish His purposes and to reveal His glory. God is good. He is the standard by which good and evil are delineated. He is incapable of evil; yet He allows free will, at times He allows evil to proceed unabated, and He regularly reveals His glory in response to or through evil. Lori's pain and suffering and exhaustion and general awfulness were evil, and God revealed His glory through them every step along her path to recovery and she is now positioned to serve God in ways she never could have accomplished before.

This causes me to consider those whose physical condition does not improve, but whom God allows to suffer until He calls them home. Sometimes terminology analogous to competition is used with respect to cancer. I have heard people described as battling the disease, cancer survivors, people who beat cancer, or people who lost to cancer, as if physical health is the ultimate victory. But we know relationship with Jesus Christ is the ultimate victory. Like Jesus during Passion Week, if we grow closer to God through our suffering, if we allow God to reveal His glory through us as we suffer, if we grow in Christ Jesus, continuing to take on His likeness, that is victory, and if He calls us home before cleansing our physical body, it is still victory.

We trust that God is truly sovereign, that He truly has all power and authority, that He loves us, that He is good, that He hears our prayers, that He responds to our prayers, and that we will do greater things than Jesus did on earth because He is with the Father in heaven (see John 14:12). Whatever you are experiencing, it is not too big for God.

Study and meditate on Scripture. Pray and seek and commune with God all the time. Allow His holy transformation and renewal of your spirit and soul so that you too may discern God's will, His good and acceptable and perfect will.

THOUGHTS TO CONSIDER

1.   Read Genesis 1. God creates the universe and everything in it, He creates order out of chaos, and everything He creates is good. When He so desires, He reaches into our realm and implements His will directly. Have you experienced, or do you see evidence of God directly implementing His will? If so, describe the situation.

2.   Read Genesis 37-50. The chapters tell Joseph's story. He is his father's favorite son, so his brothers hate him. They sell Joseph to slave traders traveling to Egypt; however, the Lord is with Joseph so he is successful and "the Lord caused all that he did to prosper in his hands" (Genesis 39:3). His master's wife lies about Joseph and the master throws Joseph in prison, where he meets two of Pharaoh's officers, his chief cupbearer, and chief baker. Through his connection with the cupbearer, Joseph eventually rises to power under Pharaoh, and he is ultimately in a position to save his family. When he speaks with his brothers he says, "Even though you intended to do harm to me, God intended it for good, in order to preserve a numerous people, as he is doing today" (Genesis 50:20).

Joseph's brothers were intent on evil and Potiphar's wife wanted to hurt Joseph, but God used their evil acts to position Joseph to save many people. How has God used your suffering to position you to help others?

3.   Read Romans 12. God's indwelling Holy Spirit transforms our spirits and souls, and renews our minds, which enables us to discern God's perfect, holy will. After writing this, Paul discusses spiritual gifts and characteristics of true association with

Christ Jesus saying, "Let love be genuine; hate what is evil, hold fast to what is good; love one another with mutual affection; outdo one another in showing honor" (Romans 12:9-10). In your personal experience, how do you discern God's perfect, holy will? Have you experienced a connection between your spiritual transformation through Christ and your love of others? Give an example.

4. Read John 6. As we consider God's will, we cannot overlook the interplay between His perfect, holy will and our faith. God's holy word says,

> Jesus said to them, "I am the bread of life. Whoever comes to me will never be hungry, and whoever believes in me will never be thirsty. But I said to you that you have seen me and yet do not believe. Everything that the Father gives me will come to me, and anyone who comes to me I will never drive away; for I have come down from heaven, not to do my own will, but the will of him who sent me. And this is the will of him who sent me, that I should lose nothing of all that he has given me, but raise it up on the last day. This is indeed the will of my Father, that all who see the Son and believe in him may have eternal life; and I will raise them up on the last day." John 6:35-40

It is God's perfect, holy will that all who see Jesus and believe in Him have eternal life, they receive His wholeness, His life abundant, His fullness, His spiritual transformation. They receive Him forever.

5. Read 1 John 2. God's holy word says,

> Do not love the world or the things in the world. The love of the Father is not in those who love the world; for all that is in the world – the desire of the flesh, the desire of the eyes, the pride in riches – comes not from the Father but from the world. And the world and its desire are passing away, but those who do the will of God live forever. 1 John 2:15-17

"Those who do the will of God live forever." How do you respond to that promise?

Portillo, Chile

41

WHO ARE EVIL

"SO I SAY TO YOU, ASK, AND IT WILL BE GIVEN YOU; SEARCH, AND YOU WILL FIND; KNOCK, AND THE DOOR WILL BE OPENED FOR YOU. FOR EVERYONE WHO ASKS RECEIVES, AND EVERYONE WHO SEARCHES FINDS, AND FOR EVERYONE WHO KNOCKS, THE DOOR WILL BE OPENED. IS THERE ANYONE AMONG YOU WHO, IF YOUR CHILD ASKS FOR A FISH, WILL GIVE A SNAKE INSTEAD OF A FISH? OR IF THE CHILD ASKS FOR AN EGG, WILL GIVE A SCORPION? IF YOU THEN, WHO ARE EVIL, KNOW HOW TO GIVE GOOD GIFTS TO YOUR CHILDREN, HOW MUCH MORE WILL THE HEAVENLY FATHER GIVE THE HOLY SPIRIT TO THOSE WHO ASK HIM!" LUKE 11:9-13

Jesus prays alone in a certain place. After He finishes, one of the disciples asks Jesus to teach them how to pray. Jesus gives the prayer template we know as the Lord's Prayer and He continues teaching about prayer. He asks the disciples to imagine themselves in a time of need, late at night, persistently knocking on a friend's door, and the friend eventually helps. Jesus continues teaching. He tells them to ask, seek and knock, and then asks them to imagine being a parent whose child requests fish or an egg. Would they give their hypothetical child a snake or a scorpion instead? Jesus continues, presuming they would give good gifts to their hypothetical children, saying, "If you then, who are evil, know how to give good gifts to your children, how much more will the heavenly Father give the Holy Spirit to those who ask him!" (Luke 11:13).

Jesus is speaking to His disciples, His closest followers, the ones being groomed to build His church, the recipients of His most intimate instruction, the fertile soil within whom seeds are growing, and Jesus describes these select few as "you then, who are evil."

When I consider evil, I rarely look in the mirror. It is easy, comforting perhaps, to consider evil as something displayed in newspaper stories and images describing and depicting faraway places and events. I see images of war and read stories about people doing horrific things to others and I lock my doors at night to protect us from evil because it is easy to think about evil as being something out there, in the darkness, in the distance. But Jesus forces me to look in the mirror and realize that I can see evil there as well.

"You then, who are evil ..." But aren't we good? Aren't we good people? The answer depends on where "good" is on the scale. Consider how Jesus views "good."

> As he was setting out on a journey, a man ran up and knelt before him, and asked him, "Good Teacher, what must I do to inherit eternal life?" Jesus said to him, "Why do you call me good? No one is good but God alone." Mark 10:17-18

According to Scripture, only God is good and every person (except Jesus) has sinned and has fallen short of God's glory (see Romans 3:23). We may seem good to ourselves when viewed through our own cloudy and flawed vision in comparison to others who we do not really know, but not when viewed in comparison to God.

This is vitally important because if we buy into the myth that we are each basically good, if we believe that I'm good and you're good, we're all good, then why should we concern ourselves with notions of salvation, redemption, the transformation available through Christ Jesus? Because if we are all good, doesn't it seem reasonable that a good, just, merciful, loving God will see that we are good? And if we are all good, then shouldn't it follow that we all gain the kingdom of heaven, eternal life, life abundant? Because we are good, right? I mean, haven't we earned that right by our goodness? But that is a myth, it is a lie, it is a deception designed by the father of lies to keep us away from Christ Jesus.

We are not good. Only God is good. We are evil and because of this ugly fact, we have only one source of hope. Every person is in need of redemption, wholeness, life abundant, eternal life, the kingdom of heaven. Every person is in need of

Christ Jesus, the only gate, the only path, the only way to God the Father.

With this in mind, I ask you to do a few things. First, when you read articles about people who have acted in horrific ways to other people, pray for the victims and their families, and pray for the perpetrators because we share the same seeds of evil that are in them, we are all in need of God's healing grace, we are all in need of spiritual transformation through the Holy Spirit. Second, as you are out in the world, continue to allow God's love, light and life to flow through you. Continue serving as a beacon of light out in the darkness, revealing God's glory to a world in need. And third, see the places you go each day as your mission field where you work on God's holy mission here on earth.

May you see others with compassion and understanding and empathy, and may God's glory continue shining through you.

Thoughts to Consider

1. Read Genesis 2 and 3. What does the account tell you about evil? As you consider evil as presented in Genesis, how does your understanding of the concept change?

2. Read Revelation 22. This is the final chapter of the Bible. As John concludes the account of His heavenly revelation an angel says, "Do not seal up the words of the prophecy of this

book, for the time is near. Let the evildoer still do evil, and the filthy still be filthy, and the righteous still do right, and the holy still be holy" (Revelation 22:10-11).

After this, Jesus says, "See, I am coming soon; my reward is with me, to repay according to everyone's work. I am the Alpha and the Omega, the first and the last, the beginning and the end" (Revelation 22:12-13). What does this make you think about evil?

3.Read Romans 7. Paul agonizes over his sinfulness, the evil lurking within him.

> For we know that the law is spiritual; but I am of the flesh, sold into slavery under sin. I do not understand my own actions. For I do not do what I want, but I do the very thing I hate.... Wretched man that I am! Who will rescue me from this body of death? Thanks be to God through Jesus Christ our Lord! Romans 7:14-15 and 24-25

Do you see parallels in your life? If so, what are specific examples?

4.Read Psalm 81. The psalmist writes,

> Hear, O my people, while I admonish you; O Israel, if you would but listen to me! There shall be no strange god among you; you shall not bow down to a foreign god. I am the Lord your God, who brought you up out of the land of Egypt. Open your mouth wide and I will fill it.

"But my people did not listen to my voice; Israel would not submit to me. So I gave them over to their stubborn hearts, to follow their own counsels. O that my people would listen to me, that Israel would walk in my ways! Then I would quickly subdue their enemies, and turn my hand against their foes. Those who hate the Lord would cringe before him, and their doom would last forever. I would feed you with the finest of the wheat, and with honey from the rock I would satisfy you." Psalm 81:8-18

How does this relate to evil?

For the Praise of His Glory

Giza, Egypt

42

Relationship & Prayer

He was praying in a certain place, and after he had finished, one of his disciples said to him, "Lord, teach us to pray, as John taught his disciples." He said to them, "When you pray, say:

Father, hallowed be your name. Your kingdom come. Give us each day our daily bread. And forgive us our sins, for we ourselves forgive everyone indebted to us. And do not bring us to the time of trial."

And he said to them, "Suppose one of you has a friend, and you go to him at midnight and say to him, 'Friend, lend me three loaves of bread; for a friend of mine has arrived, and I have nothing to set before him.' And he answers from within, 'Do not bother me; the door has already been locked, and my children are with me in bed; I cannot get up and give you anything.' I tell you, even though

HE WILL NOT GET UP AND GIVE HIM ANYTHING BECAUSE HE IS HIS FRIEND, AT LEAST BECAUSE OF HIS PERSISTENCE HE WILL GET UP AND GIVE HIM WHATEVER HE NEEDS.

"SO I SAY TO YOU, ASK, AND IT WILL BE GIVEN YOU; SEARCH, AND YOU WILL FIND; KNOCK, AND THE DOOR WILL BE OPENED FOR YOU. FOR EVERYONE WHO ASKS RECEIVES, AND EVERYONE WHO SEARCHES FINDS, AND FOR EVERYONE WHO KNOCKS, THE DOOR WILL BE OPENED. IS THERE ANYONE AMONG YOU WHO, IF YOUR CHILD ASKS FOR A FISH, WILL GIVE A SNAKE INSTEAD OF A FISH? OR IF THE CHILD ASKS FOR AN EGG, WILL GIVE A SCORPION? IF YOU THEN, WHO ARE EVIL, KNOW HOW TO GIVE GOOD GIFTS TO YOUR CHILDREN, HOW MUCH MORE WILL THE HEAVENLY FATHER GIVE THE HOLY SPIRIT TO THOSE WHO ASK HIM!" LUKE 11:1-13

We will never fully comprehend the depths of God's living word. As we study and admire and enjoy the essence of the outer layer of an onion, we realize that another layer lies beneath the first waiting to reveal new insights, a variation of pearly luminescence, a fresh new scent and new features to grasp. Beneath it is another layer and another and another. As we continue peeling deeper, the depths continue to expand. On different days in different seasons with different eyes, God's holy word continues to reveal.

Is it bad to compare God's holy word to an onion? Perhaps a mine or well that will never empty or a spouse whose nuances and depths we will never be fully know or some different analogy would be better suited for a divine topic such as this. As we continue to pursue, He continues to reveal.

Jesus' teaching in the passage above is example of this. I have long seen the first portion as a prayer template, the second as a lesson about persistence and the third as a directive to ask, seek and knock. And they are, but I recently saw a different layer to the teaching. Today, let's focus on the connection between relationship and prayer.

Jesus weaves the theme of relationship through His teaching about prayer, suggesting that prayer begins with relationship, or at least a desire to engage in relationship. As we consider approaching God in prayer, we must consider who we approach and our connection, our link, our standing with Him because we approach strangers one way and our closest friends in a different way. So we begin by considering, consciously or not, who we are to Him and who He is to us. And that initial analysis determines our approach, our words and possibly our expectations, and the character of the entire encounter.

He begins by instructing us to address God as "Father." Pause and think about that for a moment. God has incomprehensible power, authority, love and knowledge. We cannot even begin to imagine His awesomeness with our limited earthly human minds. He created everything in the universe out of nothing by speaking. He is the author of life, breathing life into each of us. He is unbound by space and time. He is truly God almighty and we will never even begin to comprehend the qualities attempted to be conveyed by the words; yet Jesus instructs us to address God as "Father."

How awesome is that? While the amazing privilege is awesome beyond words, it is also connected to daunting responsibility. Referring to God as "Father" implies that we are His children and have relationship with Him.

Before we have time to begin processing and mining the depths of that thought, Jesus changes direction and moves on. Imagine it is late at night and you need help. Who will you wake up for help? If you are stranded in the middle of nowhere with no cellphone signal, you might knock on a stranger's door for help, praying all the while that Kathy Bates' character in *Misery* does not live there. In certain dire situations we might bother a stranger late at night, but what if the need is not that sort of emergency and you have options about who to seek help from? Who will you bother late at night? Will you bother your neighbor who you wave to but don't really know? Or will you call your closest friend, the person you know will be there for you, the person you know will still be your friend even after you wake them up late at night and ask them for help. As we consider prayer, Jesus teaches us to consider God as a close friend, and because of our close relationship with Him we feel comfortable bothering Him late at night.

Jesus then instructs us to ask, seek and knock. Asking involves verbal communication, seeking involves the desire to find, and knocking involves physical action in pursuit of connection. He concludes by returning to the image of a parent-child relationship, focusing on a parent's desire to give good gifts to his or her children. If even we lowly, earthly, evil humans give good gifts to our children, "how much more will the heavenly Father give the Holy Spirit to those who ask him!" God the Father, our heavenly Father, your heavenly Father, desires to give you the best of all gifts.

Prayer presumes relationship or at least the desire to engage in relationship. As you prepare to approach God in prayer, begin by considering your relationship with Him and as you pray do so with a heart continuously asking, seeking and knocking. May you receive God as your loving heavenly Father who desires relationship with you, may you engage in the sort of relationship with Him allowing you to feel comfortable waking Him up late at night for help, may you receive the fullness of the gifts He desires to give.

Thoughts to Consider

1. Read Luke 10:21-42 and Luke 11. In two sentences set forth as Luke 10:21-22, Jesus refers to God the Father as "Father" five times. In chapter 11, as Jesus teaches about prayer, He tells us to pray to God the Father and tells us a great deal about Him. In what specific ways does Jesus present God the Father as compassionate, attentive, responsive and giving?

2. Read James 4. James connects prayer with interpersonal relationships, personal desire, God's desire for relationship with us and our humble submission to Him. Through the breadth of his writing, he connects our entire being, presence and world-

view with prayer. James writes,

> Those conflicts and disputes among you, where do they come from? Do they not come from your cravings that are at war within you? You want something and do not have it; so you commit murder. And you covet something and cannot obtain it; so you engage in disputes and conflicts. You do not have, because you do not ask. You ask and do not receive, because you ask wrongly, in order to spend what you get on your pleasures. Adulterers! Do you not know that friendship with the world is enmity with God? Therefore whoever wishes to be a friend of the world becomes an enemy of God. Or do you suppose that it is for nothing that the scripture says, "God yearns jealously for the spirit that he has made to dwell in us"? But he gives all the more grace; therefore it says,
>
>> "God opposes the proud, but gives grace to the humble."
>
> Submit yourselves therefore to God. Resist the devil, and he will flee from you. Draw near to God, and he will draw near to you. Cleanse your hands, you sinners, and purify your hearts, you double-minded. Lament and mourn and weep. Let your laughter be turned into mourning and your joy into dejection. Humble yourselves before the Lord, and he will exalt you. James 4:1-10

God yearns to dwell with us. If your entire being is connected with your prayer life and your relationship with God, what changes are necessary in your life to enable your relationship with God to grow?

3.   Read John 15. Jesus describes God the Father as the vinegrower, Jesus as the vine, children of God as branches, and fruit as God's mission on earth. Jesus uses the word "abide" eleven times in the passage. He urges us to abide in Him and His love, and to allow Him and His love to abide in us. How does our abiding in Him and His abiding in us relate to our prayer life?

4.   Read Hebrews 11. This is the faith chapter. It begins defining faith as "the assurance of things hoped for, the conviction of things not seen" (Hebrews 11:1). A few sentences later the writer says, "And without faith it is impossible to please God, for whoever would approach him must believe that he exists and that he rewards those who seek him" (Hebrews 11:6). In what ways are faith, prayer and our relationship with God connected?

For the Praise of His Glory

Seaside, Florida

43

LUKEWARM

"And to the angel of the church in Laodicea write: The words of the Amen, the faithful and true witness, the origin of God's creation:

"I know your works; you are neither cold nor hot. I wish that you were either cold or hot. So, because you are lukewarm, and neither cold nor hot, I am about to spit you out of my mouth. For you say, 'I am rich, I have prospered, and I need nothing.' You do not realize that you are wretched, pitiable, poor, blind, and naked. Therefore I counsel you to buy from me gold refined by fire so that you may be rich; and white robes to clothe you and to keep the shame of your nakedness from being seen; and salve to anoint your eyes so that you may see. I reprove and discipline those whom I love. Be earnest, therefore, and repent. Listen! I am standing at the door, knocking; if you hear my voice and open the door, I will come

IN TO YOU AND EAT WITH YOU, AND YOU WITH ME. TO THE ONE WHO CONQUERS I WILL GIVE A PLACE WITH ME ON MY THRONE, JUST AS I MYSELF CONQUERED AND SAT DOWN WITH MY FATHER ON HIS THRONE. LET ANYONE WHO HAS AN EAR LISTEN TO WHAT THE SPIRIT IS SAYING TO THE CHURCHES." REVELATION 3:14-22

A good friend recently returned from Turkey. He described the beautiful, hospitable people, and the amazing landscape, architecture, food, sounds and aromas he experienced in the region of the seven cities mentioned in Revelation. We discussed the proximity of the cities and of how being there helped him realize that the words written in Revelation were originally directed to real people in actual places struggling to live life as Christians in a world opposed to their beliefs, and that now, we share the legacy of being people to whom the words are directed.

After our conversation, I read the first few chapters of Revelation to see again what Jesus said to those churches and, once again, I am struck by His warnings. The passage at the end of chapter 3 disturbs me greatly, because Jesus' statements are directed to a church of believers who make Jesus gag by their attitude of self-sufficiency, and it stabs my soul to realize that He describes my attitude at certain times, on certain days during certain seasons. At times I think highly of myself and I feel self-sufficient and proud and I fail to realize my wretched condition.

The church in Laodicea and apparently individuals making up the church enjoy a level of prosperity and they "need nothing." The gospels are filled with Jesus teaching about money and warning about the dangers of wealth because if we are not vigilant, we will begin to trust our bank accounts more than God. We may begin to pray to the gods of the stock market to continue rising so that we may enjoy the pleasures available to us through wealth. And if our trust, faith and hope for the future are tied to those idols, where does God fit into the picture?

Jesus goes further. He explains that by the world's standards the church members in Laodicea may be wealthy; but they are actually "wretched, pitiable, poor, blind, and naked." They are church members, believers, followers of Christ, children of God; yet they are unable to see their wretched spiritual condition. They go to church while worshiping the idols of their wealth and self-sufficiency.

So I wonder, do I make Jesus want to throw up? Am I worthy of being spit out of Jesus' mouth, like a bite of awful tasting, putrid food, so bad that He wants to spit me out rather than risk upsetting His stomach if He swallows? As awful and alarming as this image is, at least it is a warning and not a foregone conclusion. Jesus warns, "I am about to spit you out of my mouth."

At this point reading the passage I pray, "Jesus, I do not want to make you throw up. What can I do? What should I do?" I am reminded of the listeners to Peter's amazing sermon preached in Jerusalem on that day of Pentecost when the Holy Spirit was unleashed. He preached to a crowd and they were convicted, and they wanted to change their ways and they asked, "What should we do?" (Acts 2:37). Peter responded by giving them the steps to follow to begin their new life in Christ Jesus. He said, "Repent, and be baptized every one of you in the name of Jesus Christ so that your sins may be forgiven; and you will receive the gift of the Holy Spirit" (Acts 2:38).

Similarly, after His startling warning, Jesus offers advice. He suggests that I buy from Jesus "gold refined by fire" so that I might be rich, and white robes to cover my naked body, and salve to anoint my eyes so that I will be able to see. Buy gold, white robes and salve from Jesus. How might I do that? Where is His market? Can I buy them online? What currency does He accept? What does He mean? Let's consider the elements of His statement.

The currency is my heart, my spirit, my soul – all of me. It is similar to God's holy word spoken through Isaiah, "Ho, everyone who thirsts, come to the waters; and you that have no money, come, buy and eat! … Listen carefully to me, and eat what is good, and delight yourselves in rich food" (Isaiah 55:1-2). We buy by desiring, drinking, eating, consuming and surrendering to Jesus.

Impurities are separated from gold by heating the solid to gold's melting point. Impurities with a higher melting point separate from the liquid as solid particles. Refining requires heat and it purifies gold. Like the beautiful hymn *Spirit of the Living God* prays, "Spirit of the living God, fall afresh on me. Melt me, mold me, fill me, use me…."[17] If we are proud, if we see ourselves as self-sufficient, if we see ourselves as somehow better than people around us, if we place our trust on things other than God, we might need a jolt, a slap in the face to remind us that we need God for every breath we take and that our worth is determined by our service to those around us. An infinite variety of means may cause the jolt, but a common one is suffering. Through suffering we gain the ability to see others with empathy, compassion and love. Through suffering we are melted, molded, filled and refined for use by God Almighty, we are purified.

How do we buy "gold refined by fire" from Jesus? We empty ourselves of us so that He might fill us, and we surrender ourselves to Him.

White robes have been cleansed in the blood of Jesus (see Revelation 7:14). They are symbols of righteousness, holiness and purity. We are cleansed in the blood of Jesus, but we must avoid wearing white robes simply to make others think we are holy. Jesus warns against this when He refers to religious leaders of His day as "whitewashed tombs," pretty and white on the outside but dead on the inside (see Matthew 23:27).

Paul writes, "I pray that the God of our Lord Jesus Christ, the Father of glory, may give you a spirit of wisdom and revelation as you come to know him, so that, with the eyes of your heart enlightened, you may know what is the hope to which he has called you…" (Ephesians 1:17-18). Through Jesus Christ we receive the Holy Spirit, and through surrender, humility and the radical transformation of our spirits and souls, we receive His compassion, wisdom, revelation and love, and we gradually gain the ability to see. The Holy Spirit is salve for our eyes.

Jesus asks His disciples to follow Him. Then He asks,

"For what will it profit them if they gain the whole world but forfeit their life? Or what will they give in return for their life?" (Matthew 16:26). What is the value of wealth if it lures us away from God?

It is frightening to realize that we might be chasing the lure without realizing it. For years my hair gradually thinned and I did not notice. Everyone I encountered could readily see my baldness, but I was oblivious to it because I never looked at the top of my head in the mirror and, as a result, I suffered a lot of painful scalp sunburns that could have easily been avoided. Is it possible, in a similar way, some of us are, in Jesus' words, "wretched, pitiable, poor, blind, and naked" and do not realize it? Is it possible that we go to church, bow before God, worship God, study His holy word and pray to Him; yet, at the same time harbor confidence in our wealth, our prosperity, our self-sufficiency, and fail to place our trust and faith and confidence in Almighty God?

If that is a possibility, I pray that I am able to heed Jesus' warning and follow His advice. I do not want to make Jesus throw up. I do not want him to spit me out of His mouth. I want to be His brother, the Father's adopted, a vessel in which His Holy Spirit dwells. If you are like me, and it is possible you have become lukewarm, let's move forward together and get on fire for Jesus.

Thoughts to Consider

1. Read Matthew 6. Matthew records the Sermon on the Mount in chapters 5-7. Jesus begins the sermon by giving the Beatitudes or blessings. The fourth blessing is "Blessed are those who hunger and thirst for righteousness, for they will be filled" (Matthew 5:6). God fills those who genuinely seek Him.

Later in the sermon Jesus discuss prayer, fasting and treasure, forcing each of us to question what do we treasure? Jesus says,

> "Do not store up for yourselves treasures on earth, where moth and rust consume and where thieves break in and steal; but store up for yourselves treasures in heaven, where neither moth nor rust consumes and where thieves do not break in and steal. For where your treasure is, there your heart will be also." Matthew 6:19-21

"Where your treasure is, there your heart will be also." What do you treasure? Where is your treasure? As you ponder the questions, do you see things in your life that need to change? If so, what specific things? What specific things will you do this week to start on the path toward change?

2. Read Isaiah 55. Speaking through the prophet Isaiah, God invites us to life abundant. Jesus says that one of the reasons He came to earth was to provide life abundant (see John 10:10), so we know it is a quality of life available through Jesus Christ. How does Isaiah's prophecy foretell the coming Messiah? In what ways does it steer us away from lukewarm existence?

3. Read I Peter I. Peter begins his letter discussing faith and suffering that refines and purifies faith. He writes,

> Blessed be the God and Father of our Lord Jesus Christ! By his great mercy he has given us a new birth into a living hope through the resurrection of Jesus Christ from the dead, and into an inheritance that is imperishable, undefiled, and unfading, kept in heaven for you, who are being protected by the power of God through faith for a salvation ready to be revealed in the last time. In this you rejoice, even if now for a little while you have had to suffer various trials, so that the genuineness of your faith – being more precious than gold that, though perishable, is tested by fire – may be found to result in praise and glory and honor when Jesus Christ is revealed. Although you have not seen him, you love him; and even though you do not see him now, you believe in him and rejoice with an indescribable and glorious joy, for you are receiving the outcome of your faith, the salvation of your souls. I Peter 1:3-9

In your experience, how has suffering refined, developed and strengthened your faith?

4. Read Malachi 3. God reveals a messianic prophecy through the prophet Malachi, saying,

> See, I am sending my messenger to prepare the way before me, and the Lord whom you seek will suddenly come to his temple. The messenger of the covenant in whom you delight – indeed, he is coming, says the Lord of hosts. But who can endure the day of his coming, and who can

stand when he appears? For he is like a refiner's fire and like fullers' soap; he will sit as a refiner and purifier of silver, and he will purify the descendants of Levi and refine them like gold and silver, until they present offerings to the Lord in righteousness. Then the offering of Judah and Jerusalem will be pleasing to the Lord as in the days of old and as in former years. Malachi 3:1-4

Christ Jesus "will sit as a refiner and purifier of silver, and he will purify…." How is He purifying you? How has your life changed since meeting and receiving His holy grace?

Glacier Bay National Park, Alaska

44

Satan's Tactics

"Hear then the parable of the sower. When anyone hears the word of the kingdom and does not understand it, the evil one comes and snatches away what is sown in the heart; this is what was sown on the path. As for what was sown on rocky ground, this is the one who hears the word and immediately receives it with joy; yet such a person has no root, but endures only for a while, and when trouble or persecution arises on account of the word, that person immediately falls away. As for what was sown among thorns, this is the one who hears the word, but the cares of the world and the lure of wealth choke the word, and it yields nothing. But as for what was sown on good soil, this is the one who hears the word and understands it, who indeed bears fruit and yields, in one case a hundredfold, in another sixty, and in another thirty." Matthew 13:18-23

The sower generously, indiscriminately tosses seeds all over the place. He throws seeds on the path, on rocky ground, among weeds and on fertile soil. He scatters seeds everywhere and some of the seeds grow into strong plants that produced an abundant crop. What happens to the seeds sown in your heart?

The parable says a lot about the sower, and the four types of places seeds land, and the abundant harvest produced by a small portion of the seeds on a small portion of the land. We can mine the depths of God's holy word and never fully comprehend the message because, well, it is God's holy word and our minds are nothing compared to His. This is one of the reasons I love reading and re-reading and praying over and meditating on God's holy word. No matter how many times I may have studied a passage, He continues to reveal new insights.

Jesus teaches a lot using parables, and Scripture records a few occasions when Jesus explains them. All of His teaching is important. All of His parables are important. But when I see Him explain a parable, I stop and pay extra attention because He takes the time to explain it, suggesting the meaning is so important, so fundamental to our lives that He does not want us to miss it. So it is with the Parable of the Sower, and as Jesus explains the parable, He describes some of the tactics Satan uses to keep us away from God.

While we often go through our days focusing exclusively on the tangible realm, Scripture screams at us to consider the spiritual realm surrounding us and dwelling within us, and to grasp its many powerful implications. Luke begins his gospel with two angelic encounters and a multitude of angels announcing the Messiah's birth, followed by Satan tempting Jesus in the wilderness (see Luke 1:11-25, 2:8-14 and 4:1-13). As He begins His ministry in Capernaum, Jesus casts unclean spirits out of man worshipping in the synagogue, and later that day Jesus heals lots of folks and "Demons also came out of many, shouting, 'You are the Son of God!'" (Luke 4:41). Demons know who Jesus is and they cower at His authority. Scripture forces us to acknowledge the spiritual realm, to consider that it influences people, and to see that Jesus is in control.

Jesus' ministry of word, deed and sign reveals the existence of spiritual battles. As He teaches and heals, He also casts out demons. Throughout His ministry the three are connected. During a sermon, Peter describes Jesus' ministry discussing, "how God anointed Jesus of Nazareth with the Holy Spirit and with power; how he went about doing good and healing all who were oppressed by the devil, for God was with him" (Acts 10:38). Jesus also directs His disciples to teach, heal and cast out demons as He sends them out as missionaries (see Matthew 10:7-8). Jesus directs the disciples to deal with demons the same way He did, and Paul describes our struggle against "spiritual forces of evil in the heavenly places" (Ephesians 6:12). Whether we realize it or not, the spiritual realm influences us, and spiritual battles are taking place.

With this in mind, consider how Jesus describes some of Satan's tactics. Seeds resting on a path fail to penetrate the surface and become bird food rather than crops. Similarly, when we hear God's holy word but fail to understand, the word fails to penetrate our hearts, and Satan snatches God's holy word away from us. Have you ever sat in church listening to someone read and explain God's holy word, and the words enter your ears and suddenly you're thinking, "What sounds good for lunch? We could go to the café, but the line will be long, and the last time we were there.…" And suddenly thoughts unrelated to God's word flood your mind and you lose track entirely and when you start listening again you have no idea what the speaker is saying? Or perhaps you sit in your reading spot and open the Bible longing to connect with God through His living word, and as soon as you read a few words you suddenly feel sleepy, unable to focus. These are but two of the ways Satan robs us of God's seeds. Sometimes our hearts are the path; at other times, we respond like rocky soil.

Suffering, grief, pain and trouble are part of the human condition. We will each experience trouble. The question is, how will we respond? God promises He is with us in our trouble (see Psalm 91), but do we believe that He truly is? When our faith is tested, will it survive? Jesus' words force us to ask, "How deep are my roots?" I know I have heard God's holy word, I believe, I have felt His joy, peace, comfort and assurance, I have seen His miraculous touch in people around me, but will my faith survive the troubles I will encounter?

I grew up in north central Oklahoma where a brisk wind often flows across the plain. There aren't many trees in that part of the world, but the ones that are there are strong. Facing the daily onslaught strengthens their trunks and branches and forces their roots to grow deep. I think of old blackjack oaks as symbols of perseverance, made strong by standing firm through wind, storms and drought encountered along the way.

When trouble arises, you might hear whispers suggesting that God has abandoned you, that He was never really with you in the first place, that you are beyond His ability to help, that His holy words are lies, or other evil thoughts. When you hear whispers like that, please know where they are coming from and ask God to make them go away and trust in His holy word and address directly the source of the whispers and demand that he leaves you alone in Jesus' holy name because you have been cleansed in the blood of Jesus. Know that God's promises are true, He is with you, He has all power and authority, He hears your prayers, and He loves you. Like the mighty oak, grow in faith through your trouble.

Thorns are all around us. They are everywhere. We invite them into our homes each time we turn on the television and see ads telling us that the only thing separating us from the perfect life we imagine is the particular product they are selling. We continuously invite thorns into our lives each time we check our social media feed and see images of perfect lives depicted in posts and the associated marketing campaigns. We are surrounded by thorns, so each seed sown in us is sown among thorns. Jesus says, "As for what was sown among thorns, this is the one who hears the word, but the cares of the world and the lure of wealth choke the word, and it yields nothing." Will we protect our seeds or will we allow them to be choked out? Will we succumb to the "lure of wealth" or grow in faith through it?

Jesus explains that the various places where seeds fall are each influenced by Satan. Spiritual forces are at work within us and around us. With this in mind, Paul urges us to put on the full armor of God, to stand firm on the Truth of God, to embrace His righteousness, maintain faith and pray all the time (see Ephesians 6:10-20). Just as God allows the wind to blow, knowing it will strengthen the mighty oak, He allows trouble so that we might grow stronger in faith and gain experiences allowing us to shine His light in new ways and to people who might otherwise never take us seriously.

Your heart is fertile soil. He has planted His seed in you with a purpose. Embrace His holy seed, allow it to grow, foster its growth, feed it with His holy word and prayer and transparent relationships with your brothers and sisters in Christ. God loves you. He is with you. May God send His angels to guard and protect you while you cherish and nurture His holy seed growing within you.

Thoughts to Consider

1. Read Psalm 91. I love the promises described in the psalm. God delivers us, protects us, and sends His angels to guard us. The psalmist writes,

> Because you have made the Lord your refuge, the Most High your dwelling place, no evil shall befall you, no scourge come near your tent. Psalm 91:9-10

I encourage you to convert Psalm 91 into your personal prayer.

2. Read Psalm 121. The psalm provides assurance of God's holy protection.

> The Lord is your keeper; the Lord is your shade at your right hand. The sun shall not strike you by day, nor the moon by night. The Lord will keep you from all evil; he will keep your life. The Lord will keep your going out and your coming in from this time on and forevermore. Psalm 121:5-8

In what specific ways do God's holy promises comfort you while you are experiencing trouble?

3. Read Mark 3. Early in Jesus' ministry in Galilee, as He taught, healed and cast out demons, crowds grew and followed Him all the time. As people responded to Him, so did demons. Mark writes,

> Whenever the unclean spirits saw him, they fell down before him and shouted, "You are the Son of God!" But he sternly ordered them not to make him known. Mark 3:11-12

Demons recognized Jesus as the Christ long before people did. God's holy word presents demons and evil spirits as real spiritual entities who interact with Jesus, respect His authority and obey His commands. Demons and evil spirits exist, but they only function within limits imposed by God. God is in control. Does this cause your perspective of evil influences to change?

If so, in what way?

4. Read Matthew 13. Jesus tells the Parable of the Sower in the first nine verses. He explains the parable in verses 18-23. Between the passages involving the specific parable, the disciples ask Jesus why He teaches through parables. Jesus answers, "To you it has been given to know the secrets of the kingdom of heaven, but to them it has not been given" (Matthew 13:11). Some have eyes to see and ears to hear, others do not. Using words from the prophet Isaiah, Jesus explains that people unable to understand the message have shut their eyes and have allowed their hearts to harden.

Through Isaiah, God urges them to turn that He might heal them. Jesus continues saying,

> Truly I tell you, many prophets and righteous people longed to see what you see, but did not see it, and to hear what you hear, but did not hear it. Matthew 13:17

As you read the Parable of the Sower and Jesus' explanation, how do you respond to Jesus' statements regarding parables in general?

Randy L Allen

Dead Sea, Israel

45

God's Purpose

On the third new moon after the Israelites had gone out of the land of Egypt, on that very day, they came into the wilderness of Sinai. They had journeyed from Rephidim, entered the wilderness of Sinai, and camped in the wilderness; Israel camped there in front of the mountain. Then Moses went up to God; the Lord called to him from the mountain, saying, "Thus you shall say to the house of Jacob, and tell the Israelites: You have seen what I did to the Egyptians, and how I bore you on eagles' wings and brought you to myself. Now therefore, if you obey my voice and keep my covenant, you shall be my treasured possession out of all the peoples. Indeed, the whole earth is mine, but you shall be for me a priestly kingdom and a holy nation. These are the words that you shall speak to the Israelites. Exodus 19:1-6

God promised Abraham would be the father of nations who would live in the Promised Land (see Genesis 12:1-3 and 15:18-20), and God acted on His promise. He heard the cries of His people, delivered them from bondage in Egypt and led them toward the Promised Land. In the passage above, they take a break from their journey to rest at Mount Sinai, God's holy mountain, and commune with God Almighty.

God brought them to His holy mountain for a reason. As God explains the purpose behind His action, He begins by asking His people to recognize His holy hand at work in their lives, to see and remember what He has already done for them and to believe and trust that He will continue to act. He brought them to Mount Sinai so that they might hear and obey His voice, experience His glory and be His treasured possession. God wanted His people to engage in relationship with Him and to move forward as "a priestly kingdom and a holy nation."

God delivered His people from bondage with a purpose in mind. Peter, writing to followers of Christ dispersed around northern Asia Minor, explains that God delivered them, and by implication you and me, from bondage for the same reason: He desires relationship with us, He calls us to move forward as His representatives, and He calls us to Him to be His treasured possession. Just as He led the Israelites to meet Him at the holy mountain, God urges us to "Come to him ... to be a holy priesthood, to offer spiritual sacrifices acceptable to God through Jesus Christ" (1 Peter 2:4-5).

What does a holy priesthood, a holy nation, a priestly kingdom look like? I imagine a bunch of people seeking God, desiring relationship with God, living in communion with God, serving Him, treating others, even strangers, with hospitality and compassion and love. I imagine a community whose distinctive characteristic is God's holy light, life and love revealed through their actions.

I commonly hear folks bemoan the disunity, lack of civility and caustic attitude woven through public discourse across our nation. At times we seem to be a society governed by mob mentality rather than civil debate, exchange of differing viewpoints based on facts, and sincere pursuit of a better society for all. As we discuss thoughts such as these, I conclude that this is one of the fundamental points of the good news of Jesus Christ. While we must vigilantly defend and protect our freedom, true change occurs one heart at a time through Christ Jesus. Can you imagine a society characterized by peace, unity, compassion, hospitality and love – a holy priesthood?

Jesus says, "Peace I leave with you; my peace I give you. I do not give to you as the world gives. Do not let your hearts be troubled and do not be afraid" (John 14:27). In his song *Imagine*, John Lennon sang,

> Imagine all the people living in peace, you
> You may say I'm a dreamer
> But I'm not the only one
> I hope some day you'll join us
> And the world will be as one.

Lennon's imagined world sounds like a realm characterized by Christ Jesus' peace and unity. It sounds like a holy priesthood.

Today we typically use the word "priest" to describe a person employed by a religious institution, but in the passage above the word does not refer to occupation. It denotes lifestyle and character. A society comprised entirely of people employed by the church, managing offerings and sacrifices would not sustain itself, but a community of holy people living in communion with God and revealing His love while they are out in the world working other occupations is certainly sustainable.

God calls us to be holy, pure and righteous, but I continue to ponder what that looks like. What do holy people look like? How do we identify a holy priesthood existing in our presence? In the Sermon on the Mount, Jesus says,

> You will know them by their fruits. Are grapes gathered from thorns, or figs from thistles? In the same way, every good tree bears good fruit, but the bad tree bears bad fruit. A good tree cannot bear bad fruit, nor can a bad tree bear good fruit. Every tree that does not bear good fruit is cut down and thrown into the fire. Thus you will know them by their fruits. Matthew 7:16-20

And on the evening of the Last Supper Jesus says,

> "I give you a new commandment, that you love

one another. Just as I have loved you, you also should love one another. By this everyone will know that you are my disciples, if you have love for one another." John 13:34-35

A holy priesthood would be a society of people characterized by compassionate, loving service, by good fruit, by holiness. God's holy word explains that holy people live holy lives and behave righteously, and sinful people behave sinfully:

> Little children, let no one deceive you. Everyone who does what is right is righteous, just as he is righteous. Everyone who commits sin is a child of the devil; for the devil has been sinning from the beginning. The Son of God was revealed for this purpose, to destroy the works of the devil. 1 John 3:7-8

If it is true that each of us is a sinner, that we all fall short of God's glory and that no one is holy except God, how do the concepts fit within the duality of the passage? We are each a sinner, but when the Holy Spirit convicts us of sin in our lives, do we repent or do we continue acting in ways that, through His holy conviction, we know to be inconsistent with His will for our lives? Ideally, we are each on the path moving toward God, toward holiness, perfection and sanctification, but I know I have far to go. Participating in a holy priesthood does not require perfection; it requires continued movement forward along the path toward God.

"The Son of God was revealed for this purpose, to destroy the works of the devil." In a world bearing elements of disharmony, as we seek peace and unity, it is nice to see the truth presented in Scripture, that Jesus came to destroy the devil's work and to give us His peace.

God delivers people from bondage for a purpose. He has plans for you and me. Throughout Scripture, God explains that He delivers people from bondage so that they, we, you might enjoy relationship with Him. God explains this time and time again. He delivered His people from bondage in Egypt and guided them to His holy mountain so that they might commune with Him. He begged them to hear His voice and to be His people and to be a kingdom of priests, a holy nation. Peter returns to this image and explains that God delivers you and me from bondage for the same reason: He desires relationship with us. Just as God urged the Israelites to meet Him at the holy mountain, He urges us to "Come to him … to be a holy priesthood, to offer spiritual sacrifices acceptable to God through Jesus Christ" (1 Peter 2:4-5)

May the Body of Christ be characterized by unity, peace and compassionate loving service. May we be one and may we each be united as one with God in the same way the Father, Son and Holy Spirit is one. May you continue seeking Him, desiring Him, and allowing Him to reveal His glory through you.

Thoughts to Consider

1. Read Matthew 28. Matthew concludes his gospel writing,

> And Jesus came and said to them, "All authority in heaven and on earth has been given to me. Go therefore and make disciples of all nations, baptizing them in the name of the Father and of the Son and of the Holy Spirit, and teaching them to obey everything that I have commanded you. And remember, I am with you always, to the end of the age." Matthew 28:18-20

Jesus instructs the disciples to go, make, baptize and teach. Specifically, He instructs disciples to go everywhere to make disciples, baptizing them and "teaching them to obey everything that I have commanded you." Jesus spoke to a specific group of eleven people now known as His disciples. Do you think the statement applies to us? As He calls the eleven to go and make disciples, does the same call apply to the disciples they make? Why or why not? Does this passage influence your view of your purpose?

2. Read John 14. John records the events of the Last Supper beginning with chapter 13 and continuing through chapter 17. So chapter 14 includes a portion of Jesus' teaching during the Last Supper. At verse 12 Jesus says,

> Very truly, I tell you, the one who believes in me will also do the works that I do and, in fact, will do greater works than these, because I am going to the Father. John 14:12

He begins the statement saying, "Very truly, I tell you...." This means He is about to say something very important. After saying that Jesus says that each person who believes in Jesus will do the works that Jesus did while on earth. The statement is absolute. It is not conditional. It is not limited to certain people who believe. Rather, each person who believes will do the works He did.

We each should ask ourselves whether we believe. If we do, what are we doing that Jesus did? Do these questions influence your understanding of your purpose?

3. Read Matthew 5. Immediately after giving the Beatitudes, Jesus discusses salt and light saying, "You are the salt of the earth... You are the light of the world... let your light shine before others, so that they may see your good works and give glory to your Father in heaven" (Matthew 5:13-16). How does the passage influence your thinking regarding purpose?

4. Read Joshua 1. Shortly after Moses' death, Joshua prepares to lead the Israelites across the Jordan River into the Promised Land. As he prepares, God says,

> Be strong and courageous; for you shall put this people in possession of the land that I swore to their ancestors to give them. Only be strong and very courageous, being careful to act in accordance with all the law that my servant Moses commanded you; do not turn from it to the right hand or to the left, so that you may be successful wherever you go. This book of the law shall not depart out of your mouth; you shall meditate on it day and night, so that you may be careful to act in

accordance with all that is written in it. For then you shall make your way prosperous, and then you shall be successful. Joshua 1:6-8

God urges Joshua to follow God's holy word and to act in accordance with God's direction because that is the key to living a good life. How does this passage influence your thoughts regarding purpose?

Randy L Allen

Laguna del Inca, Portillo, Chile

46

TRANSCENDENCE

What shall I do with you, O Ephraim? What shall I do with you, O Judah? Your love is like a morning cloud, like the dew that goes away early. Therefore I have hewn them by the prophets, I have killed them by the words of my mouth, and my judgment goes forth as the light. For I desire steadfast love and not sacrifice, the knowledge of God rather than burnt offerings. Hosea 6:4-6

Thus says the Lord of hosts, the God of Israel: Add your burnt offerings to your sacrifices, and eat the flesh. For in the day that I brought your ancestors out of the land of Egypt, I did not speak to them or command them concerning burnt offerings and sacrifices. But this command I gave them, "Obey my voice, and I will be your God, and you shall be my people; and walk in the way I command you, so that it may be well with you. Jeremiah 7:21-23

> "YOU HAVE HEARD THAT IT WAS SAID TO THOSE OF ANCIENT TIMES, 'YOU SHALL NOT MURDER;' AND 'WHOEVER MURDERS SHALL BE LIABLE TO JUDGMENT.' BUT I SAY TO YOU THAT IF YOU ARE ANGRY WITH A BROTHER OR SISTER, YOU WILL BE LIABLE TO JUDGMENT..." MATTHEW 5:21-22

As the Soviet Union collapsed in 1990, I had the opportunity to visit Berlin, Moscow and other parts of Europe feeling shockwaves from the fall. I rented a sledgehammer for a few minutes to knock off a chunk of the Berlin wall – a terrific souvenir. Moscow was filled with an uneasy energy. Hotel security officials warned about venturing outside alone explaining that police payroll had not been met and even if they were paid, the Ruble was so devalued their pay would have been worthless, so they were unlikely to respond. Stores were empty; unemployment soared; young women called hotel rooms all night begging for a meal. To the extent taxi drivers could be viewed as market indicators, the market's preferred currency was either US Dollars or Marlboro cigarettes. The foundations of society had not collapsed – for the most part people still respected the legal systems in place, they drove on the correct side of the street, mass looting was not happening, people still openly traveled streets, electricity still flowed through power lines, stores were open with limited hours and nearly empty shelves – but there was a sense that the system was on the verge of morphing into chaos and a cloud of uncertainty, concern and worry filled the air as everyone watched their life's savings lose all value, wondered whether they would have food to eat tomorrow, and wondered what would fill the power vacuum created by the government's collapse.

At first glance it may seem counterintuitive, but laws and systems to enforce them are necessary for freedom. I recently read an article about a family living in the rubble of what was previously their apartment in a war-torn city. They had no food and no water, and venturing outside was risky. In desperation, two young men carried buckets to a nearby water source and as they filled the containers both were killed. The family remained in a desperate, vulnerable position, subjected to the whims of people with firepower. The fabric of society was torn, justice had disappeared, peace had been replaced by fear and chaos, and they had no freedom.

Just laws are necessary for freedom and functioning society, but they are merely foundational. They establish minimum standards necessary for society to function. Through the prophets and throughout the New Testament we see God calling His people to transcend the law, to receive His spiritual transformation and move to a holy condition such that the letter of the law is no longer meaningful to them. Jesus begins the Sermon on the Mount by giving the Beatitudes, the promise of God's special blessing on people in need. Jesus then states two amazing proclamations: "You are the salt of the earth" and "You are the light of the world" (see Matthew 5:13-14). He doesn't urge them to be salt and light, He proclaims that they are salt and light.

Immediately after that amazing introduction, Jesus

begins His call to transcendence by saying, "Do not think that I have come to abolish the law or the prophets; I have come not to abolish but to fulfill.... For I tell you, unless your righteousness exceeds that of the scribes and Pharisees, you will never enter the kingdom of heaven" (Matthew 5:17 & 5:20).

We need laws, but they set the floor. Jesus calls us to transcend and He describes what this looks like through a series of statements, each beginning with something similar to "You have heard it said ... but I say to you...." With each statement Jesus urges us to transcend customary behavior, to move beyond mere action toward spiritual transformation, holiness, sanctification, perfection, with hearts so filled with the Holy Spirit that we live out His love without thinking about the law, so filled with the Holy Spirit that our human nature is replaced with His righteousness and our lives embody and reveal His love, His glory, His life, His light. We truly become His salt and light out in the world, making a difference in lives around us.

Jesus chooses a handful of examples encouraging us to consider the condition of our hearts and whether, by focusing on certain aspects of our lives, we are able to identify things in our hearts separating us from God. He discusses anger, urging us to quickly seek reconciliation if we become angry with another, because anger, even if it is not acted on and we keep it bottled up inside, separates us from God and harms our relationships with others. So if we experience anger with another, we need to forgive, seek reconciliation and re-establish unity (see Matthew 5:21-26).

Jesus discusses adultery, urging us to see that lusting for

another, except within the bonds of marriage, separates us from God, taints our view of others and harms our relationships. He discusses divorce, oaths and retaliation and in each instance, He encourages us to seek reconciliation with everyone, and to build unity within the Body of Christ and unity between each of us and God (see Matthew 5:27-42).

Then He takes this imperative a step further saying, "You have heard that it was said, 'You shall love your neighbor and hate your enemy.' But I say to you, love your enemies and pray for those who persecute you, so that you may be children of your Father in heaven; for he makes his sun rise on the evil and on the good, and sends rain on the righteous and on the unrighteous" (Matthew 5:43-45).

First, let's be clear, the Law of Moses does not say, "hate your enemy." It is not in the law, but apparently it was an expression that some people commonly said at the time. With that out of the way, let's consider the core of the statement – Jesus' directive for us to love our enemies and to pray for those who persecute us. Jesus urges us to transcend and throughout the teaching he urges us to avoid situations and thoughts and behavior that separate us from other people and from God, and to seek reconciliation quickly when our thoughts or actions cause separation. Here He pushes the thought to its extreme – loving an enemy.

If you were the family in that war torn city whose sons and brothers were killed while attempting to get buckets of water for their family, would you be able to love the people who killed them? Would you be able to pray for them? Jesus knows that reconciliation is so important, He calls us to do so. He knows that seeds of anger and hatred separate us from God and from one another, and we must eliminate them from our lives. If we do not, they will hinder and block our relationship with God and they will steal love from our hearts and they will create roots of disunity in our souls.

How has someone harmed you? How have you harmed others? Jesus urges you to seek reconciliation with them as soon as possible. He urges us to transcend above the requirements of law, to transcend above the way most people act in society, to transcend above cultural norms. He urges us to allow the Holy Spirit to invade our spirits and souls in such a way that we are transformed by His indwelling and we embody His love and life and light and we allow His glory to be revealed through us.

May you continue seeking God in every aspect of your life.

Thoughts to Consider

1.　Read Jeremiah 10. The prophet discusses "the signs of the heavens" (Jeremiah 10:2), people's "stupid and foolish" desire to worship idols (Jeremiah 10:8), and God's transcendent majesty. As to God, the prophet writes,

> It is he who made the earth by his power, who established the world by his wisdom, and by his understanding stretched out the heavens. When he utters his voice,

there is a tumult of waters in the heavens, and he makes the mist rise from the ends of the earth. He makes lightnings for the rain, and he brings out the wind from his storehouses. Jeremiah 10:12-13

How do you describe God's transcendent majesty?

2. Read Romans 8 and 1 Corinthians 15. God is majestic. The words pure, divine, holy, almighty and sovereign refer exclusively to God. Through Christ Jesus, as we grow closer to Him we let go of fleshly desires and worldly loves, and our spirits and souls are transformed into His image. Near the end of chapter 8 Paul writes,

> We know that all things work together for good for those who love God, who are called according to his purpose. For those whom he foreknew he also predestined to be conformed to the image of his Son, in order that he might be the firstborn within a large family. And those whom he predestined he also called; and those whom he called he also justified; and those whom he justified he also glorified. Romans 8:28-30

And near the end of chapter 15 he writes,

> The first man was from the earth, a man of dust; the second man is from heaven. As was the man of dust, so are those who are of the dust; and as is the man of heaven, so are those who are of heaven. Just as we have borne the image of the man of dust, we will also bear the image of the man of heaven. 1 Corinthians 15:47-49

Consider the changes that have taken place within you since meeting Jesus. How have you taken on the image of Christ? What needs to change for you to take another step toward Him?

3. Read John 17. On the evening of the Last Supper before walking to Gethsemane to pray, Jesus prays this amazing prayer recorded as John 17. He prays for Himself, then He prays for the disciples, and then He prays for each person who will come to believe through the disciples, which includes us. It amazes me that Jesus prayed for us, particularly at that time, when His moments were nearing the end. As He prays He says,

> I am not asking you to take them out of the world, but I ask you to protect them from the evil one. They do not belong to the world, just as I do not belong to the world. Sanctify them in the truth; your word is truth. As you have sent me into the world, so I have sent them into the world. And for their sakes I sanctify myself, so that they also may be sanctified in truth.... I made your name known to them, and I will make it known, so that the love with which you have loved me may be in them, and I in them." John 17:15-19 & 26

Growing in holiness or sanctification is another way of saying we take on the image of Christ Jesus. Jesus prays for us to "be sanctified in truth" and for God's love and Christ Jesus Himself to fill us. This is the culmination of spiritual transformation in and through Christ Jesus. As you ponder that message, what do you think?

For the Praise of His Glory

Seaside, Florida

47

Faith

Now faith is the assurance of things hoped for, the conviction of things not seen. Indeed, by faith our ancestors received approval. By faith we understand that the worlds were prepared by the word of God, so that what is seen was made from things that are not visible. Hebrews 11:1-3

By faith Abraham obeyed when he was called to set out for a place that he was to receive as an inheritance; and he set out, not knowing where he was going. By faith he stayed for a time in the land he had been promised, as in a foreign land, living in tents, as did Isaac and Jacob, who were heirs with him of the same promise. For he looked forward to the city that has foundations, whose architect and builder is God. By faith he received power of procreation, even though he was too old — and Sarah herself was barren — because he considered him faithful who

HAD PROMISED. THEREFORE FROM ONE PERSON, AND THIS ONE AS GOOD AS DEAD, DESCENDANTS WERE BORN, "AS MANY AS THE STARS OF HEAVEN AND AS THE INNUMERABLE GRAINS OF SAND BY THE SEASHORE." HEBREWS 11:8-12

BY FAITH ABRAHAM, WHEN PUT TO THE TEST, OFFERED UP ISAAC. HE WHO HAD RECEIVED THE PROMISES WAS READY TO OFFER UP HIS ONLY SON, OF WHOM HE HAD BEEN TOLD, "IT IS THROUGH ISAAC THAT DESCENDANTS SHALL BE NAMED FOR YOU." HE CONSIDERED THE FACT THAT GOD IS ABLE EVEN TO RAISE SOMEONE FROM THE DEAD — AND FIGURATIVELY SPEAKING, HE DID RECEIVE HIM BACK. HEBREWS 11:17-19

As I drove to work this morning, I heard a tragic story on the radio. After his wife left, a man suddenly found himself alone picking up the pieces, caring for two young boys and moving forward. He cried out to God for help, but when he saw no evidence of God answering his prayers, he lost faith. As his bitterness and pain and anger with God grew, he concluded that God does not exist and he stopped praying and he was no longer angry with God, only with himself for having believed that sort of fantasy.

The man believed enough to cry out to God, but then he lost faith. We each experience times when our faith is tested. Storms will blow. The question is not whether they will come, but how will we respond? How strong is our faith? How deep are our roots?

God's holy word tells us, "faith is the assurance of things hoped for, the conviction of things not seen" (Hebrews 11:1) and "faith comes from what is heard, and what is heard comes through the word of Christ" (Romans 10:17). It is by faith in God's holy word that we believe with complete certainty that God is who He claims to be, that His word is true, that He is all powerful, that He is love, that He loves us, and that He hears and listens to and responds to our prayers.

We know all this, but at times we pray and we see no response. At times our faith is tested because our connection with God has faded like a poor cellphone signal and it feels as if our prayers go unheard, as if the ceiling is blocking their transmission, and we feel distant from God. In times like that, how will we respond? Scripture is loaded with examples of people suffering, enduring trials, waiting on God, feeling distant from God, crying out to God and growing in faith as they wait. David cries out to God saying,

> "My God, my God, why have you forsaken me? Why are you so far from helping me, from the words of my groaning? O my God, I cry by day, but you do not answer; and by night, but find no rest." Psalm 22:1-2

By the end of the psalm, we see that his faith grew through the process. Even Jesus Christ felt distant from God, quoting God's holy word penned by David at Psalm 22:1 while hanging on the cross, but He trusted God's promises. Job suffered through torment but after it all he said to God, "I had heard of you by the hearing of the ear, but now my eyes see you" (Job 42:5). His relationship with God and his faith grew through the process.

Sometimes our faith is tested while we wait on God. We grow impatient. We want things to happen according to our schedule, fulfilling our expectations, accomplishing our plans. But God sees all, knows all, loves each of us, and is implementing the perfect plan in His perfect time. Abram (aka Abraham) heard God. God promised Abram saying,

> "I will make you into a great nation, and I will bless you; I will make your name great, and you will be a blessing. I will bless those who bless you, and whoever curses you I will curse; and all the peoples on earth will be blessed through you." Genesis 12:2-3

What an amazing promise! In response, Abram packed up and headed out and when he reached Canaan, God told him this was the land God would give his descendants (see Genesis 12:7), but there were problems – Abram was 75 years old with no children and the land of Canaan was suffering famine. So he and his family left for a while. They went to Egypt to wait out the famine and later returned. Twenty-four years later, Abram was 99, he still lived in a tent and his wife had not conceived a child. When God asked Abram to follow Him, Abram packed up and followed, and then he waited and waited and when he was 100 years old, his son Isaac was born.

Finally, after waiting a long, long time, Abram (now Abraham) had a son and God's promise to make him "into a great nation" seemed within the realm of possibility; yet sometime later, when Isaac was old enough to travel a distance with his father and ask questions about sacrifice (see Genesis 22:1-19), God tested Abraham by asking him to sacrifice Isaac. And Abraham obeyed. Abraham was faithful. After years of waiting, trusting God, knowing that God is faithful and true, God sent Abraham to offer Isaac as a sacrifice, and Abraham obeyed and just before Abraham plunged his knife into Isaac, God called off the horrific mission and provided a ram instead. Abraham put aside everything else – his personal hopes and dreams, his love for his son, his desire to have a family – and followed God, trusted God and believed God above all else. Possibly he trusted that God would raise Isaac from the dead or perform some other miracle, we do not know, but we know Abraham placed all his trust and confidence and hope in the Lord God Almighty.

We also know that ultimately, God fulfills His promises. He is faithful. His faith endures even when ours falters. But He does so in His time, not ours. If you have been crying out to God but you do not see evidence of His response and He feels distant from you, please know that He is with you, He hears your prayers, He loves you, and His promises are true.

What storm is blowing through your life? May it strengthen your faith, may it force your roots deeper into God's holy word, deeper into prayer, deeper into the Holy Spirit, may your relationship with Christ Jesus grow, and may you weather the storm and use the experience to serve God in new and glorious ways.

Thoughts to Consider

1.	Read Genesis 15, 18:1-15, 21:1-7 & 22:1-19. God makes a covenant with Abram promising his descendants will be as numerous as the stars in the sky (see Genesis 15:5). Abram and Sarai had no children, and as they advanced in age they must have wondered whether God's covenant was true. Finally, when Abram (aka Abraham) was 100 years old, Isaac was born (see Genesis 21:1-7). They had prayed and waited, for years after God made His covenant, and finally God delivered the first step, and in the next chapter God asks Abraham to sacrifice Isaac, his only son. And Abraham obeyed. Do you see parallels to God's sacrifice of His only Son?

Abraham's willingness to obey God demonstrates His faithfulness. How does God's willingness to sacrifice His only Son demonstrate His faithfulness?

2.	Read Ephesians 2. God loves us and by His holy grace offers us His loving gift of grace. We do not deserve it. We can never earn it. He loves us and offers His gift of life to us even while we were "dead through the trespasses and sin" (Ephesians 2:1). Here's the thing ... while we are saved by faith and faith alone, faith begins with God not us. If it began with us we might be able claim that we earned salvation as a result of our faith, which is not the case. Faith is a gift from God, His holy gracious, loving gift. God's holy word says, "For by grace you have been saved through faith, and this is not your own doing; it is the gift of God – not the result of works, so that no one may boast" (Ephesians 2:8-9). How does the thought that faith begins with God alter your view of our faith?

3.   Read Romans 10. At verse 8, Paul quotes Deuteronomy 30:11-14 saying, "The word is near you, on your lips and in your heart" (that is, the word of faith that we proclaim) ...." He then discusses justification by faith and the source of faith. As to the latter he writes, "So faith comes from what is heard, and what is heard comes through the word of Christ" (Romans 10:17).

Faith comes by hearing, from God's holy word, through God's word and through Christ Jesus. In what ways has this been true in your experience?

For the Praise of His Glory

Massadona, Colorado

48

A Public Service Warning

"You are the salt of the earth; but if salt has lost its taste, how can its saltiness be restored? It is no longer good for anything, but is thrown out and trampled under foot.

"You are the light of the world. A city built on a hill cannot be hid. No one after lighting a lamp puts it under the bushel basket, but on the lampstand, and it gives light to all in the house. In the same way, let your light shine before others, so that they may see your good works and give glory to your Father in heaven. Matthew 5:13-16

"Beware of practicing your piety before others in order to be seen by them; for then you have no reward from your Father in heaven. So whenever you give alms, do not sound a trumpet

BEFORE YOU, AS THE HYPOCRITES DO IN THE SYNAGOGUES AND IN THE STREETS, SO THAT THEY MAY BE PRAISED BY OTHERS. TRULY I TELL YOU, THEY HAVE RECEIVED THEIR REWARD. BUT WHEN YOU GIVE ALMS, DO NOT LET YOUR LEFT HAND KNOW WHAT YOUR RIGHT HAND IS DOING, SO THAT YOUR ALMS MAY BE DONE IN SECRET; AND YOUR FATHER WHO SEES IN SECRET WILL REWARD YOU.

"AND WHENEVER YOU PRAY, DO NOT BE LIKE THE HYPOCRITES; FOR THEY LOVE TO STAND AND PRAY IN THE SYNAGOGUES AND AT THE STREET CORNERS, SO THAT THEY MAY BE SEEN BY OTHERS. TRULY I TELL YOU, THEY HAVE RECEIVED THEIR REWARD. BUT WHENEVER YOU PRAY, GO INTO YOUR ROOM AND SHUT THE DOOR AND PRAY TO YOUR FATHER WHO IS IN SECRET; AND YOUR FATHER WHO SEES IN SECRET WILL REWARD YOU.

"WHEN YOU ARE PRAYING, DO NOT HEAP UP EMPTY PHRASES AS THE GENTILES DO; FOR THEY THINK THAT THEY WILL BE HEARD BECAUSE OF THEIR MANY WORDS. DO NOT BE LIKE THEM, FOR YOUR FATHER KNOWS WHAT YOU NEED BEFORE YOU ASK HIM. MATTHEW 6:1-8

God came to earth as a man – fully human and fully God. Jesus is God. He is the Word, the Truth, the Way, the Life. He is the Light of the world. He gave up the glory that He knew before creation to come to earth on a multifaceted mission. He came that we might have life in abundance, He came to deliver eternal life, He came to preach and teach and reveal God's glory and to demonstrate how people should live. During His brief earthly ministry, He also issued a number of commands or directives telling us how we should behave. Recognizing that He is God, we should pay special attention to His directives.

The passages above are from the Sermon on the Mount. They contain three positive directives (Jesus tells us to do certain things) and five negative directives (Jesus tells us not to do certain things). As to the positive, Jesus tells us to "let your light shine before others, so that they may see your good works and give glory to your Father in heaven" (Matthew 5:16); He tells us to "beware of practicing your piety before others in order to be seen by them" (Matthew 6:1); and He tells us to "go into your room and shut the door and pray to your Father who is in secret" (Matthew 6:6). In successive breaths during a single sermon Jesus tells us to let our light shine so that other people will see our good works and to avoid practicing piety to be seen by others. Isn't that potentially contradictory?

As with many things, it has to do with the condition of our hearts. When we perform good works or pray or fast, what are we seeking? Are we seeking God or praise from other people?

To gain context, let's consider the negative directives. Jesus says, "So whenever you give alms, do not sound a trumpet before you, as the hypocrites do in the synagogues and in the streets, so that they may be praised by others" (Matthew 6:2). Helping the poor is presumed. It is good and something we should do, but what is our motivation? Do we perform good acts as a show, to enhance our social standing, to present ourselves in a way that will cause others to think we are better than we really are? The word hypocrite has its roots in performance, like actors performing on stage, pretending to be someone they are not. Do we selectively choose times and places to help people in need ensuring the spotlight shines brightly on us, or do we help because God's love flowing through us gives us eyes to see others as beings created in God's image and we need to help them without regard to who sees? Are we seeking praise from others or are we seeking God?

Next, Jesus turns His attention to prayer saying, "And whenever you pray, do not be like the hypocrites; for they love to stand and pray in the synagogues and at the street corners, so that they may be seen by others" (Matthew 6:5). Prayer is presumed. It is good. We should pray continuously, seeking God, communing with God, growing in relationship with God, and as we lead lives of prayer we pray in private, we pray in public, we pray all the time everywhere, and that is good. But if we make a big, theatrical production of our prayers, performing so that others will see us praying and view us in a holy light and think we are better than we are, if that is our motivation then our enhanced social standing will be our only reward – we will receive exactly what we sought. In the same way, if we pray genuinely seeking God, communing with God, growing in relationship with God, we will receive what we seek. Jesus' warning makes me consider whether my motivation is God-centered or self-centered.

Jesus continues discussing prayer saying, "When you are praying, do not heap up empty phrases as the Gentiles do; for they think that they will be heard because of their many words" (Matthew 6:7). Prayer is a conversation with God. It should be honest and transparent, and we should be on guard so that it does not become an opportunity to impress others with our eloquence or anything else. Again, what are we seeking?

Jesus warns us. He urges us to beware of our motivation when we do good works, when we pray, when we fast, suggesting we should be careful during all our public interaction. In fact, Jesus hyperbolically underscores the two points regarding prayer telling us to go to our room, close the door and pray privately. If we struggle praying honestly, transparently, genuinely seeking God in settings where others can see us, avoid those situations and pray privately.

In the same sermon, in successive breaths, Jesus tells us that we are the light of the world and urges us to let our light shine before others so that they may see our good works, and then He warns against practicing acts of piety to be seen by others. So which is it? The key lies in the phrase "to be seen by others" (Matthew 6:1). Jesus is not commanding us to avoid public displays of loving action; in fact, He calls us to do just that. He commands us to avoid doing acts of love "to be seen by others." Why are we acting in the first place? What motivates us? What are we seeking? Are we seeking God or praise from others?

May you continue seeking Him, desiring Him, growing in relationship with Him, allowing His holy transformation to occur in you, and allowing His light, life and love to be revealed through you while you are out in the world.

Thoughts to Consider

1.   Read Matthew 23. Jesus blasts religious leaders for their hypocrisy. He describes them as hypocrites six times in seven paragraphs. He begins telling His listeners to do what religious leaders tell them to do, but not to act the way they act. As He gives examples of what they do wrong He says, "They do all their deeds to be seen by others; for they make their phylacteries broad and their fringes long" (Matthew 23:5). Then He says, "All who exalt themselves will be humbled, and all who humble themselves will be exalted" (Matthew 23:12). They acted to perform for others, not necessarily to serve God. Can you think of times you may have acted similarly?

2.   Read Luke 18. Beginning at verse 9, Jesus tells a parable involving a religious leader and a tax collector. As you read the parable, please keep in mind that the gospels discuss tax collectors as such bad actors that they need their own separate category of sinfulness. For example, Matthew describes Jesus eating with "many tax collectors and sinners" (Matthew 9:10). Apparently simply saying "sinners" would not convey the point.

So the parable presents a religious leader who prays loudly in the temple boasting of his good deeds, and a tax collector standing far off beating his breast and begging God for mercy. Jesus concludes saying, "I tell you this man [the tax collector] went home justified rather than the other; for all who exalt themselves will be humbled, but all who humble themselves will be exalted" (Luke 9:14). The one who fasted twice a week, tithed, faithfully went to church, regularly prayed, wore the right clothing and held himself out as religious was rebuked while tax collector was justified. In the parable the distinguishing factor was humility.

We are each sinner. Not a single one of us deserves God's grace, not through regular church attendance, tithing, fasting, praying or anything else we can do. God offers His holy, loving grace as a gift that we receive through Christ Jesus by faith. As you consider your sin, your brokenness, your pain and suffering, your separation from God, can you relate to the tax collector? As you consider your regular church attendance, giving, Bible study, prayer life and good works, have you ever found yourself looking down on others who might not work as hard as you do at their faith? In light of the parable, can you think of things you should change in your heart?

3.   Read Psalm 34. Several passages above discuss exaltation. The psalmist urges us to keep our focus on God and to exalt God, because as we focus on Him it is impossible to exalt ourselves. The psalm begins,

> I will bless the Lord at all times; his praise shall continually be in my mouth. My soul makes its boast in the Lord; let the humble hear and be glad. O magnify the Lord with me, and let us exalt his name together.
> Psalm 34:1-3

May we each follow the psalmist's lead, and may we join together exalting God's holy name.

Randy L Allen

Utah

49

GOOD TREES

"Either make the tree good, and its fruit good; or make the tree bad, and its fruit bad; for the tree is known by its fruit. You brood of vipers! How can you speak good things, when you are evil? For out of the abundance of the heart the mouth speaks. The good person brings good things out of a good treasure, and the evil person brings evil things out of an evil treasure. I tell you, on the day of judgment you will have to give an account of every careless word you utter; for by your words you will be justified, and by your words you will be condemned." Matthew 12:33-37

Chapter 12 of Matthew's gospel describes events of one particular Sabbath. Jesus walks through a wheat field, picking and eating grain. During a subsequent exchange with religious leaders, He declares Himself to be "lord of the Sabbath" (Matthew 12:8). He then enters a synagogue and heals a man's hand, which causes further discussion with religious leaders about Sabbath customs.

As Jesus leaves the synagogue, a crowd follows and Jesus cures "all of them" (Matthew 12:15) and then He cures a man who had been rendered mute and blind by a demon (see Matthew 12:22). In response to the final healing, which involved casting out demons, religious leaders accuse Jesus of being an agent of Satan. Jesus responds saying that their position makes no sense – Satan would not remove demons, as that would be contrary to his plans. Jesus continues saying, "But if it is by the Spirit of God that I cast out demons, then the kingdom of God has come to you" (Matthew 12:28).

Immediately following this exchange, Jesus states the passage first quoted above and the religious leaders ask Jesus for a sign to confirm His authority. Jesus had just healed a man in the synagogue, cured everyone in need in the crowd that followed Him, and cast a demon from a person. It seems that religious leaders saw Jesus heal in the synagogue and cast out the demon because they complain to Jesus about the acts; yet they ask Jesus for a sign that would confirm His authority. What more did they hope to see?

In the middle of this story involving Jesus revealing God's glory, revealing the kingdom of God to everyone with eyes to see, and religious leaders being so hung up on matters relating to Sabbath customs that they were unable to see the kingdom of God as it was revealed to them, Jesus discusses good trees bearing good fruit and bad trees bearing bad fruit. Given this context, what is He saying?

God's holy word frequently uses the image of fruit to help us understand the kingdom of God and our role as part of it. Jesus says, "I am the vine, you are the branches. Those who abide in me and I in them bear much fruit, because apart from me you can do nothing" (John 15:5). In the context of the teaching, we see fruit equating to good deeds, loving service, tangible evidence of Jesus' holy light revealed through us through our loving action.

Earlier, in the Sermon on the Mount, Jesus said,

> Beware of false prophets, who come to you in sheep's clothing but inwardly are ravenous wolves. You will know them by their fruits. Are grapes gathered from thorns, or figs from thistles? In the same way, every good tree bears good fruit, but the bad tree bears bad fruit. A good tree cannot bear bad fruit, nor can a bad tree bear good fruit. Every tree that does not bear good fruit is cut down and thrown into the fire. Thus you will know them by their fruits. Matthew 7:15-20

And before that, as John the Baptist taught about repentance, baptized in the wilderness and paved the way for Jesus, religious leaders went to the wilderness to be baptized by him. John greeted them saying,

> You brood of vipers! Who warned you to flee from the wrath to come? Bear fruit worthy of repentance. Matthew 3:7-8

Just as fruit of the Spirit is tangible evidence of His holy transformation of our spirits and souls (see Galatians 5:22-23), the fruit we produce is tangible evidence of who we really are. Jesus' word choice implies change.

Jesus says, "make the tree good, and its fruit good… For out of the abundance of the heart the mouth speaks. The good person brings good things out of a good treasure." Just as fruit of the Spirit is tangible evidence of His holy transformation of our spirits and souls, the fruit we produce is tangible evidence of who we really are. Jesus' word choice implies change. He says, "*make* the tree good, and its fruit good." Something makes the tree good and as a result it produces good fruit. Something makes the person good, causes the person to do good deeds, and fills his or her heart with good treasure.

What causes good? We know that what God creates is good (see Genesis 1:31). We know that only God is good (see Luke 18:19). We know that, apart from God, we are each evil (see Colossians 1:21-23). God the Father, Jesus Christ, the Holy Spirit is at the heart of everything good, and spiritual transformation through Him lies at the root of the gospel and is our only hope of embodying any amount of holiness. Jesus Christ offers redemption, new life, life abundant and total spiritual transformation, makes trees good, and builds up good treasure in hearts.

No matter where you might be today, please know that

Christ Jesus is with you, offering you His life and His transformation so that, through His indwelling, you are able to produce the best fruit ever. May you continue moving along the path toward Christ Jesus.

Thoughts to Consider

1. Read Matthew 12. In the passage first set forth above Jesus says,

> For out of the abundance of the heart the mouth speaks. The good person brings good things out of a good treasure, and the evil person brings evil things out of an evil treasure. I tell you, on the day of judgment you will have to give an account of every careless word you utter; for by your words you will be justified, and by your words you will be condemned." Matthew 12:34-37

Jesus connects the condition of our hearts and our words, and then says, "by your words you will be justified, and by your words you will be condemned." God's holy word tells us we are justified by faith (see Romans 3:28, Romans 5:1, Galatians 2:16, Galatians 3:24 and others). So which is it? Are we justified by faith or our words? While a superficial reading may suggest the statements are potentially contradictory, they are not because the root of each is in our heart. Faith lies in our heart and our words reveal the condition of our hearts, so the statements are consistent.

How do you read the passages? Is this argument compelling? Why or why not?

2. Read Romans 10. After connecting righteousness with belief in Christ Jesus (see Romans 10:4), God's holy word says,

> But the righteousness that comes from faith says, "Do not say in your heart, 'Who will ascend into heaven?'" (that is, to bring Christ down) "or 'Who will descend into the abyss?'" (that is, to bring Christ up from the dead). But what does it say?
>
> > "The word is near you, on your lips and in your heart"
>
> (that is, the word of faith that we proclaim); because if you confess with your lips that Jesus is Lord and believe in your heart that God raised him from the dead, you will be saved. For one believes with the heart and so is justified, and one confesses with the mouth and so is saved. Romans 10:6-10

Righteousness is connected to belief in Christ Jesus, which results from faith and reveals itself by words flowing from our lips. Our words reveal the condition of our hearts.

When I hear people use God's holy name or Jesus Christ's holy name as a curse, it grieves me for a myriad of reason, not the least of which is the words reveal the speaker's separation from God. I am similarly grieved when people speak caustic, angry, argumentative words to one another, because the attitude and heart condition revealed by the words are contrary to fruit of the Spirit.

In your experience, how are words connected to your heart condition?

3. Read Galatians 5. As the Holy Spirit transforms our spirits and souls, we take on His characteristics and they reveal their existence in ways other people notice. Paul refers to the characteristics as fruit of the Holy Spirit writing,

> By contrast, the fruit of the Spirit is love, joy, peace, patience, kindness, generosity, faithfulness, gentleness, and self-control. There is no law against such things. And those who belong to Christ Jesus have crucified the flesh with its passions and desires. If we live by the Spirit, let us also be guided by the Spirit. Let us not become conceited, competing against one another, envying one another. Galatians 5:22-26

As you grow in relationship with Christ Jesus and as His indwelling transforms you, how has the fruit of the Holy Spirit been revealed through you?

4. Read Genesis 1. God spoke light into existence (see Genesis 1:3). God spoke the sky into existence (see Genesis 1:6-8). God spoke and land and water were separated (see Genesis 1:9). God spoke and plants, living creatures and humans came into existence. God's word is powerful. When He speaks things happen. In what specific ways do your words have power?

Inlet to Lake San Cristobal, Colorado

50

BOND OF PEACE

> I THEREFORE, THE PRISONER IN THE LORD, BEG YOU TO LEAD A LIFE WORTHY OF THE CALLING TO WHICH YOU HAVE BEEN CALLED, WITH ALL HUMILITY AND GENTLENESS, WITH PATIENCE, BEARING WITH ONE ANOTHER IN LOVE, MAKING EVERY EFFORT TO MAINTAIN THE UNITY OF THE SPIRIT IN THE BOND OF PEACE. THERE IS ONE BODY AND ONE SPIRIT, JUST AS YOU WERE CALLED TO THE ONE HOPE OF YOUR CALLING, ONE LORD, ONE FAITH, ONE BAPTISM, ONE GOD AND FATHER OF ALL, WHO IS ABOVE ALL AND THROUGH ALL AND IN ALL. EPHESIANS 4:1-6

Think of a time when you laughed so hard your body hurt. Who were you with? Think of times when you felt true happiness, joy, wholeness in your soul. Who did you share the experiences with? We are designed in God's image to be relational, and genuine, transparent, mutual loving relationships are fundamental to God's design. We share wholeness, joy, happiness, grief and sorrow through genuine, loving relationships.

God is all about unity. The Holy Trinity presents an example of unity that we cannot quite wrap our simple brains around, and Jesus prays that we might be one in the same way the Holy Trinity is united (see John 17:21). As believers, we are each components of a single Body of Christ, a single gathering, unified through the Holy Spirit in the bond of peace. As we each grow closer to God, we grow closer to one another and, ideally, the Body of Christ reveals God's glory to the world.

Because God is all about unity, Satan is all about tearing us apart. He seeks to separate us from God and break apart genuine, loving, transparent relationships where trust is warranted. He wants to cloud transparency and remove our ability to trust one another and replace genuine love with an artificial version of it. Satan prowls like a lion seeking to destroy us and everything good in our lives (see 1 Peter 5:8).

As they shared the meal now known as the Last Supper, Jesus taught the disciples lesson after amazing lesson. He got up from the meal, removed His outer clothing, washed the disciples' feet and taught about loving service. He commanded the disciples to love one another as Jesus loved them. He taught about the Holy Spirit and, using several different images, He desperately tried to help them (and us) understand the connection that exists between God the Father, Jesus Christ, the Holy Spirit, each individual believer, and the collective community of believers (see John 13-16).

Jesus dwells in the Father and the Father dwells in Him. The words Jesus speaks are the Father's words and the works

Jesus does are the Father's works. Jesus Christ dwells in the Holy Spirit and the Holy Spirit dwells in Him. Jesus Christ and the Holy Spirit dwell in each believer, and each believer dwells in Him. And the members of the community of faith share a unique, heavenly, spiritual connection.

Our faith and our spiritual connections with God and with one another develop in synchronized harmony. As our connections with God strengthen, as our relationship with God grows, our faith matures. The reverse is also true, and as we allow God into our spirits and souls, and as we allow His holy transformation, ideally, we reveal His light, which may be perceived by others as characteristics known as fruit of the Spirit.[1]

In the two remarkable sentences set forth above, Paul merges these thoughts. He begs us to live with "all humility and gentleness, with patience, bearing with one another in love, making every effort to maintain the unity of the Spirit in the bond of peace." It is Jesus Christ and the Holy Spirit dwelling within us who give us His Spirit of love, peace, humility and unity, and it is His light and life flowing through us that has been described as fruit.

Peter urges us forward on the same path writing, "Now that you have purified your souls by your obedience to the truth so that you have genuine mutual love, love one another deeply from the heart" (1 Peter 1:22). The transformation of our spirits and souls leads to "genuine mutual love," the essence of unity.

---

1   God's holy word describes the fruit of the Spirit as follows: "By contrast, the fruit of the Spirit is love, peace, patience, kindness, generosity, faithfulness, and self-control" (Galatians 5:22-23).

During His last evening of teaching, before surrendering to death on the cross, during His final hours, He urgently taught about the spiritual connections we share. We are connected to God through faith, through the indwelling Holy Spirit, through Jesus Christ, and we experience unity with the Body of Christ. And I firmly believe that Satan actively seeks to destroy our links – our links with God and our links with one another. And on that evening 2,000 years ago Jesus prayed for us and for our unity.

After the Last Supper, Jesus prayed. John records the prayer as chapter 17 of his gospel. It is an amazing, chapter-long prayer that Jesus prays before walking to the Garden of Gethsemane where He surrendered to authorities. He begins by praying for Himself. Then He prays for the disciples. After that, He prays for us. As He prays He says,

> "I ask not only on behalf of these, but also on behalf of those who will believe in me through their word, that they may all be one. As you, Father, are in me and I am in you, may they also be in us, so that the world may believe that you have sent me." John 17:20-21

Later that evening, after all His teaching, after teaching about the links connecting the Holy Trinity and the Holy Trinity to each of us and the collective body of believers, He prays for unity. He prays that we, the body of believers, will be joined together as one in the same way the Father, Son and Holy Spirit is one. And He prays for unity, not just so that we might know the glory and pleasure associated with dwelling in God and experiencing Him and knowing Him, but so that the world might believe that Jesus is who He claims to be.

God's holy word says, "There is one body and one Spirit, just as you were called to the one hope of your calling, one Lord, one faith, one baptism, one God and Father of all, who is above all and through all and in all" (Ephesians 4:4-6). By discussing the inter-dwelling between the Father, the Son, the Holy Spirit and each believer, and Jesus as the point of access and the embodiment of God the Father, Jesus clearly presents the link, the connection between the Holy Trinity, between each of us and the Holy Trinity, and between the members of the Body of Christ. We are all linked with God and with each other.

God fills you with His holy power. Arm yourself with His holy word, protect yourself with the strength of your faith, cloak yourself in prayer. May you continue to grow in Christ Jesus, may you continue to surrender yourself to the indwelling Holy Spirit, may you continue to know the joy, happiness, comfort and peace of genuine loving relationships, and may God protect our bond of peace.

Thoughts to Consider

1. In its most basic sense, the concept of peace is the absence of conflict in regard to relations between people, or perhaps more accurately, the absence of factors causing conflict.[18] The Hebrew word shalom is translated in English as peace and in Greek as the word transliterated "eirene." How-

ever, shalom means much more than mere absence of conflict; it means wholeness, well-being and harmony. It is tied to the concepts of prosperity, security, safety and health. When used as a greeting or farewell, it is intended to promote harmony. Paul wrote "eirene" when he penned the words first quoted above in Greek, and he imbedded the concepts of shalom in his message.

In the passage first set forth above, Paul urges us to make "every effort to maintain the unity of the Spirit in the bond of peace." Does the concept of shalom alter your understanding of the passage? If so, how?

2.   Jesus is known as the Prince of Peace (see Isaiah 9:6). On the evening of the Last Supper Jesus said,

> I have said these things to you while I am still with you. But the Advocate, the Holy Spirit, whom the Father will send in my name, will teach you everything, and remind you of all that I have said to you. Peace I leave with you; my peace I give to you. I do not give to you as the world gives. Do not let your hearts be troubled, and do not let them be afraid. John 14:25-27

After His resurrection He used the greeting, "Peace be with you" (John 20:19, 21&26), and at one point He said,

> "Peace be with you. As the Father has sent me, so I send you." When he had said this, he breathed on them and said to them, "Receive the Holy Spirit." John 20:21-22

He connects His peace with the Holy Spirit, and He promises

His peace. Is true peace available apart from the Holy Spirit?

3.   Read 2 John. The short epistle is thirteen verses long. John begins writing,

> The elder to the elect lady and her children, whom I love in the truth, and not only I but also all who know the truth, because of the truth that abides in us and will be with us forever:
>
> Grace, mercy, and peace will be with us from God the Father and from Jesus Christ, the Father's Son, in truth and love. 2 John 1-3

Jesus is the truth (see John 14:6). He abides in us (see John 15:4). He promises to be with us forever (see Matthew 28:20). And through Him, God's grace, mercy and peace are with us. No matter what you are facing, no matter what you have experienced, God's grace, mercy and peace are with you!

4.   Read 1 Peter. As discussed above, Jesus greeted disciples saying, "Peace be with you." Paul urges us to facilitate bonds of peace, and Peter demonstrates this by saying hello and goodbye in terms of peace, shalom, eirene.   He begins his first epistle writing,

> Peter, an apostle of Jesus Christ,
>
> To the exiles of the Dispersion in Pontus, Galatia, Cappadocia, Asia, and Bithynia, who have been chosen and destined by God the Father and sanctified by the Spirit to be obedient to Jesus Christ and to be sprinkled with

his blood:

> May grace and peace be yours in abundance. 1 Peter 1:1-2

He concludes the epistle writing,

> Through Silvanus, whom I consider a faithful brother, I have written this short letter to encourage you and to testify that this is the true grace of God. Stand fast in it. Your sister church in Babylon, chosen together with you, sends you greetings; and so does my son Mark. Greet one another with a kiss of love.
>
> Peace to all of you who are in Christ. 1 Peter 5:12-14

I realize the greeting and farewell merely set the stage for our actual conduct with one another, and that words may not accurately represent our heart; however, do you think words of peace influence our hearts? Why or why not?

For the Praise of His Glory

Canyonlands National Park, Utah

51

SIGNS, WONDERS AND BELIEF

THEN THEY BROUGHT TO HIM A DEMONIAC WHO WAS BLIND AND MUTE; AND HE CURED HIM, SO THAT THE ONE WHO HAD BEEN MUTE COULD SPEAK AND SEE. ALL THE CROWDS WERE AMAZED AND SAID, "CAN THIS BE THE SON OF DAVID?" BUT WHEN THE PHARISEES HEARD IT, THEY SAID, "IT IS ONLY BY BEELZEBUB, THE RULER OF DEMONS, THAT THIS FELLOW CASTS OUT THE DEMONS."
MATTHEW 12:22-24

PHILIP SAID TO HIM, "LORD, SHOW US THE FATHER, AND WE WILL BE SATISFIED." JESUS SAID TO HIM, "HAVE I BEEN WITH YOU ALL THIS TIME, PHILIP, AND YOU STILL DO NOT KNOW ME? WHOEVER HAS SEEN ME HAS SEEN THE FATHER. HOW CAN YOU SAY, "SHOW US THE FATHER? DO YOU NOT BELIEVE THAT I AM IN THE FATHER AND THE FATHER IS IN ME? THE WORDS THAT I SAY TO YOU I DO NOT SPEAK ON MY OWN; BUT THE FATHER WHO DWELLS IN ME DOES HIS WORKS. BELIEVE ME THAT I AM IN THE FATHER AND THE FATHER IS IN ME;

BUT IF YOU DO NOT, THEN BELIEVE ME BECAUSE OF THE WORKS THEMSELVES. JOHN 14:8-11

Then Jesus, again greatly disturbed, came to the tomb. It was a cave, and a stone was lying against it. Jesus said, "Take away the stone." Martha, the sister of the dead man, said to him, "Lord, already there is a stench because he has been dead four days." Jesus said to her, "Did I not tell you that if you believed, you would see the glory of God?" So they took away the stone. And Jesus looked upward and said, "Father, I thank you for having heard me. I knew that you always hear me, but I have said this for the sake of the crowd standing here, so that they may believe that you sent me." When he had said this, he cried with a loud voice, "Lazarus, come out!" The dead man came out, his hands and feet bound with strips of cloth, and his face wrapped in a cloth. Jesus said to them, "Unbind him, and let him go." Many of the Jews therefore, who had come with Mary and had seen what Jesus did, believed in him. But some of them went to the Pharisees and told them what he had done. So the chief priests and the Pharisees called a meeting of the council, and said, "What are we to do? This man is performing many signs. If we let him go on like this, everyone will believe in him, and the Romans will come and destroy both our holy place and our nation." …

So from that day on they planned to put him to death. John 11:38-48 and 53

Beginning with converting water into wine at a wedding celebration (see John 2) and continuing until He blessed the disciples with a miraculous catch of fish (see John 21), Jesus' ministry revealed God's glory in many ways including miraculous signs, wonders, loving deeds and authoritative teaching. John testifies that he wrote his gospel based on his personal experience with Jesus (see John 19:35 & 21:24), and then says, "But there are also many other things that Jesus did; if every one of them were written down, I suppose that the world itself could not contain the books that would be written" (John 21:25). While Jesus Christ was on earth in fully human form, God's glory flowed through Him, revealed by works too numerous to record.

Philip ate, traveled and lived with Jesus, and studied under and followed Him for years. He likely witnessed many of Jesus' works; he likely experienced God's glory flowing through Jesus in remarkable ways day after day. After all their time together, after living an amazing collection of remarkable experiences, on the evening of the Last Supper, Philip said, "Lord, show us the Father, and we will be satisfied" (John 14:8), indicating all the previous revelations of God's glory flowing through Jesus were not enough to support Philip's faith, trust and belief. He needed more.

In essence Jesus says, at that moment, there was no more; Philip simply needed to believe. He says, "Believe me ... but if you do not, then believe me because of the works themselves" (John 14:11). Jesus urges Philip to believe on the basis of their relationship, the totality of Philip's experiences with Jesus, but if that is not enough, believe on the basis of having seen God's works flow through Jesus.

Philip had years of personal experiences with Jesus, yet he struggled to believe. We have so much more than Philip had at that moment. We have what the prophets of the Old Testament longed to possess, we have what the disciples longed to experience – we have Jesus' Spirit dwelling within us. Pause for a moment and let that sink in. Think about what makes a person who they really are – their personality, character, wit, sense of humor, memories, ability to think, emotions. The characteristics comprising the essence of a person are spiritual. We have His Spirit within us! We also have the body of God's holy word; we have truth describing some of God's works in the world performed through Jesus Christ; we have an amazing collection of God's promises to us; and we have our personal experiences with Jesus Christ who dwells within us. We have felt Him lift the veil from our eyes as we read His holy word. We have prayed and felt His holy presence as we breathe Him into our hearts. We have experienced His blessing as He answers our prayers. We know He is here and active. We know that He is love and He loves us.

But is that enough to support your faith, your trust, your belief?

When Jesus healed people and cast demons out of people and raised people from the dead and multiplied loaves and fish and performed other amazing signs and wonders, some saw what God did through Jesus and believed in Jesus while others saw the same events yet failed to believe.

Religious leaders were the people who should have been closest to God, striving to be near God, striving to represent God on earth. Their occupation was studying and teaching God's holy word, but when they heard that Jesus cast demons out of a blind and mute person who was suddenly able to see and speak, they accused Jesus of performing the good deed through the power of Satan (see Matthew 12:22-24). And when they heard that Jesus raised Lazarus from the dead, they plotted to kill Him (see John 11:46-47).

Seeing does not always lead to believing but believing leads to seeing. Jesus urged Philip to believe so that he might see. Do you believe? Do you believe that Jesus continues to reveal His signs and wonders around us? Ask God to open your eyes to see His glory as He reveals Himself around you today. Ask God to use you as His instrument today so that others may see Him through you.

May God continue to reveal His glory through you.

Thoughts to Consider

1. Read Matthew 15 & 16:1-12. Matthew tells stories of many people encountering Jesus and responding to Him. Some know exactly who He is. Others cannot see Him as the Messiah. Poor, sick, demon-possessed Gentiles saw Him, believed and were healed. However, religious leaders simply could not

see Him. They were spiritually blind.

Chapter 14 describes Jesus feeding five thousand men and many uncounted women and children with five loaves and two fish. The chapter describes Jesus ordering a storm to stop and it obeys, and He heals lots and lots of people in Gennesaret. Chapter 15 begins with religious leaders questioning Jesus. They had traveled from Jerusalem to meet Him and Jesus responds to their questions saying,

> "You hypocrites! Isaiah prophesied rightly about you when he said: 'This people honors me with their lips, but their hearts are far from me; in vain do they worship me, teaching human precepts as doctrines.'" Matthew 15:7-9

In response to her mother's faith, He cures a Canaanite girl before traveling to the Sea of Galilee, where He sat at the top of a mountain healing great crowds of people and feeding four thousand men and lots of uncounted women and children with seven loaves and two fish. Many, many, many people, great crowds of people saw Him and believed and were healed.

But religious leaders were blind to His truth. They saw healing, they heard about the miracles, but they simply could not believe what they heard about was from God. Chapter 16 begins with religious leaders asking Jesus to show them a sign so that they might believe.

God's glory shines around us. I pray that we have eyes to see. I pray that we are not blind to spiritual truth. I pray that we are not today's version of Pharisees, unable to see the truth.

2.   Read 2 Corinthians 4. Paul begins the chapter acknowledging that some people reject the gospel of Jesus Christ. He explains that he preaches the truth; however, Satan blinds some people to the "light of the gospel of the glory of Christ, who is the image of God" (2 Corinthians 4:4). He continues discussing his amazement that God chooses to shine His glory through ordinary people. Our bodies are ordinary fragile vessels wasting away, yet God chooses to shine His glory through us. This extraordinary, indescribable treasure resides in and flows through us! How awesome is that?

He concludes the chapter contrasting our physical frailty with God's glory saying,

> So do not lose heart. Even though our outer nature is wasting away, our inner nature is being renewed day by day. For this slight momentary affliction is preparing us for an eternal weight of glory beyond all measure. 2 Corinthians 4:16-17

We live in a dark and evil world. We are exposed to disease, illness, aging, trauma, and violations of every sort. No matter what you are going through, do not lose heart because your spirit and soul are being renewed and strengthened and filled day by day. And when we, like Paul, explain the gospel of the glory of Christ Jesus to people who simply cannot see the truth, please do not take it personally. God's holy word tells us that Satan causes some people to be blind to the truth of Christ Jesus.

How do you respond to the messages of this chapter?

3.	Read 1 John 2. John presents a few important theological points. He explains that Christ Jesus died for the sins of the whole world. With that in mind, he urges us to love everyone; and he explains that walking in the light equates to loving everyone and hating another indicates we are still in darkness. He then writes,

> But whoever hates another believer is in the darkness, walks in the darkness, and does not know the way to go, because the darkness has brought on blindness." 1 John 2:11

Light symbolizes God. Darkness symbolizes separation from God, and the darkness brings on spiritual blindness.

God's holy word explains that "faith comes from what is heard, and what is heard comes through the word of Christ" (Romans 10:17). If spiritual blindness is the result of separation from God and faith is the result of listening to His holy word, we must continue telling everyone about God the Father, Christ Jesus and the Holy Spirit because eventually they will gain eyes to see.

4.	Read Revelation 3. Jesus gives messages to the churches in Sardis, Philadelphia and Laodicea. As part of His message to the church in Laodicea He says,

> So, because you are lukewarm, and neither cold nor hot, I am about to spit you out of my mouth. For you say, 'I am rich, I have prospered, and I need nothing.' You do not realize that you are wretched, pitiable, poor, blind and naked. Revelation 3:16-17

Their wealth and comfort have made them spiritually blind. Their material blessings have made them spiritually blind. That sends chills down my spine. How about you?

For the Praise of His Glory

Seaside, Florida

52

A Thorn for Humility

On behalf of such a one I will boast, but on my own behalf I will not boast, except of my weaknesses. But if I wish to boast, I will not be a fool, for I will be speaking the truth. But I refrain from it, so that no one may think better of me than what is seen in me or heard from me, even considering the exceptional character of the revelations. Therefore, to keep me from being too elated, a thorn was given me in the flesh, a messenger of Satan to torment me, to keep me from being too elated. Three times I appealed to the Lord about this, that it would leave me, but he said to me, "My grace is sufficient for you, for power is made perfect in weakness." So, I will boast all the more gladly of my weaknesses, so that the power of Christ may dwell in me. Therefore I am content with weaknesses, insults, hardships, persecutions, and calamities for the sake of Christ; for whenever I am weak, then I am strong. 2 Corin-

For the Praise of His Glory

THIANS 12:5-10

The final sentence is a remarkable statement of contentedness. Paul is content with everything, even persecutions and calamities endured for the sake of Jesus Christ, and he seeks weakness so that the power of the Holy Spirit may be made perfect in him. How might we find contentedness while suffering insults, hardship, persecution and calamities for the sake of Jesus Christ? The key to Paul's frame of mind, the foundation of his faith is his relationship with God.

The Scripture reading is the second portion of a paragraph. Paul begins the paragraph discussing boasting and saying, "nothing is to be gained by it" (2 Corinthians 12:1). He continues describing an event that happened fourteen years earlier to a person, presumably Paul, during which he was transported to heaven and granted the amazing privilege of seeing and hearing the glory of heaven. He was "caught up into Paradise and heard things that are not to be told, that no mortal is permitted to repeat" (2 Corinthians 12:4).

We can imagine what Paul might have experienced based on the descriptions of heavenly revelations provided by Isaiah, Ezekiel and John, but Paul was not permitted to repeat his revelation, and besides that, he did not want anyone to think better of him. He was granted an amazing gift from God and he was careful not to discuss it in a way that would direct any focus on Paul – he wanted to keep everyone's focus on Jesus Christ.

It is in this context that Paul mentions another gift, his

thorn, designed to keep him "from being too elated." Paul knew that God had the power and authority to take the thorn away from him – God had healed many in response to Paul's prayers, people even passed around Paul's handkerchiefs believing they possessed healing qualities – but after Paul prayed three times for God to take away the thorn he heard God say, "My grace is sufficient for you, for power is made perfect in weakness."

God knew that Paul had experienced God's glory in remarkable ways and Paul was at risk of allowing his amazing experiences to go to his head, so God allowed Paul to keep his thorn as a gift for humility. Paul refers to the condition tormenting him as a "thorn," but we do not know what the condition was. It was possibly a lingering physical ache, pain or illness. It might have been a person who served as "a messenger of Satan to torment" him, an unholy desire or something entirely different. And that is part of the beauty of God's holy word – we do not know the specific identity of Paul's thorn, so there is no limit to parallels in our lives.

Think about your encounters with God the Father, with Jesus Christ, with the Holy Spirit. Think about the times you have been reading God's holy word and the message comes to life, the times you have prayed and you felt His Holy Presence burning deep within your soul, the times you have been caught up worshiping and you felt goose bumps of joy, the times when His Holy Presence was so near you could touch, smell and feel Him, the times when in the ears of your spirit you heard Him speaking to you, the times when you have prayed and suddenly God placed the right person in your path. Think of the quiet, ordinary moments when God's glory is suddenly revealed in a new way. Isn't it amazing that the eternal, infinite, almighty, holy, pure, divine One, the Creator of all things, the Author of life continuously grants you the gift of holy grace?

Whether or not you have experienced the sort of heavenly vision that God granted Paul, you have probably experienced God's blessing in remarkable ways. As a result of His holy gift of grace in each of our lives, we are each at risk of allowing our relationship with Him to go to our heads. If you are experiencing a thorn, follow Paul's example and ask God to take it away, and if it lingers, perhaps it is, like Paul's thorn, a gift for humility.

God says, "My grace is sufficient for you, for power is made perfect in weakness." How is power made perfect in weakness? Electric power is made better by improved consistency, battery power is made better by longer life, and athletic power and military power are made better by additional strength. In the world, power is not improved by weakness, but in God's kingdom power is made perfect through our weakness.

Jesus promises, "you will receive power when the Holy Spirit has come upon you" (Acts 1:8). We received the power of the Holy Spirit when He came upon each of us. Through weakness, brokenness, suffering and pain we seek God, we desire God, we discover the ability to trust God, we find humility, we rely on His power rather than our own. His power is perfect. Weakness strengthens our connection to His perfect power. Through weakness we discover His strength.

I pray that God grants each of us His holy blessing of contentedness. May you find His rest, His peace, His holy comfort in every aspect of your life in a new and refreshed way.

Thoughts to Consider

1.   Read Daniel 10. Daniel's final revelation is recorded in chapters 10-12. He encounters an angel who was called away from battling in the spiritual realm to serve as messenger to Daniel with the specific mission of helping him "understand what is to happen to your people at the end of days" (Daniel 10:14). The angel was fighting a battle and Michael came to take over, allowing the angel to leave and meet with Daniel. And the angel says he will return to the battle after fulfilling his mission with Daniel. We often discuss battles taking place in the spiritual realm. We read Paul's description of the armor of God and discuss spiritual warfare (see Ephesians 6:10-20), but to hear an angelic warrior mention his battle and explain the need for reinforcement corroborates and adds texture to the thought. Battles really are being fought in the spiritual realm.

As Daniel enters the spiritual state in which he is able to interact with the angel, he says, "My strength left me, and my complexion grew deathly pale, and I retained no strength. Then I heard the sound of his words; and when I heard the sound of his words, I fell into a trance, face to the ground" (Daniel 10:9). The angel touched Daniel and through the touch he gained strength.

How do you respond to the account in Daniel of spiritual battles, of God's messenger and of angelic strengthening?

2.   Read I Corinthians 2. Writing to his friends in Corinth, Paul begins chapter 2 writing,

> When I came to you, brothers and sisters, I did not come proclaiming the mystery of God to you in lofty words or wisdom. For I decided to know nothing among you except Jesus Christ, and him crucified. And I came to you in weakness and in fear and in much trembling. My speech and my proclamation were not with plausible words of wisdom, but with a demonstration of the Spirit and of power, so that your faith might rest not on human wisdom but on the power of God. I Corinthians 2:1-5

When Paul first arrived in Corinth as a preacher proclaiming God's holy word, he did not have a big following there (see Acts 18). He met Anquila and Priscilla and they formed a tentmaking business together, and he preached in the synagogue for a period of weeks before they began to oppose his message. Then Paul started preaching in houses, in the streets, in the market and probably in the tent shop. He stays eighteen months and the church in Corinth gradually forms.

In his letter to his friends in Corinth he says that he came to them "in weakness and in fear and in much trembling" (I Corinthians 2:3). He trusted God's power, He trusted the Holy Spirit, He trusted God's truth, not his own wisdom or persuasive skills. He allowed himself to be a mere vessel through which God was able to operate.

How did the thorn enable him to maintain the level of humility necessary to allow God to truly use him? Consider your thorns. How might they enable you to serve God?

3.   Read Ephesians 3. After explaining the purpose of the church and the eternal purpose carried out through Jesus Christ (see Ephesians 3:10-12), Paul prays for his readers. As you read his prayer, notice his references to strength and power. He prays,

> For this reason I bow my knees before the Father, from whom every family in heaven and on earth takes its name. I pray that, according to the riches of his glory, he may grant that you may be strengthened in your inner being with power through his Spirit, and that Christ may dwell in your hearts through faith, as you are being rooted and grounded in love. I pray that you may have the power to comprehend, with all the saints, what is the breadth and length and height and depth, and to know the love of Christ that surpasses knowledge, so that you may be filled with all the fullness of God.
>
> Now to him who by the power at work within us is able to accomplish abundantly far more than all we can ask or imagine, to him be glory in the church and in Christ Jesus to all generations, forever and ever. Amen. Ephesians 3:14-21

He prays that God will strengthen us and fill us with His power as Christ Jesus dwells within us and we are being "rooted and grounded in love." God empowers us and fills us as we become lower and less. How does this relate to your experience?

4.   Read Acts 1. Just before ascending to heaven, Jesus says to the disciples,

> "It is not for you to know the times or periods that the Father has set by his own authority. But you will receive power when the Holy Spirit has come upon you; and you will be my witnesses in Jerusalem, in all Judea and Samaria, and to the ends of the earth." Acts 1:7-8

Through Jesus we receive the Holy Spirit and He comes with power. May you fully receive His holy gift of loving grace, may you be fully transformed by Him, may you allow His life, love and light to flow through you changing the world around you, Amen.

Randy L Allen

For the Praise of His Glory

Massadona, Colorado

Randy L Allen

About the Author

Photo by Savannah Smith

    I am married to Lori and thankful that she continues to put up with me. We have two children, both of whom are married (Elizabeth to Hunter, and Henry to Meagan), and one grandson, Carson.

    I serve as associate pastor at First United Methodist Church in Tuscaloosa, Alabama and managing partner of Druid Capital Partners in Northport, Alabama, and enjoy quiet time with family, Yolo boarding on Lake Tuscaloosa, participating in CrossFit over lunch (an elderly version), praying in the Sanctuary with close friends and strangers, praying alone in the backyard, and studying, talking about and writing about God's holy word.

    This is my second book of devotionals. The first is titled *God's Glory Revealed: 52 Devotionals*.

Inner Passage, Alaska

San Juan Range, Colorado

NOTES

If you would like to receive future devotionals, please sign up for emails at

https://RandyLAllen.com

1	Alter, Robert (2019). The Hebrew Bible: A Translation with Commentary, Volume 3, The Writings. New York: W.W. Norton & Company, p.123.

2	"Every Child Is an Artist. The Problem Is How to Remain an Artist Once He or She Grows Up," Quote Investigator (online), https://quoteinvestigator.com/2015/03/07/child-art/#return-note-10748-2

3	Newton, John, "Amazing Grace." The United Methodist Hymnal: Book of United Methodist Worship. The United Methodist Publishing House (1989), Hymn 378.

4	Genesis 1:27

5	Isaiah 41:10

6	Jeremiah 29:11

7	Jeremiah 31:3, John 3:16, Romans 5:8 (among others)

8	Isaiah 43:1

9	Id

10	Id

11	1 John 3:1

12	Romans 8:29, Hebrews 2:11

13	Ephesians 1:14

14	Acts 1:8; Ephesians 3:16-19

15	Isaiah 41:10